# BURLINGTON
## THROUGH TIME

## ROBERT J. COSTA

AMERICA THROUGH TIME®

AMERICA THROUGH TIME is an imprint of Fonthill Media LLC

Fonthill Media LLC
www.fonthillmedia.com
office@fonthillmedia.com

First published 2014

ISBN 978-1-62545-055-5

Typeset in Mrs Eaves XL Serif Narrow
Printed and bound in England

Connect with us:
www.twitter.com/USAthroughtime
www.facebook.com/AmericaThroughTime

AMERICA THROUGH TIME® is a registered trademark of
Fonthill Media LLC

# INTRODUCTION

'Rich Past, Bright Future' was the town slogan when Burlington, Mass.. commemorated its 175th anniversary in 1974. In some ways this still holds true for the town today. The history of the area, however, dates to the founding of the state of Massachusetts and the nation itself. Woburn, established in 1642, was the tenth town founded in the colony of Massachusetts Bay. Several of the founding fathers of Woburn settled in the area named 'Shawshin', a variation of the name used by the Native Americans who inhabited the region for hundreds of years before the coming of the English settlers in

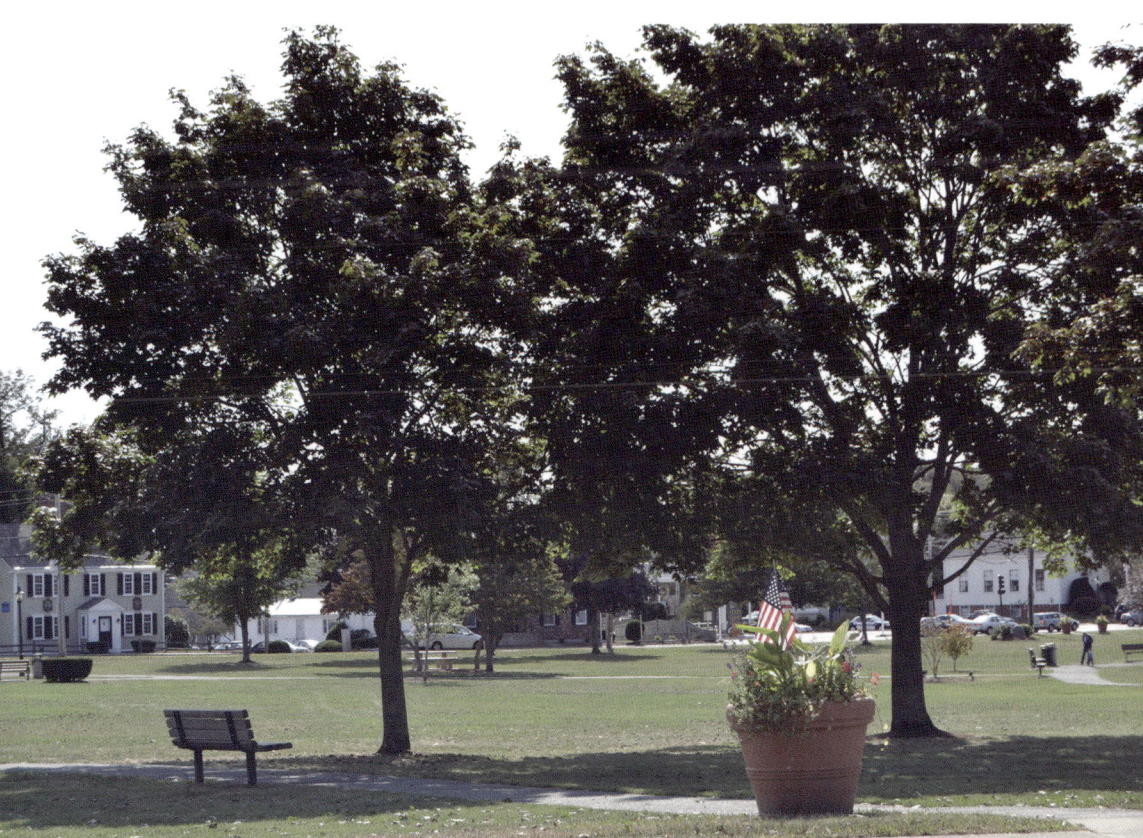

1620. Men such as Francis and John Wyman, Edward Winn and others established large farms and homesteads in the area that encompasses the present town of Burlington. The population grew steadily. In the year 1730, the Second Parish of Woburn was created, and, on February 28, 1799 the town of Burlington was incorporated.

The new town's population grew slowly throughout the nineteenth and mid-twentieth centuries, with great emphasis on agriculture, dairy, ham and market garden crops. Many fine farms, with distinctive barns dotted the town. The Walker, Crawford, McIntire, Patterson and Reed are notable examples. The completion of Route 128 and the creation of the town's Water Department in the early 1950s began a transformation. Because of its geographic location and country ambiance the population grew from the early sixties to 1975 (peak app. 25,000) as many young families moved from troubled urban centers to the safe confines of the 'country'. Farms gave way to the development of Burlington from a quintessential rural landscape with many Colonial Era houses and barns, reminding the residents of our connection to history and heritage, into the mixed-use development site it has become today.

*Previous page:* The Town Common, part of the Heritage Trail marker, reflects our historic past.

*Opposite page:* 'The best room' of the Samuel Sewall mansion built in 1732. Artifacts on display include a portrait of Judge Samuel Sewall, the sword of Revd John Marrett, and table and chairs used by John Hancock and Samuel Adams.

# CONTENTS

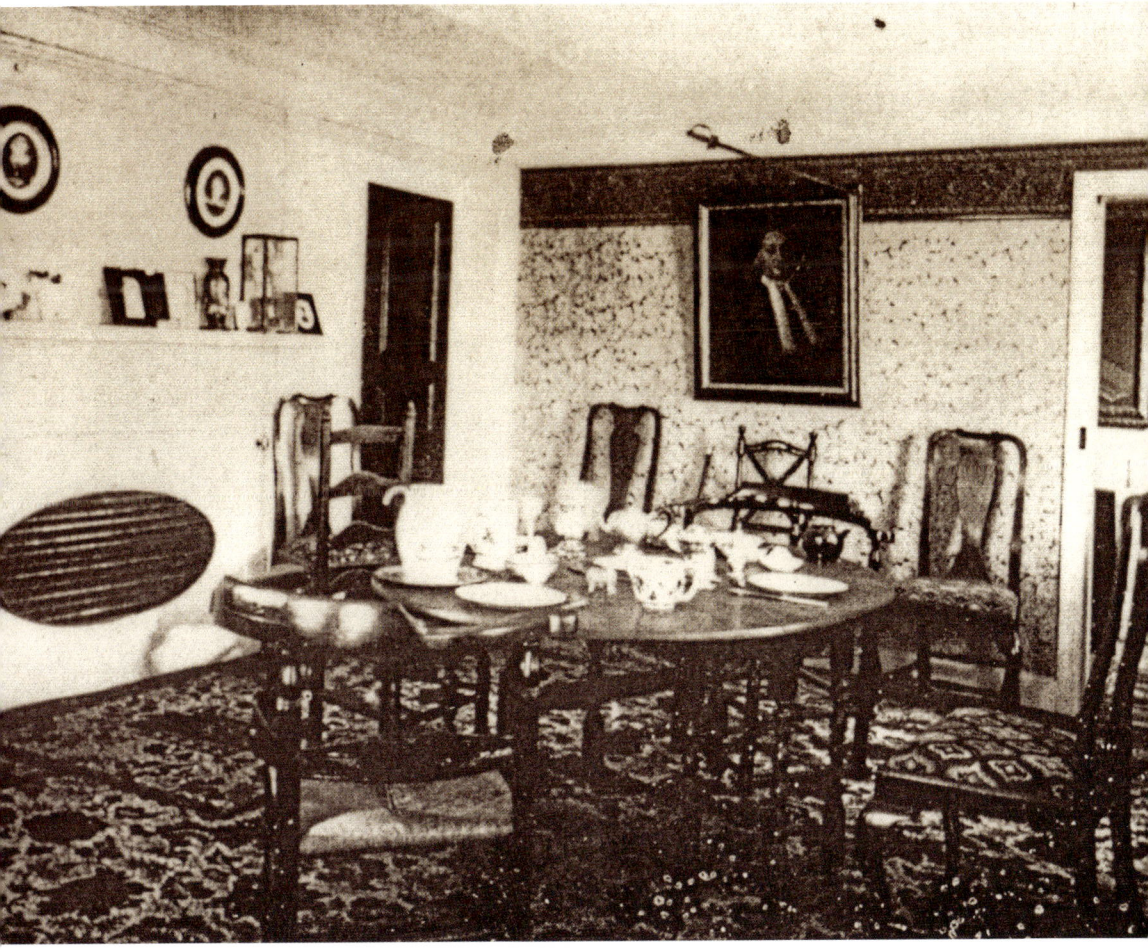

# ACKNOWLEDGMENTS

The author would like to acknowledge the following individuals, organizations and publications for assistance in the creation of this work:

The Burlington Town Archives for scans of historic images from the John E. Fogelberg collection, Toni Faria of the Burlington Historical Commission, John Goff's publication, *Historic Preservation Survey of Burlington 1999*, and longtime History teachers Jan Costa and Donna Fairbanks for their help in making this work possible. Inspiration for the book came, in part, from the many Burlington students that embraced the study of local history, several of whom have become leaders, business men/women and residents in the community.

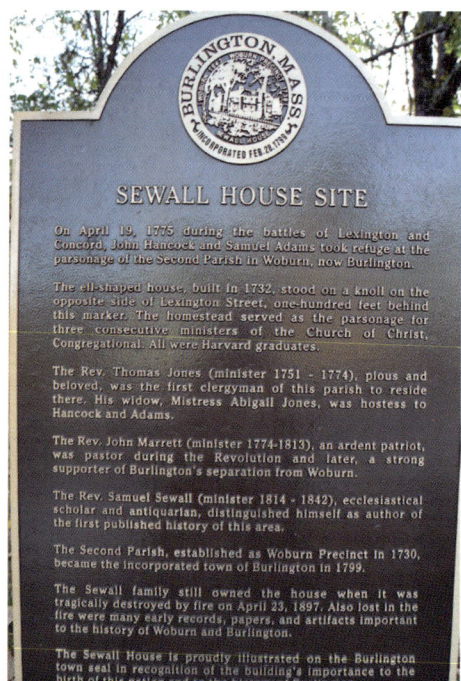

*Left:* The bronze marker, sponsored by the Social Studies Department of Burlington High School indicating the site of the Sewall Mansion on Lexington Street.

*Opposite page:* The Civil War drum, diary and watch—artifacts that are part of the Burlington Historical Museums collection.

# Section 1

# The Burlington Heritage Trail

On April 19, 1976, the Burlington Heritage Trail was dedicated in conjunction with the celebration of the nation's Bicentennial. The Burlington Garden Club, in co-operation with the Burlington Historical Commission, organized the project. Local artists designed and painted signs for each of the ten stops, as well as an illustrated map. New awareness regarding local history and its connection to our nation's history was prevalent for a time in 1975–1976. John E. Fogelberg, Burlington's town historian, had published in 1974 the first comprehensive study of the town with his book, *Burlington: Part of a Greater Chronicle*, that "Greater Chronicle" being the history of our nation.

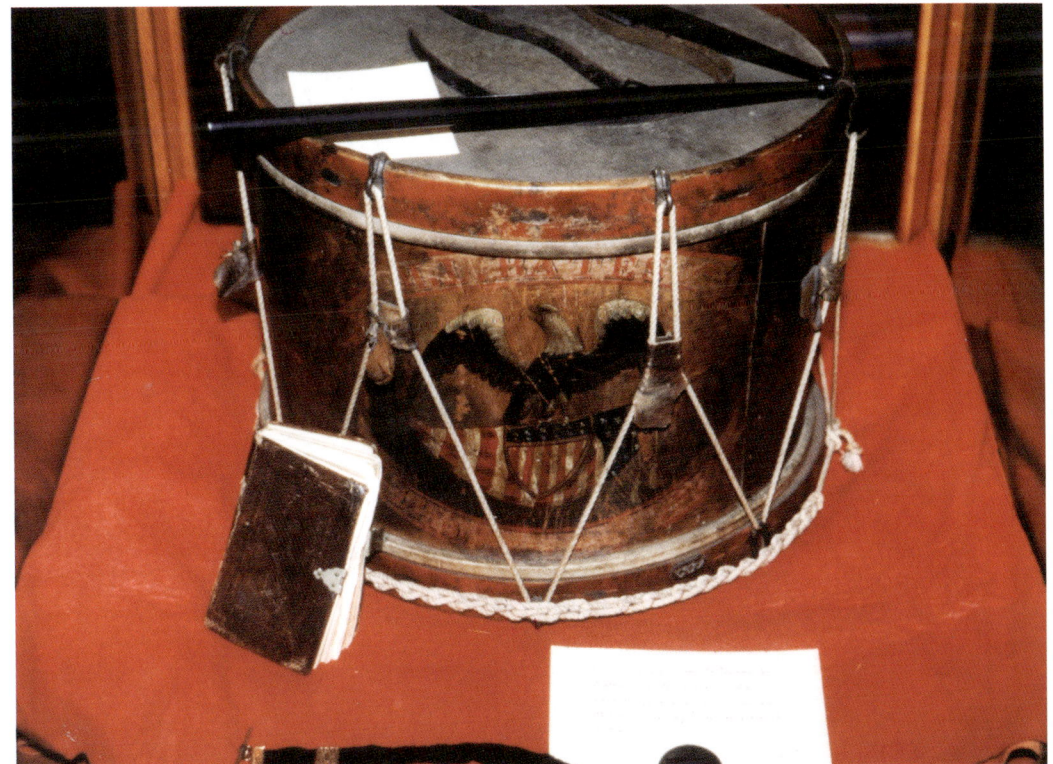

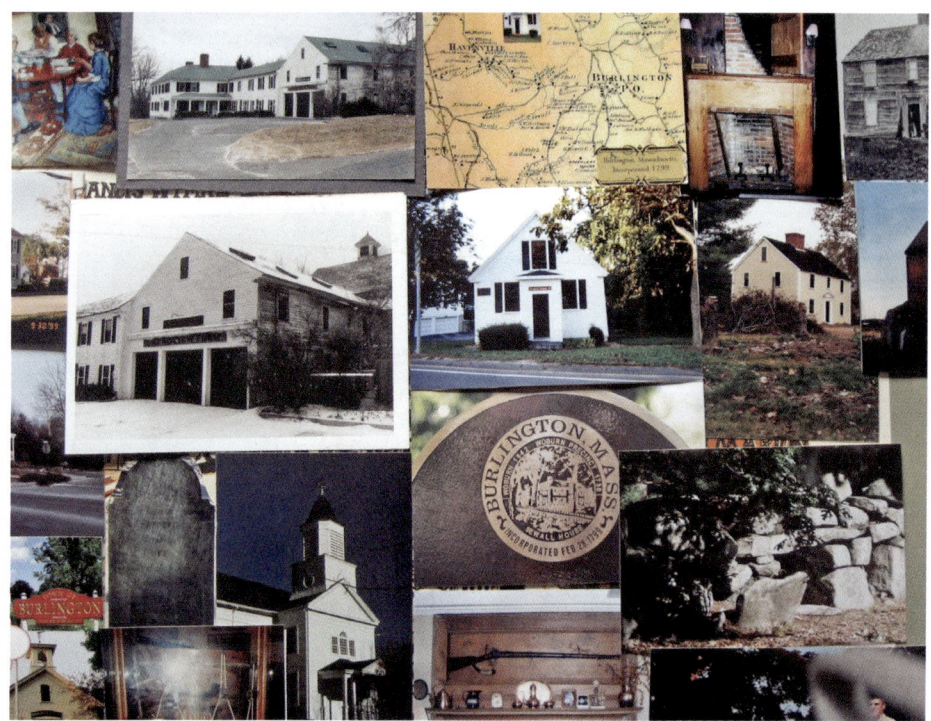

**BURLINGTON HERITAGE TRAIL:** The Trail consists of ten significant historic sites throughout the town, covering the four points of the compass. At the time of the Revolutionary War, Burlington was part of Woburn. Men and women from Woburn's Second Parish had notable roles in the battles that began the American Revolution; Lexington and Concord. (SCAN + IMAGE RJC)

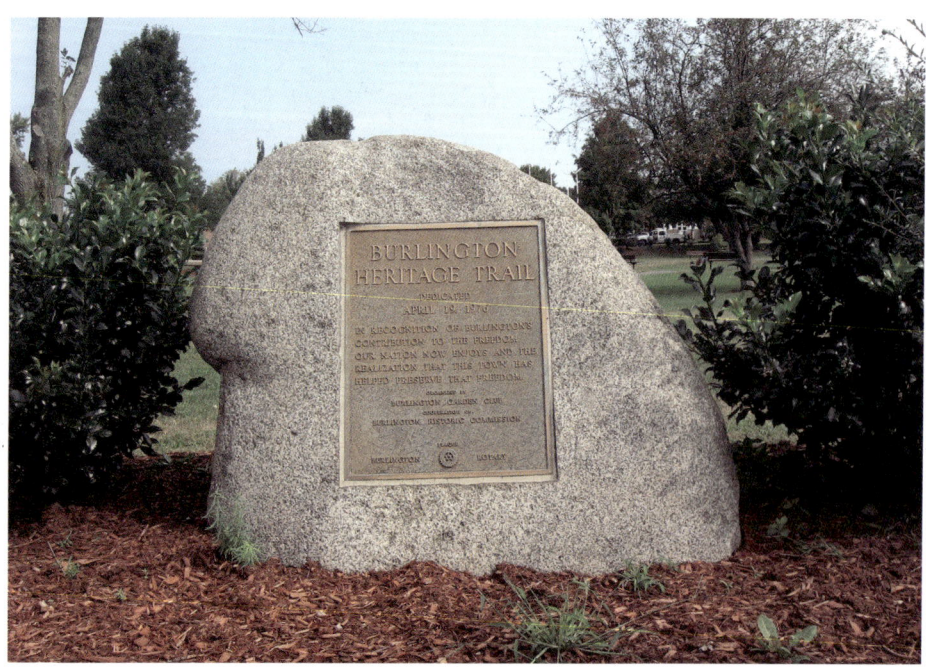

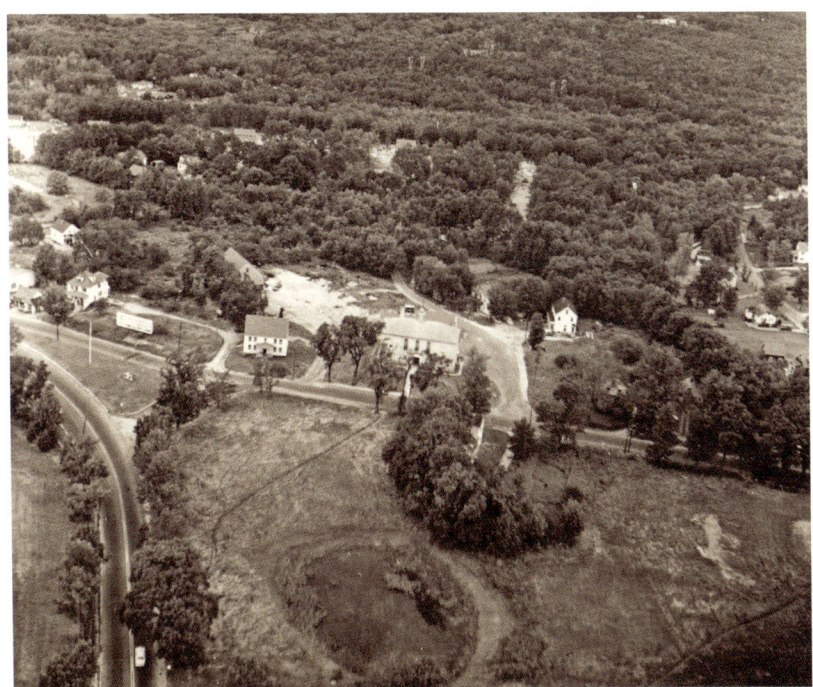

**BURLINGTON TOWN COMMON AERIAL:** It may surprise the reader that Burlington's Town Common wasn't always the public place it is today. From its settlement in the 1730s to the early 1960s, most of the Common was privately owned land, consisting of dwellings and small businesses. In the 1950s we see vast tracks of forested land with the Wood Tavern and the Second Town Hall visible. It was quite a different scene by 1975. (BTA SCANS)

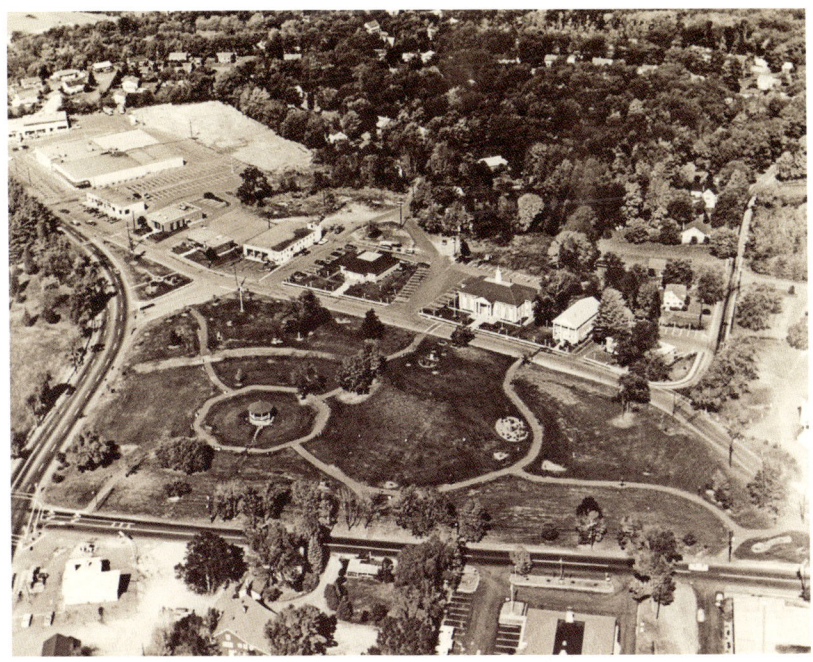

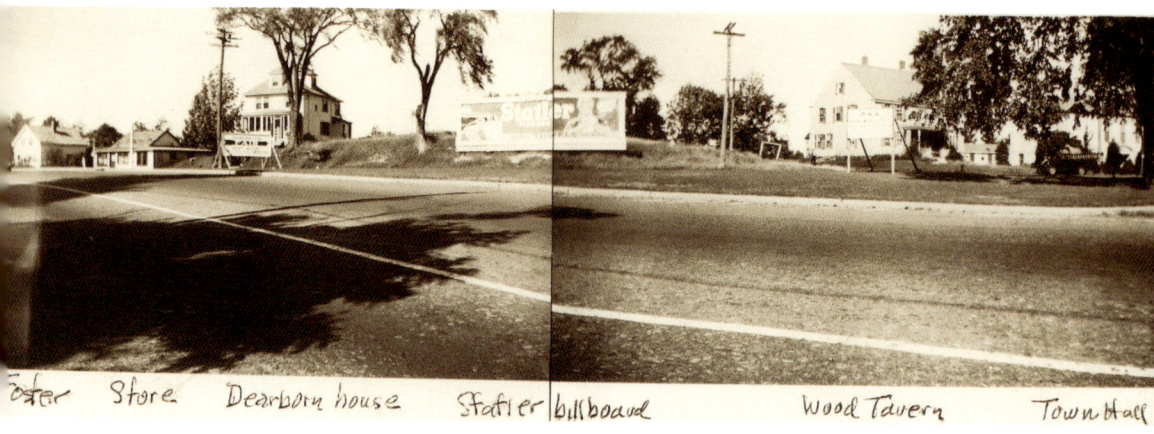

Foster  Store  Dearborn house  Statler | billboard  Wood Tavern  Town Hall

COMMON PANORAMA TOUR:  Burlington's Common developed through the early twentieth century with a blacksmith shop, the Second Town Hall, Silas Cutler's General Store, the historic Wood Tavern and several private residences occupying the area. In the 1930s Burlington even featured a billboard, in this case, advertising Statler Tissues. By 1960 all the buildings had been demolished. Today, the area is the heart of the town's political and public service sectors and a popular meeting place for various activities that bring the people of Burlington together. (BTA SCANS)

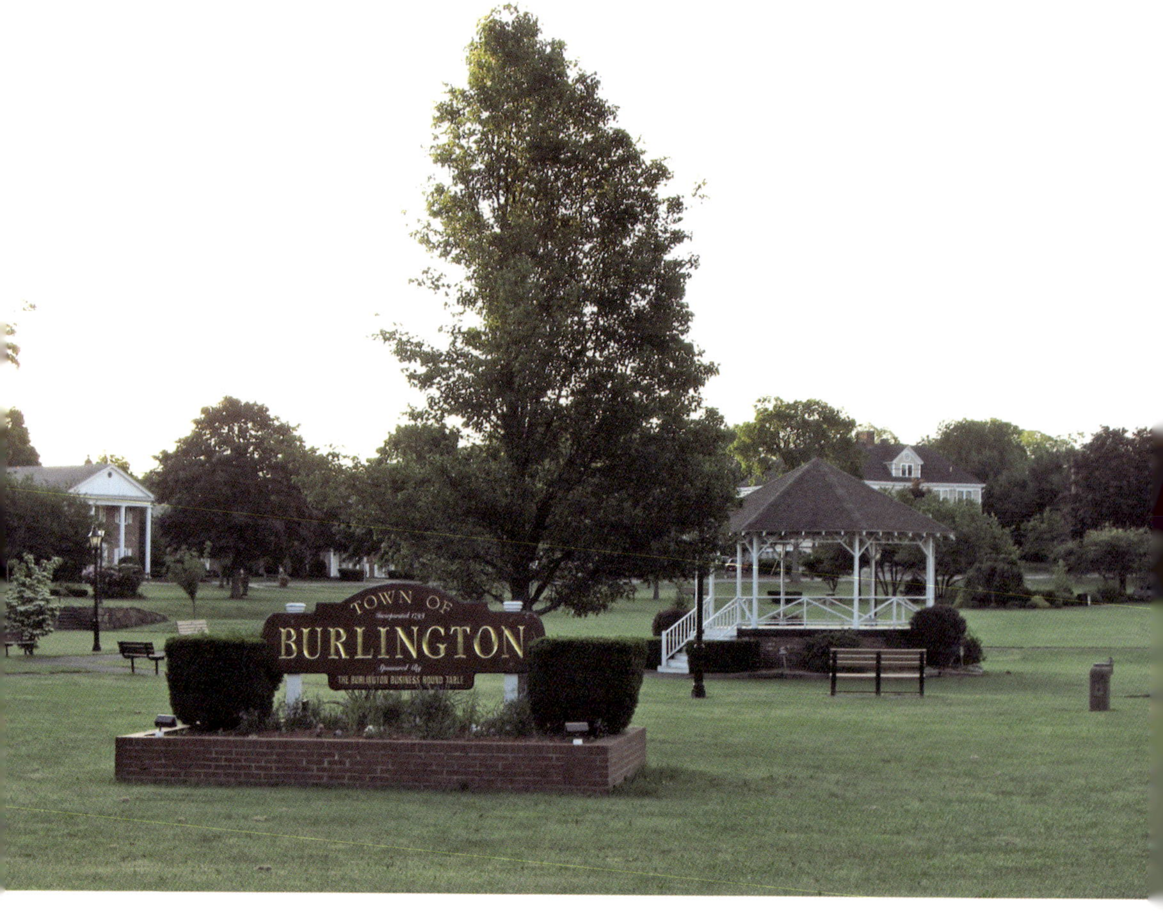

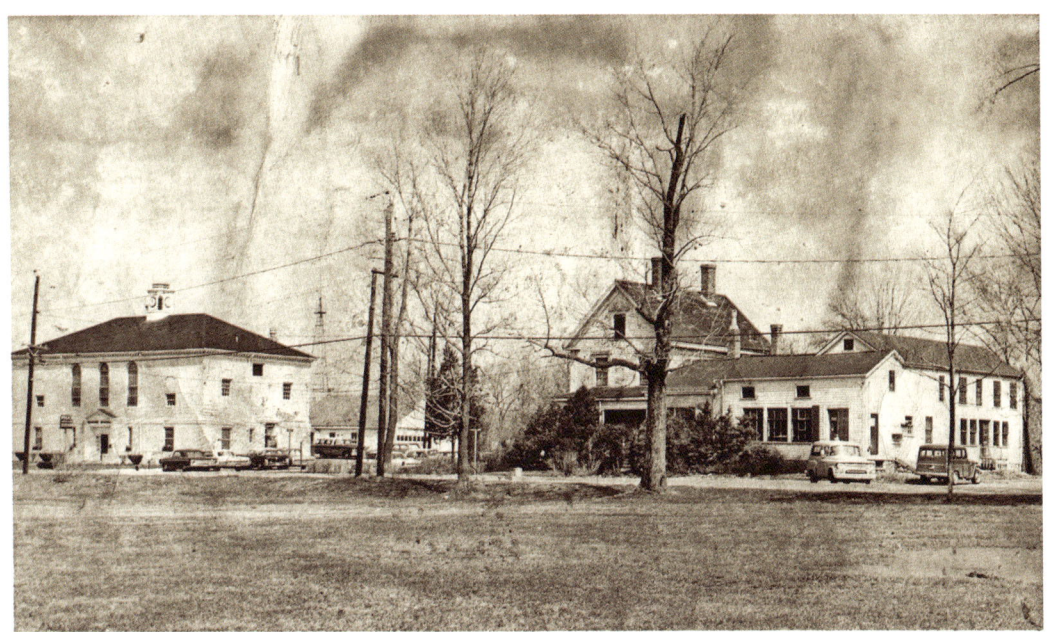

**COMMON/"MAIN STREET":** On Main Street, Burlington in the mid-twentieth century you could visit the Second Town Hall, which also housed the Police Department, stop at the General Store, or study at the Union School. Main Street is now called Center Street and connects to Cambridge Street at the "Triangle". It is the vital center of the town in 2013, used by many residents in many ways. Government, Police and Fire protection, financial and legal services are all located around the town common. (BTA SCAN) (RJC/IMAGE)

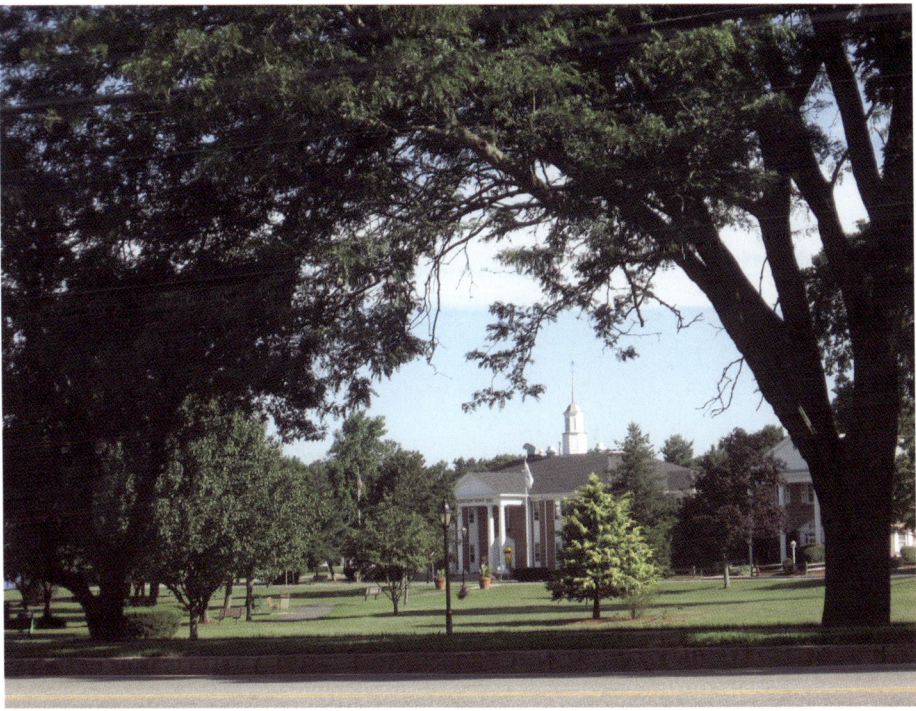

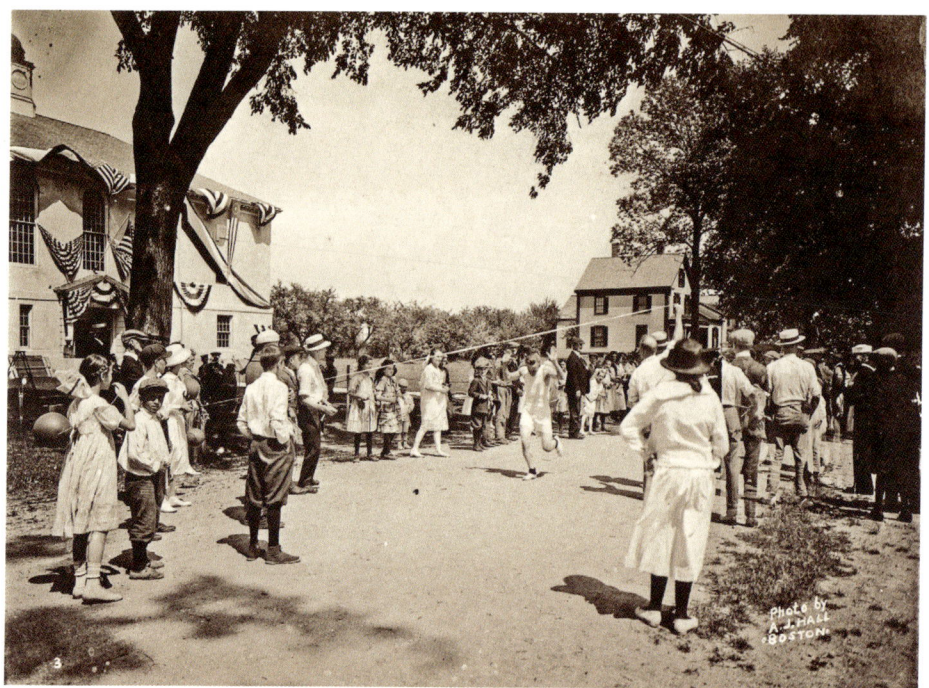

MAIN STREET/CENTER STREET: In 1919 Burlington celebrated the return of her soldiers from the battles of the First World War. The stately elm trees that graced this part of the Common were lost in the Hurricane of 1938. Since the beginning of the twentieth century, community gatherings on the Town Common have been a long, proud tradition. Whether for patriotic celebrations, proms, weddings, concerts or community events, Burlington's Town Common is the place to be. (BTA SCAN) (RJC/IMAGE)

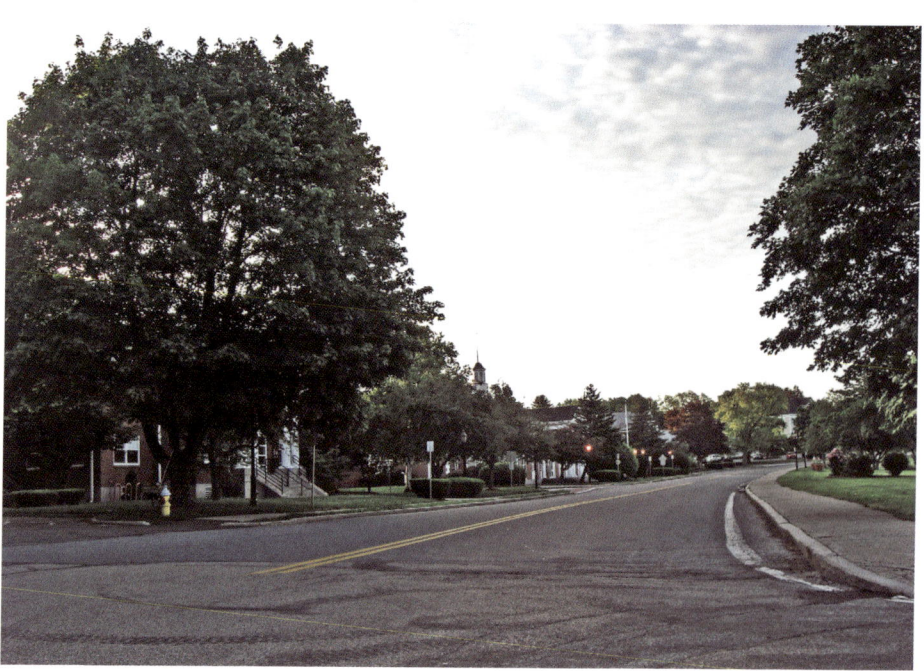

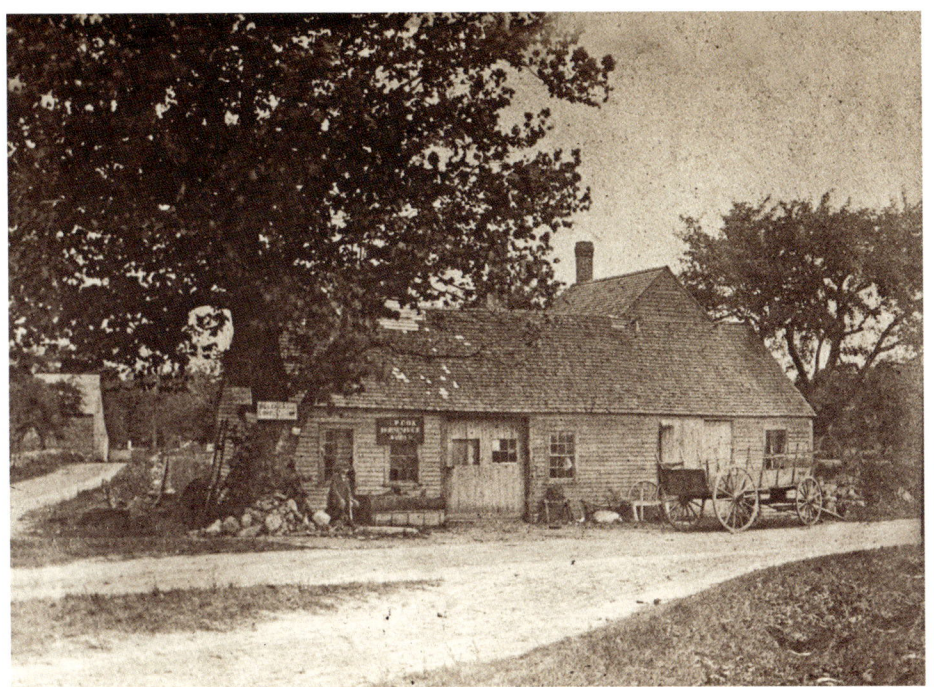

THE BLACKSMITH SHOP: Iron making was one of the first industries started by the settlers of the thirteen colonies. Virtually every New England town had a village blacksmith who provided many necessary farm implements and tools. Burlington's blacksmith shop was located at the corner of Bedford Street and Main Street, now called Center Street. Notable local blacksmiths were Solomon Trull and Richard Alley. According to archival sources, Richard J. Alley ran the shop from 1842 until the 1890s. The weathervane atop the Burlington Public Museum is credited to this man. (BTA SCAN) (RJC/IMAGE)

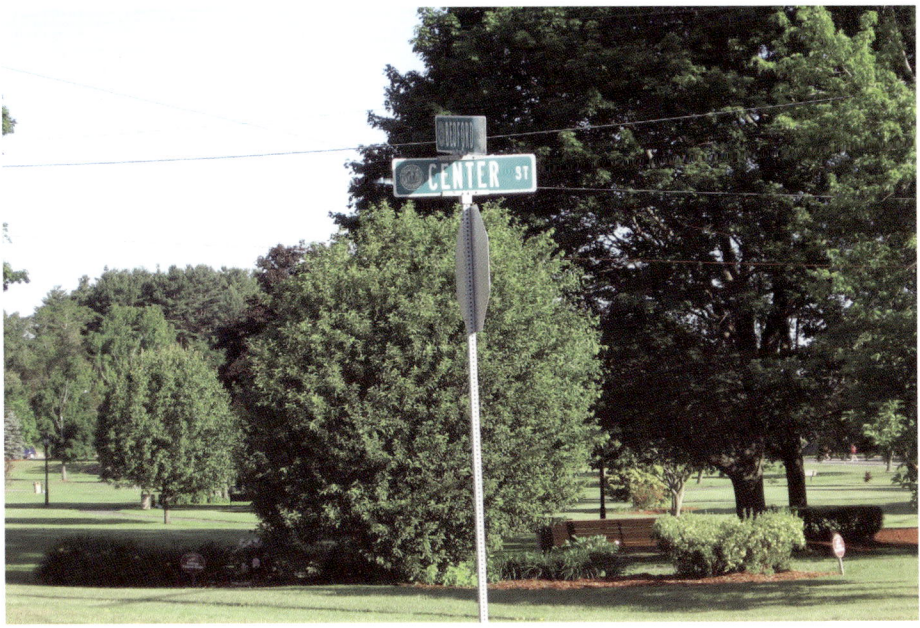

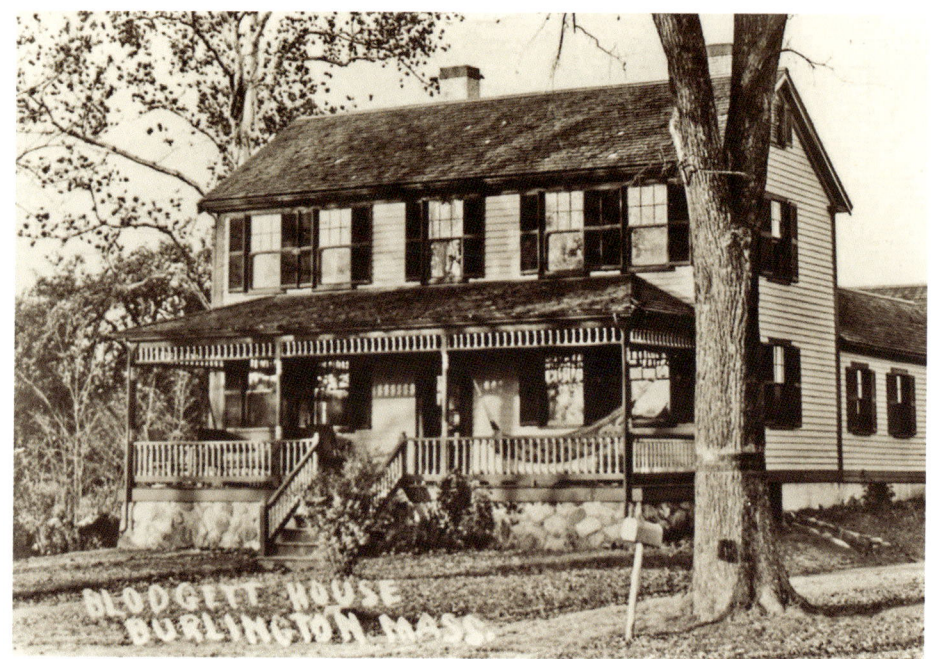

**W. E. CARTER HOUSE:** One of the private homes that once stood on the Town Common was the W. E. Carter house, located on the corner of Center and Sears Streets, where the Colonial Building stands now. It was built prior to 1850 by Albert Wood and was once the home of Addie Blodgett. W. E. Carter ran a shoe heel company on nearby Cambridge Street. By the early 1900s the Town Common was cleared of private buildings. (BTA SCAN) (RJC/IMAGE)

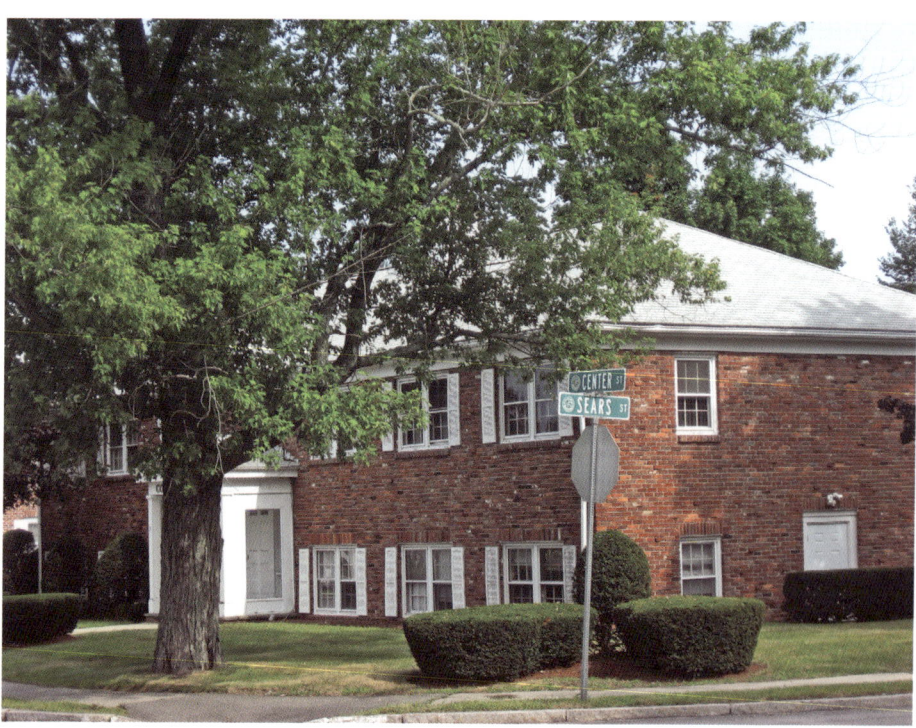

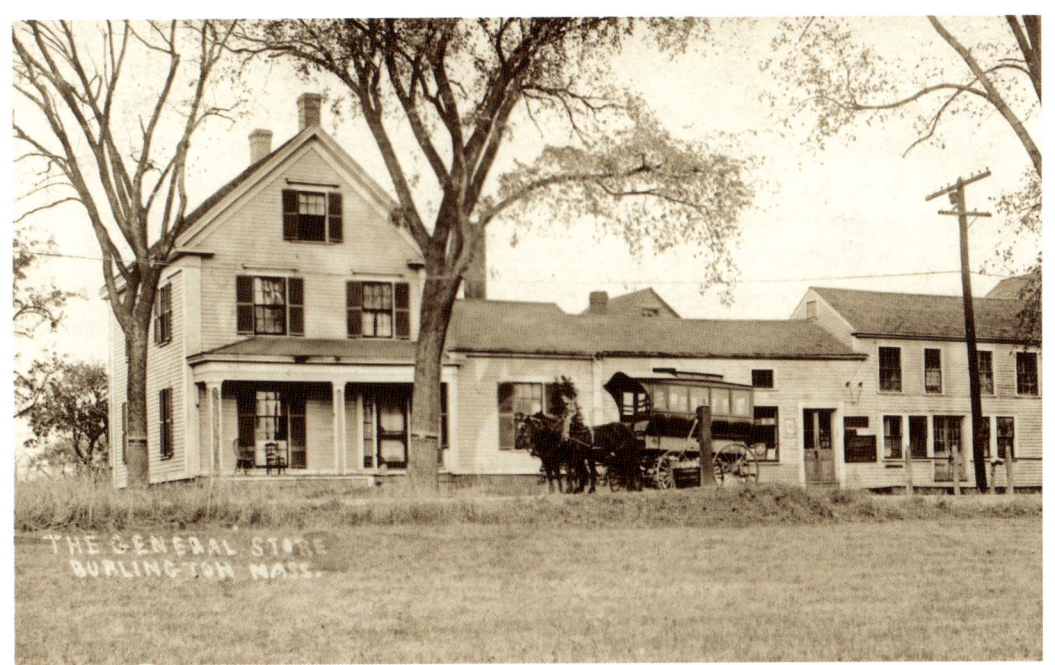

SILAS CUTLER GENERAL STORE: The General Store was an essential component of small New England towns and served a variety of important functions. The Silas Cutler General Store, also called the Dodge House, was originally located where the Town Hall Annex is today but was later moved. The "Barge", seen in the lower right of the *c.* 1900 image was Burlington's first school bus. It was also used by the local mail carrier. The General Store operated until the 1940s when it was razed to make way for the third Town Hall in 1968. (BTA SCAN) (RJC/IMAGE)

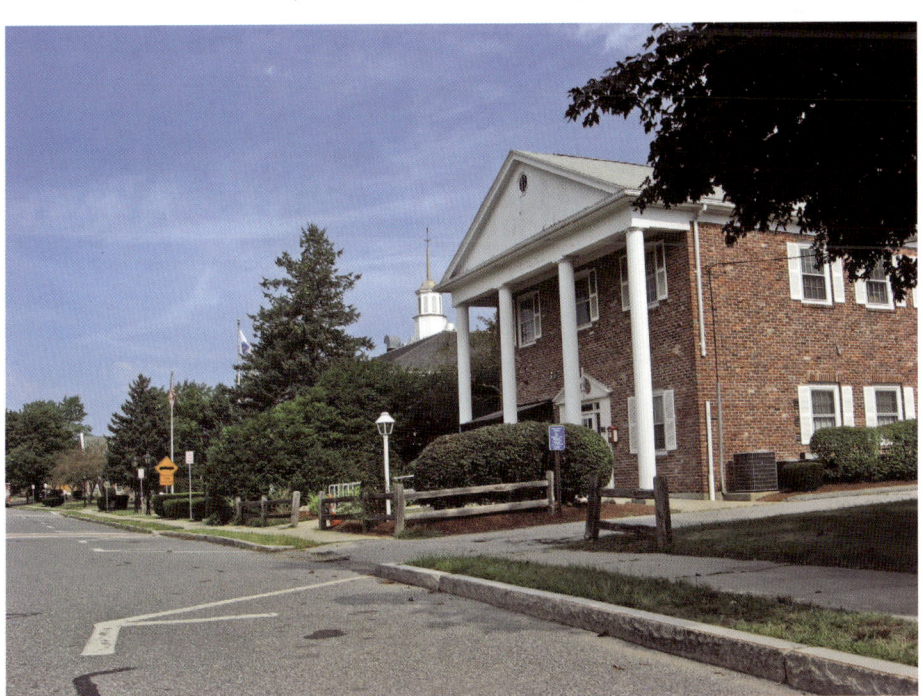

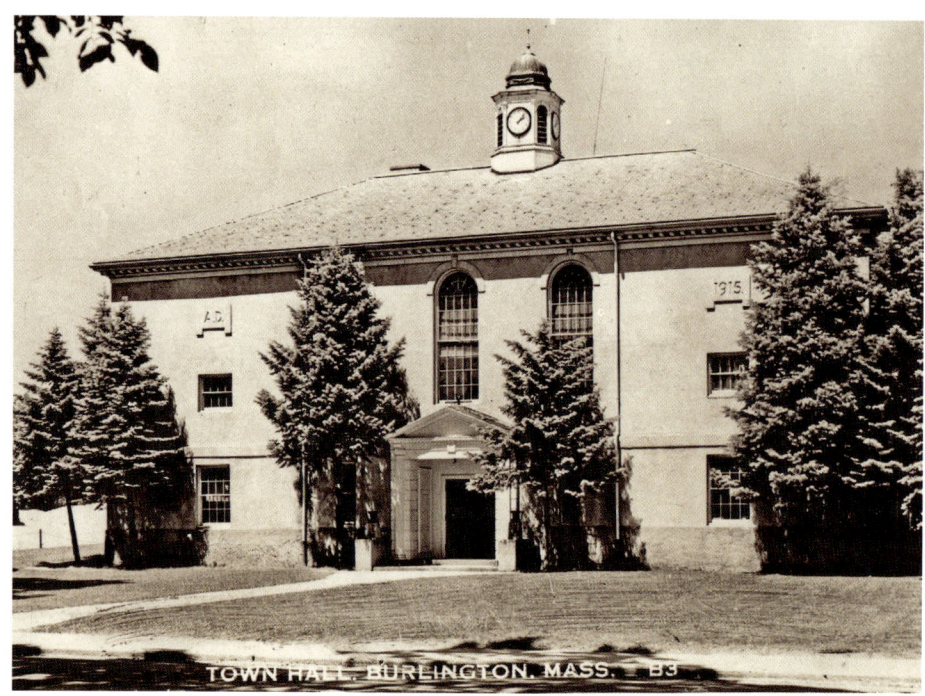

TOWN HALL. BURLINGTON, MASS. B3

THE SECOND TOWN HALL/ANNEX: Burlington's Second Town Hall was built in 1915 to replace the "Town House" which burned to the ground in 1902. It was a two-story stucco building with an auditorium that occupied the second level. The structure also had an office for the selectmen and a vault for storage. The Police Department was located here for a time, prior to the construction of a new building for the men in blue. The distinctive and functional Second Town Hall was demolished in 1969, and Town Hall Annex now stands at its former site.

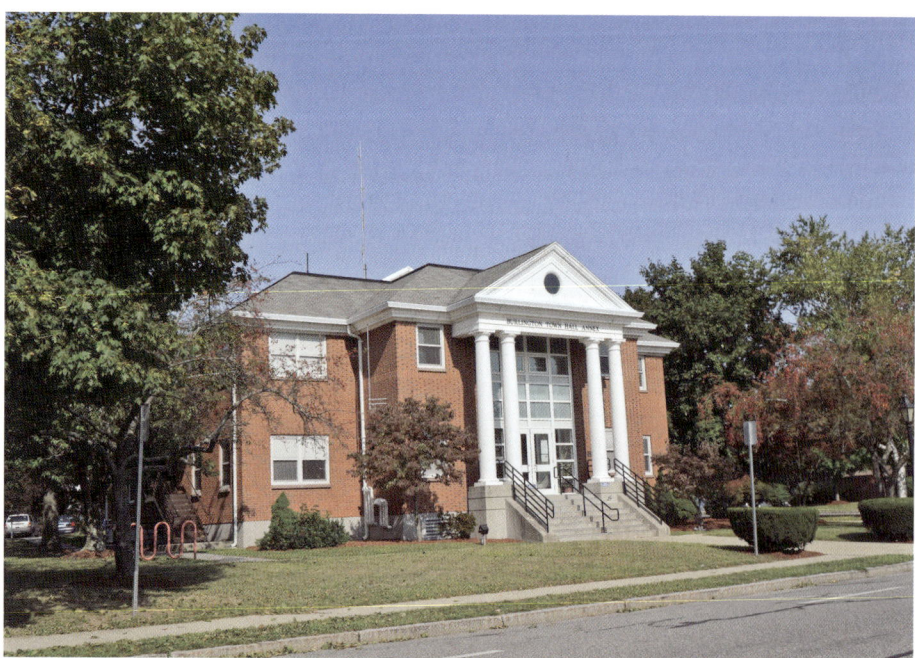

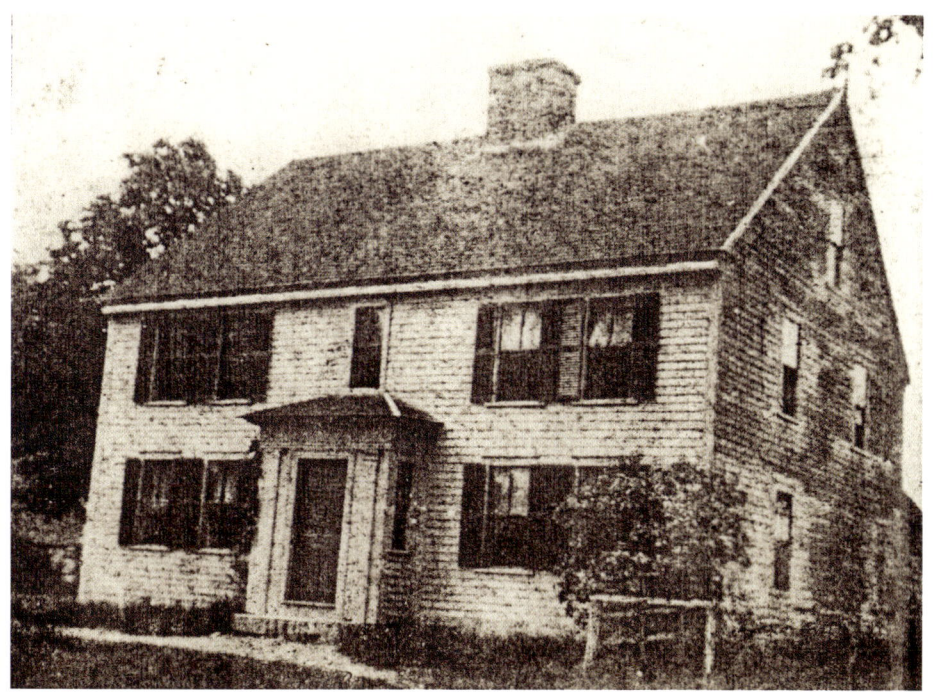

THE CAPTAIN JOHN WOOD TAVERN: Veteran of the French and Indian Wars in the 1750s, member of the militia from the 2nd Precinct at the Battles of Lexington and Concord in 1775 and one of the founding fathers of the town of Burlington in 1799, Captain John Wood was a true patriot and leader. Born in Woburn's Second Parish or Precinct in 1740, he joined the local militia at age sixteen and served in the French and Indian War and later the American Revolution. Captain Wood built his house in the center of town in 1764. (Scan BTA) (RJC/IMAGE)

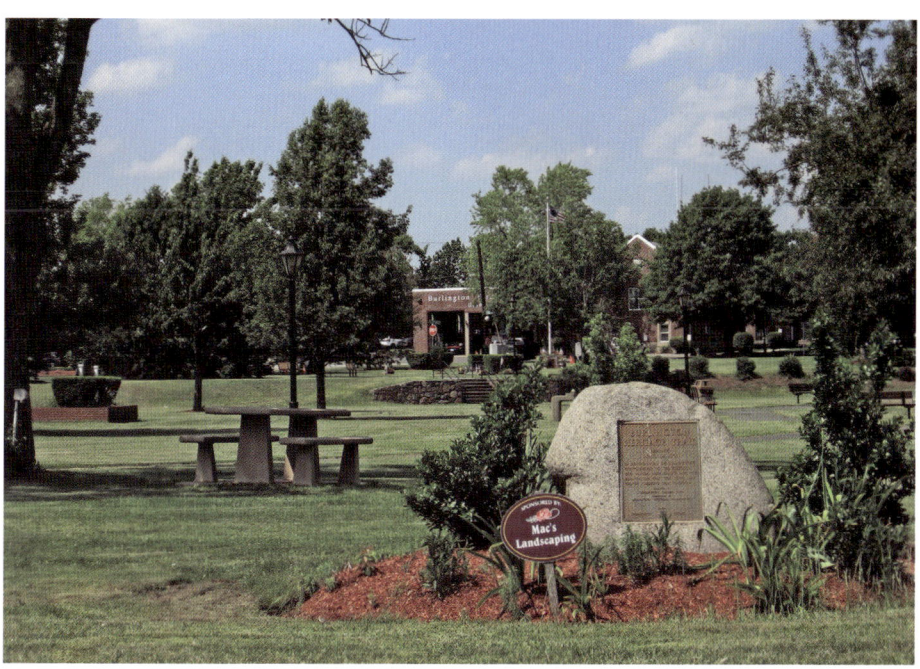

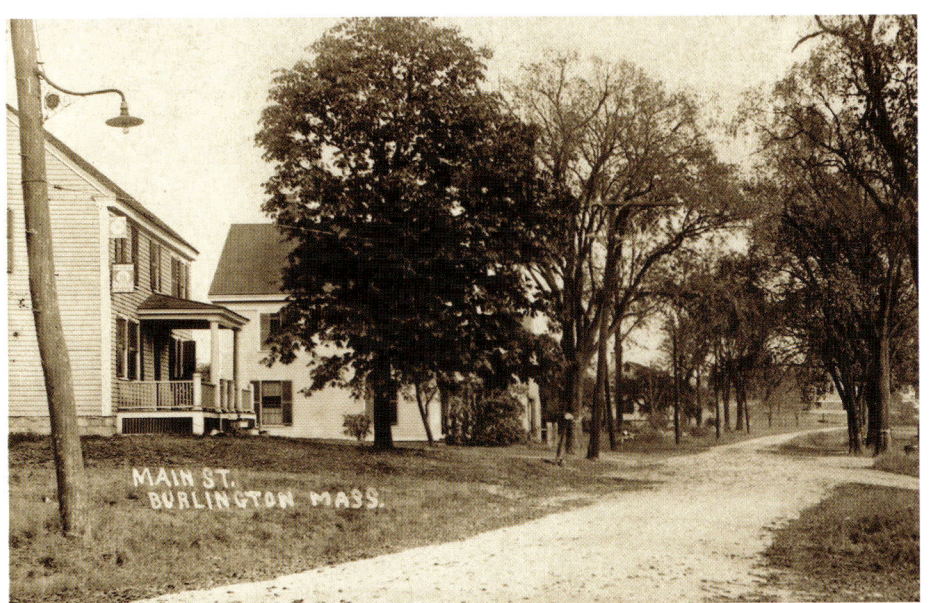

**MAIN STREET/WOOD TAVERN:**  The Wood Tavern has a close historical connection to the very founding of the town of Burlington that was incorporated on February 28, 1799. Captain Wood operated a tavern at his home after the American Revolution. It was here, on March 18, 1799, that the new town of Burlington celebrated its creation with a town-wide banquet held in the second story "social hall". By 1957 the town had acquired the property and later razed the tavern. In 1959 a new fire station was built on the site and later renovated to its current configuration. (SCAN/BTA) (RJC/IMAGE)

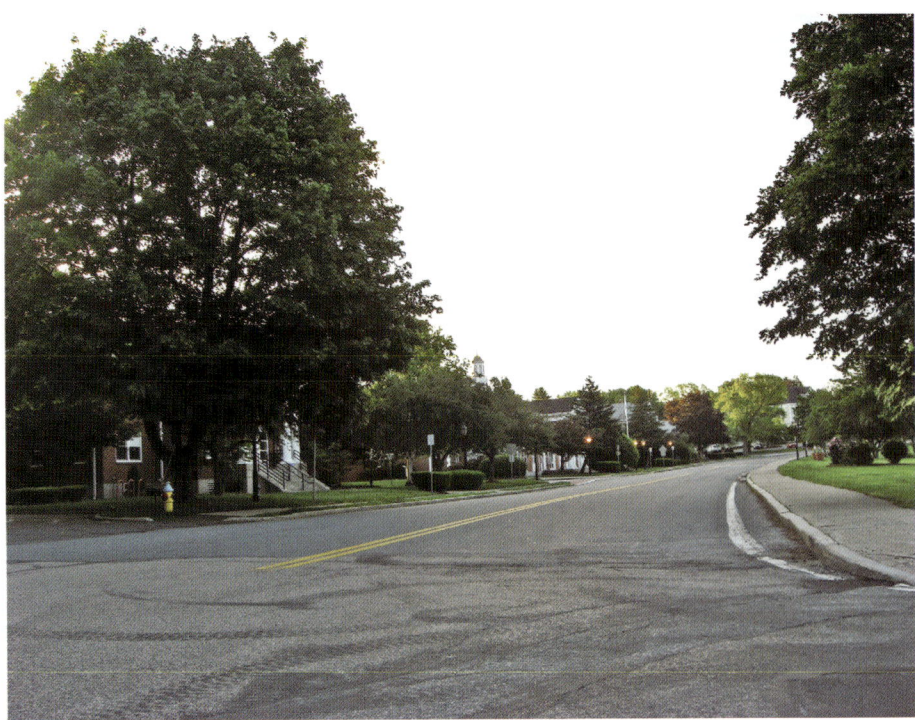

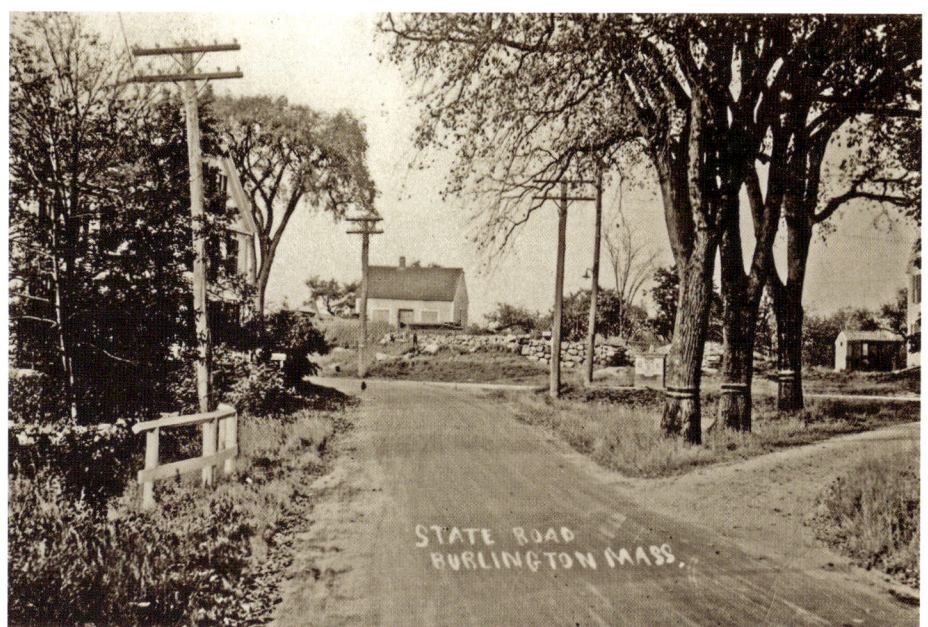

"THE TRIANGLE": The three great elm trees you see on the right in the *c.* 1900 image stood at the intersection of Cambridge Street, Center Street and Olympian Way at a spot locally called "the Triangle." The town scales were once located here, a vital necessity to a small agricultural community. The large elm on the left shades the Gleason-Bennet-Simonds House, a large complex with a barn and separate connected farmhouse. The Burlington Garden Club maintains a connection with our agricultural past with their yearly plantings in the "Triangle". (SCAN/BTA) (RJC/IMAGE)

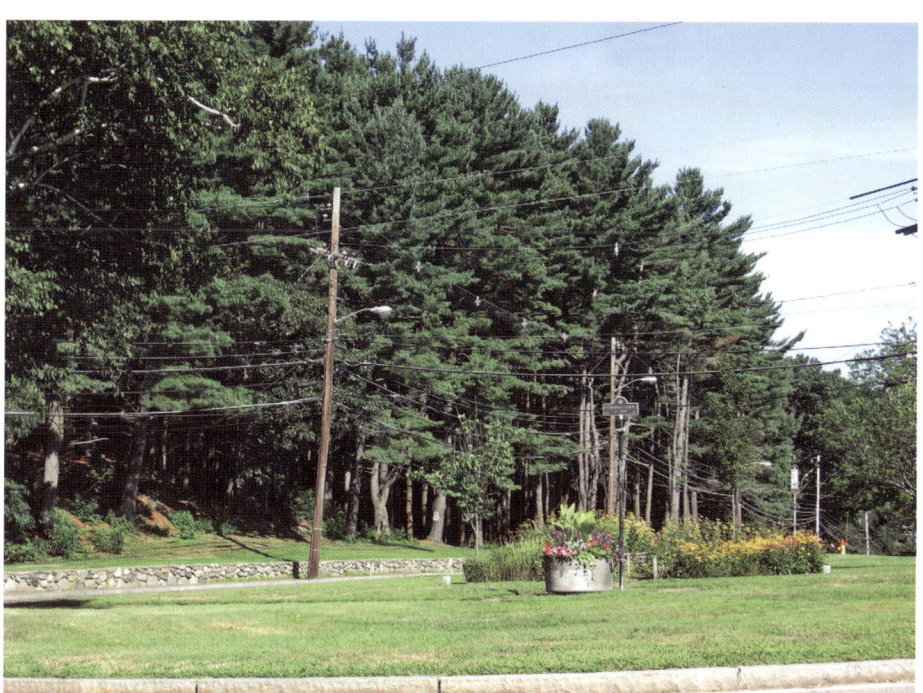

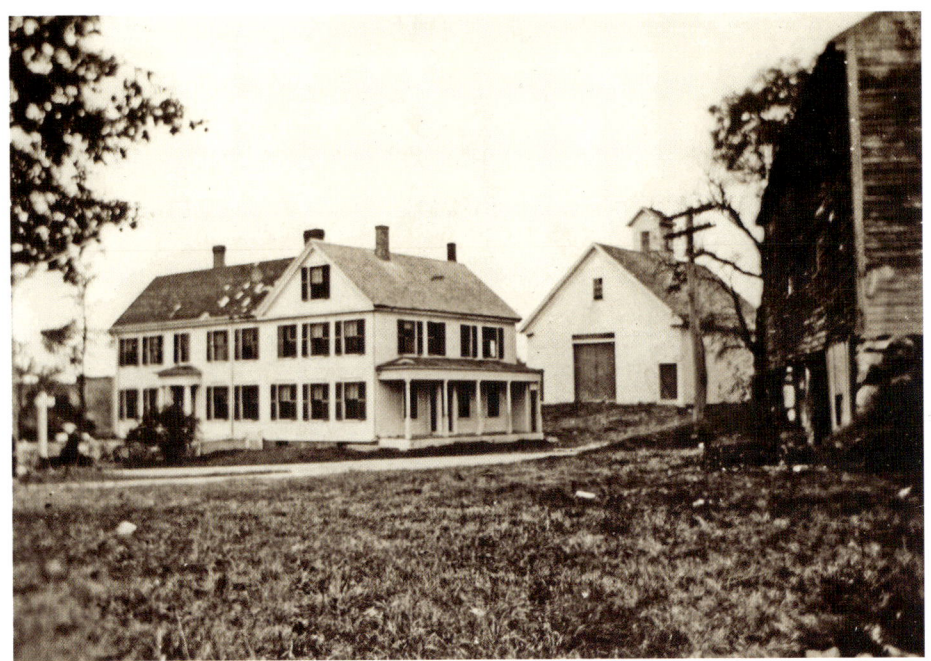

**THE GLEASON-BENNETT-SIMONDS HOUSE:** The extensive farm complex, the Simonds House, was built prior to 1851 and originally stood on a sharp curve on Cambridge Street across from today's Olympian Way. In 1920 the State widened and straightened Cambridge Street and the house was split in two and moved. The town library was once located in this section, in the center of the pre-1920 image. The barn pictured in the rear was also moved. (SCAN/BTA) (RJC/IMAGE)

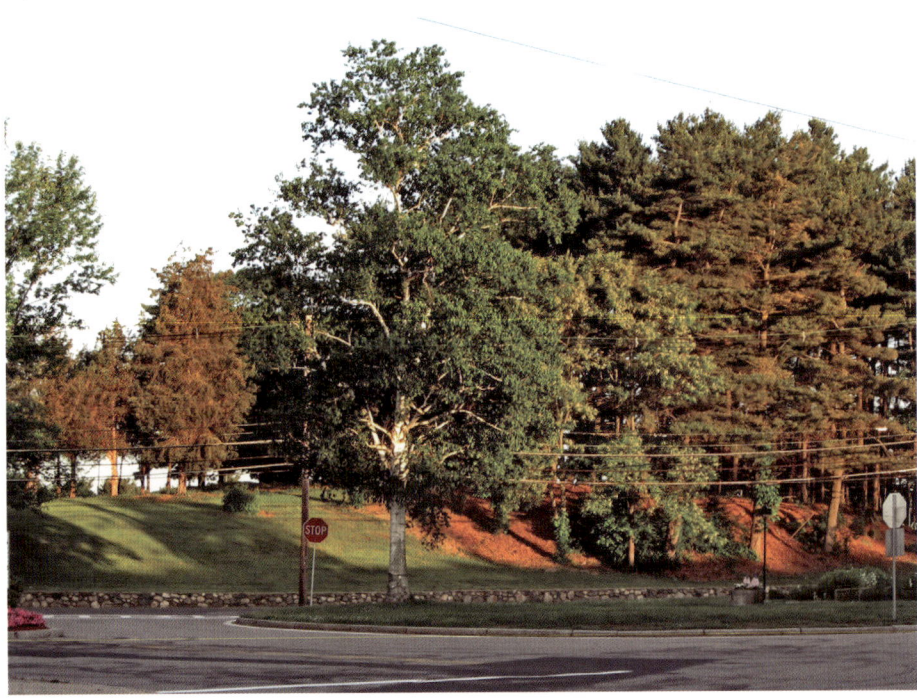

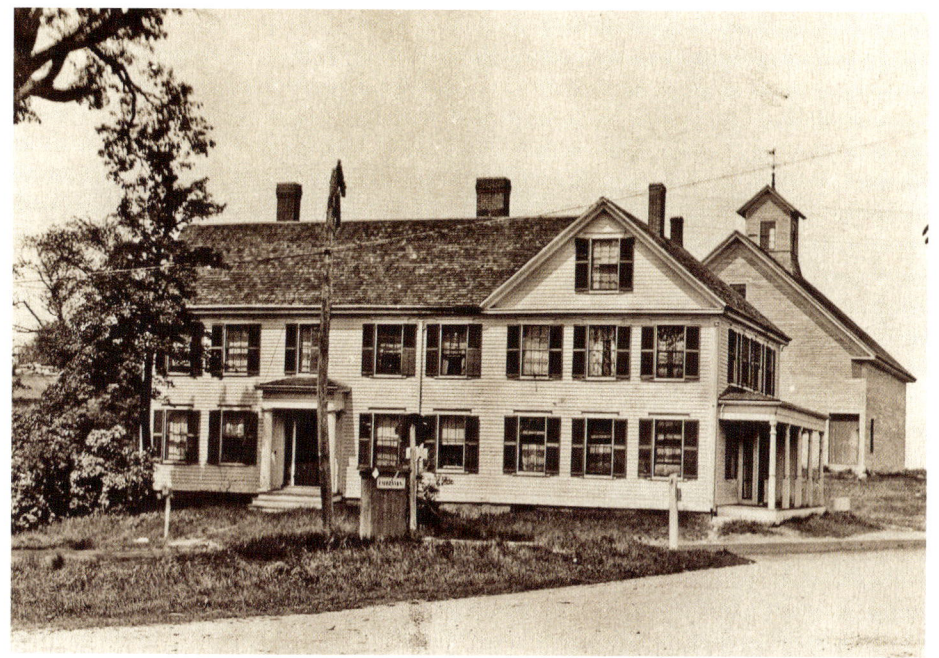

**SIMONDS HOUSE:** This imposing combination of various architectural styles once housed Burlington's Post Office and Library. In the early image, the box in the center was for mail. Marshall Simonds, one of the most generous benefactors in town history, purchased "the Block" as it was known, sometime prior to his death in 1905. The half of the house that was moved to Mill Street stands proudly today as a private home. (SCAN/BTA) (RJC/IMAGE)

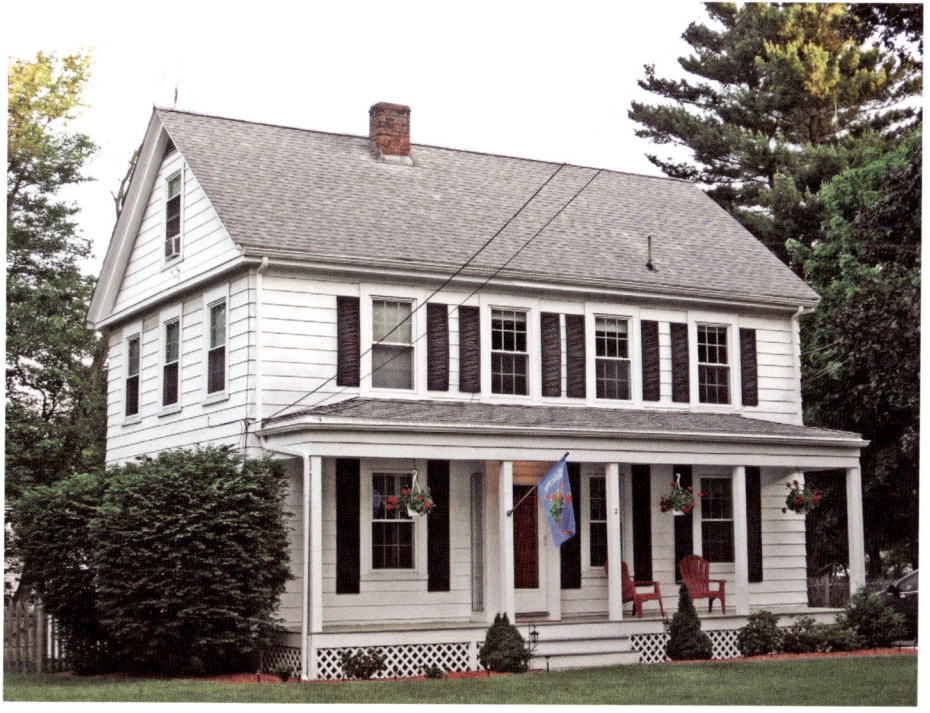

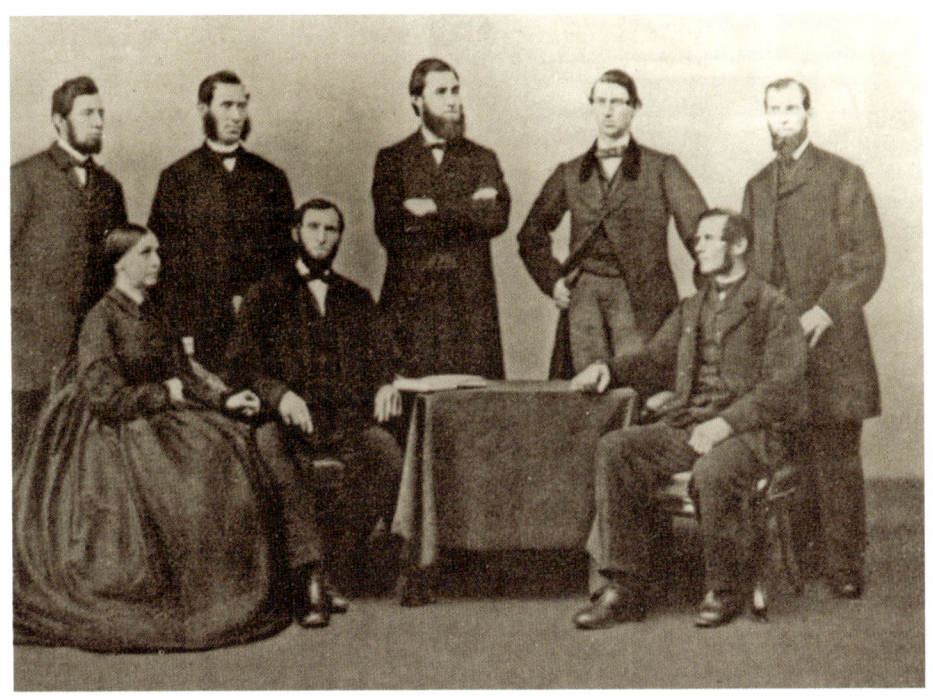

THE SIMONDS FAMILY: Marshall Simonds is featured standing, second from the left in this family photograph. After earning a fortune in western real estate and business, Marshall returned to the place of his birth, purchased a large farm complex off the Common, and later moved to Woburn. Marshall Simonds died in 1905 and in his will bequeathed to the town of his birth his house, barn, land and a sum of money. Today many Burlington residents enjoy the beautiful Simonds Park, above the site of the old homestead. (SCAN/BTA) (RJC/IMAGE)

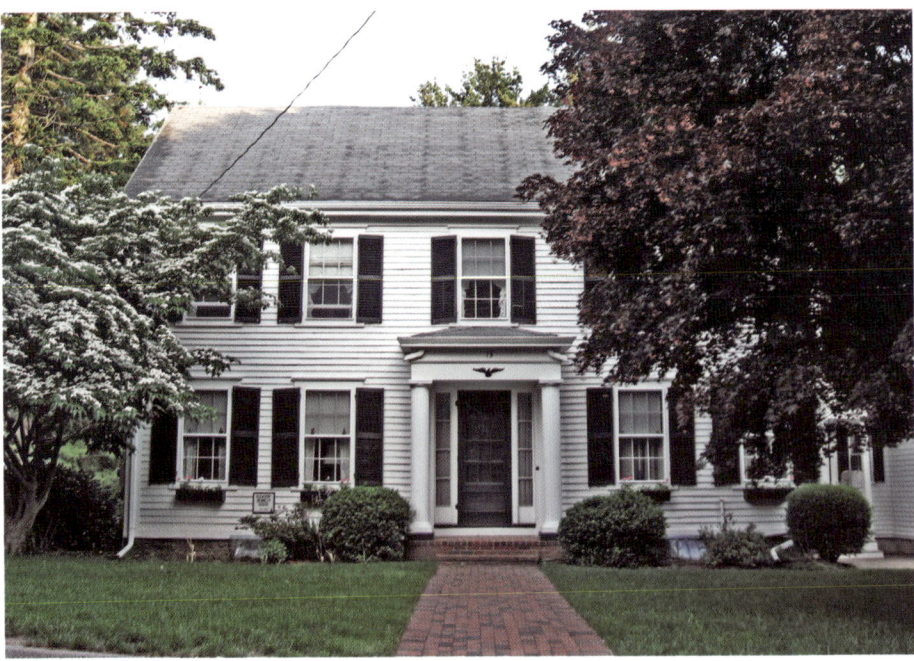

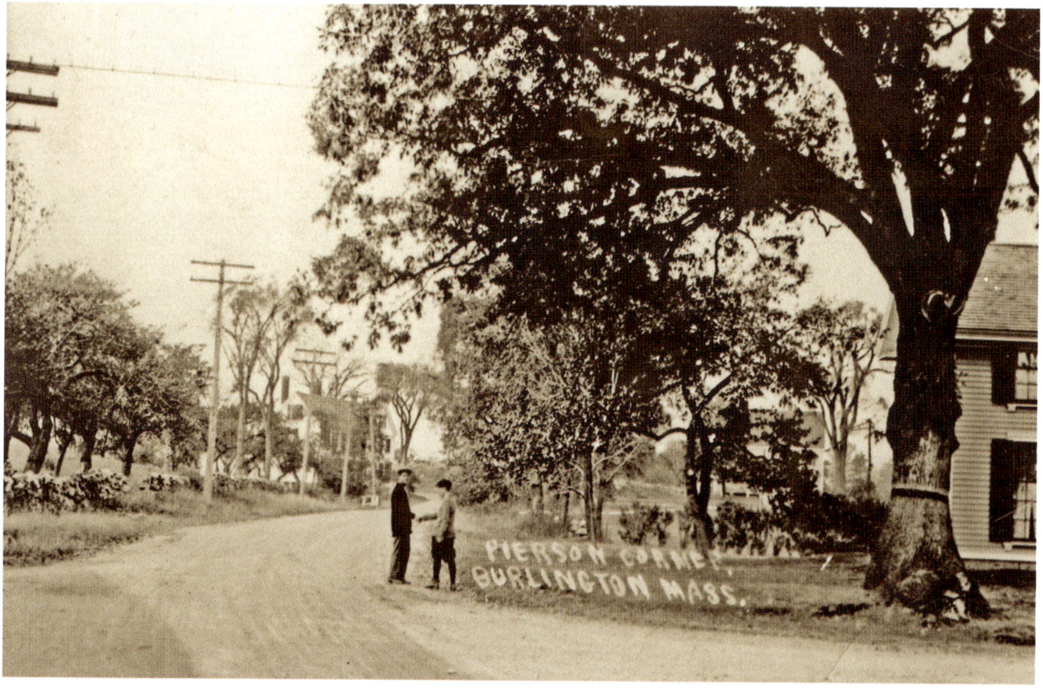

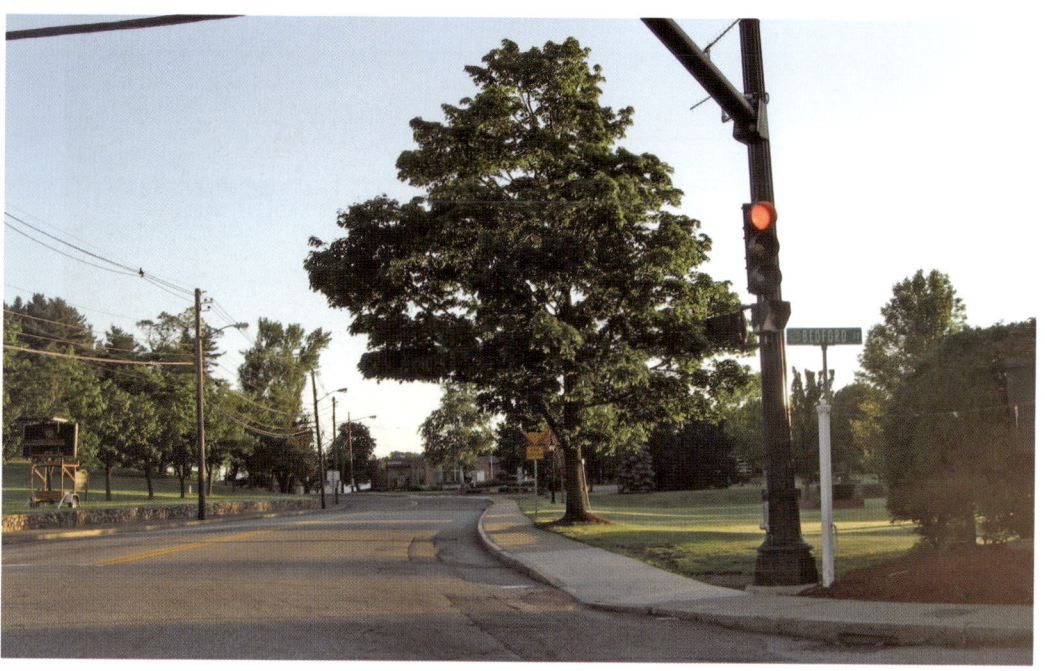

"PIERSONS CORNER": The Pierson-Symmes house once stood on the Town Common, on the corner of Bedford and Cambridge Street. The house was built sometime between 1827–1864 and later moved to Sears Street. This ancient road was laid out by the Puritan settlers in the 1630s to connect Boston with the "frontier" settlements of Woburn and Billerica. Known over the years as Up Street, Cambridge Street, State Road or Route 3A  it is today one of the busiest roads in Burlington. (SCAN/BTA) (RJC/IMAGE)

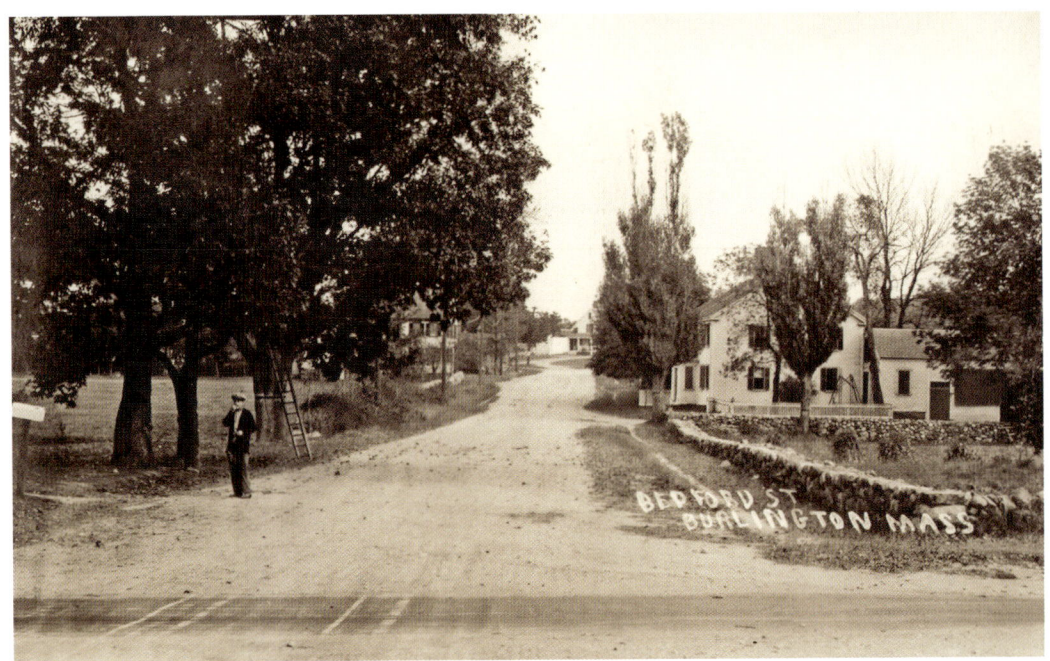

**BEDFORD/CENTER STREETS:** Streetcars on tracks once ran down this road, the intersection of Bedford Street and the State Road (Route 3A) *c.* 1900. In both images the Grand View Farm is visible in the center back. In the early image, the building on the Common (left) is the Prescott House, which was moved before 1950 to 36 Bedford Street. The General John Walker House is seen on the right in both photographs. (SCAN/BTA) (RJC/IMAGE)

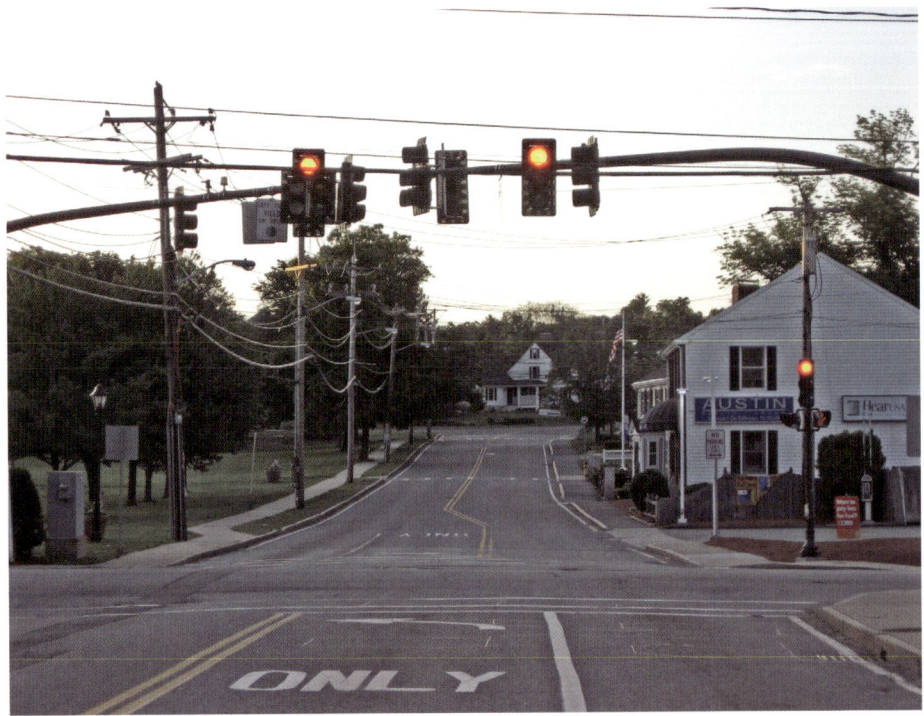

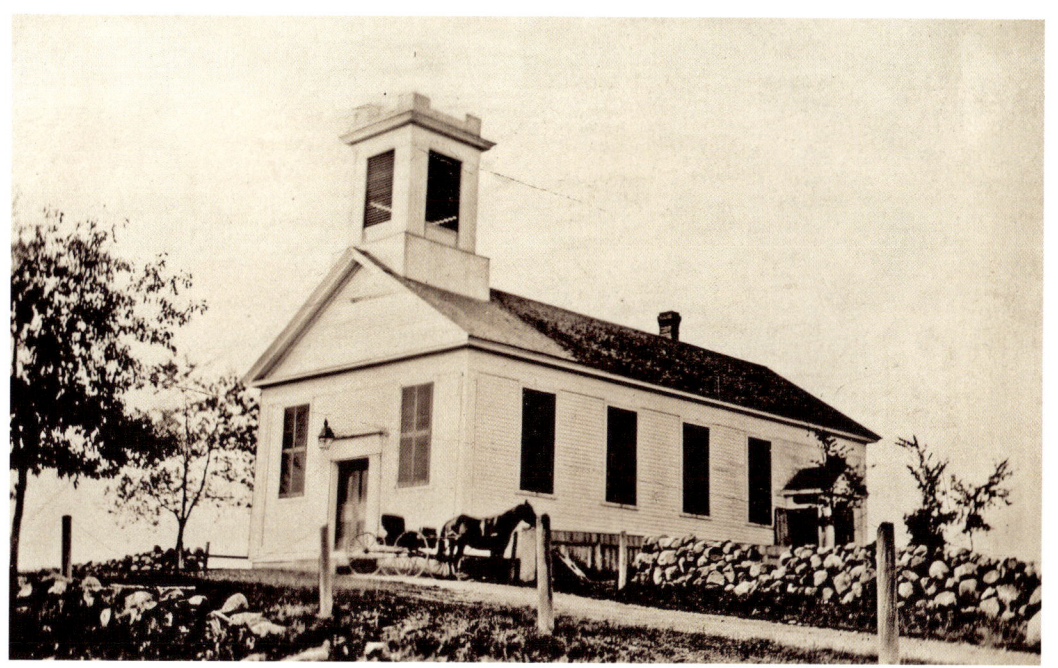

**TOWN HOUSE 1844:** "Forrest Field Hill" is the location of several significant historic structures that once stood and, in some cases, still stand today. Burlington's first town hall or "Town House" was built in 1844 atop the hill, on land now occupied by the town's Simonds Park. Many historical artifacts and documents were housed here. The Town House was also the center of activity for political and town wide social events. In May of 1902, the Town House burned to the ground and many valuable historical items and records were lost. (SCAN/BTA) (RJC/IMAGE)

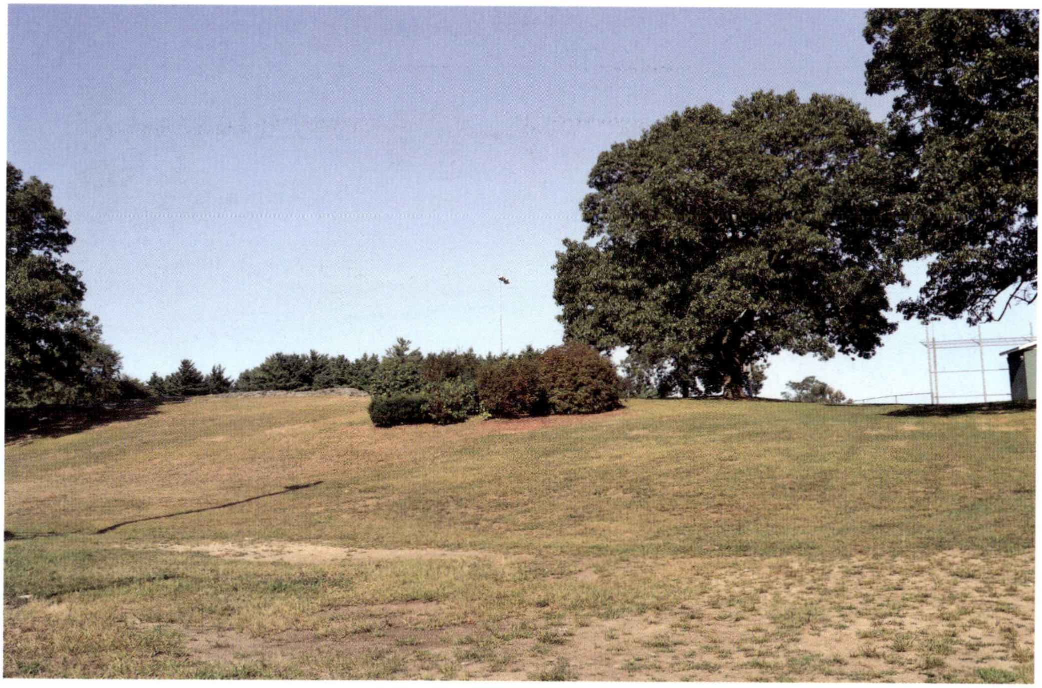

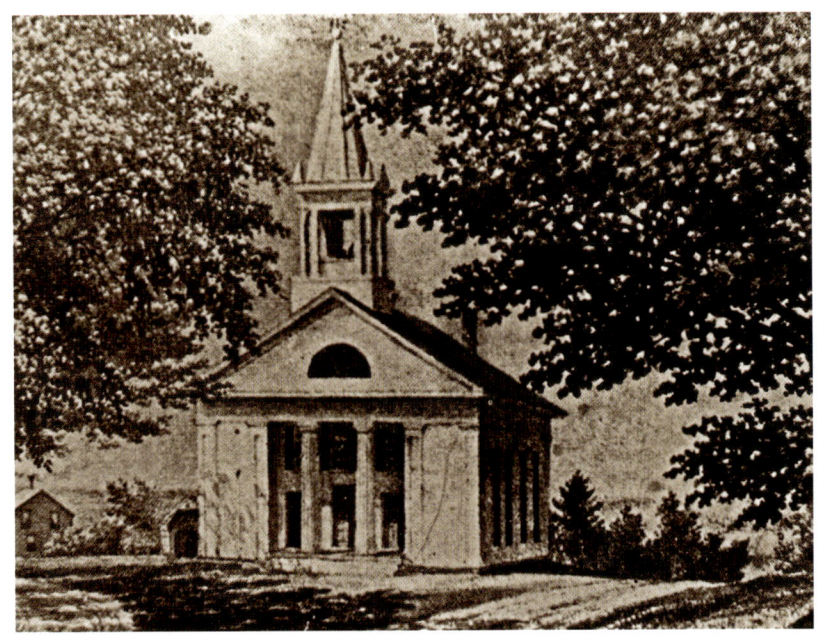

**SECOND PARISH MEETING HOUSE/1846:** When the area was separated from Woburn in 1730 to become the Second Parish, the need for a Meeting House arose. On July 23, 1732, the Second Parish Meeting House was raised atop Forrest Field Hill. Dating to Puritan days, the "meeting house" was not only the epicenter of the town's religious life, but also the center of early New England town government. In the illustration, the United Church of Christ Congregational, as it is known today, reflects its remodeling done in 1846. A steeple was added as well as Greek Revival style columns. (SCAN/RJC) (RJC/IMAGE)

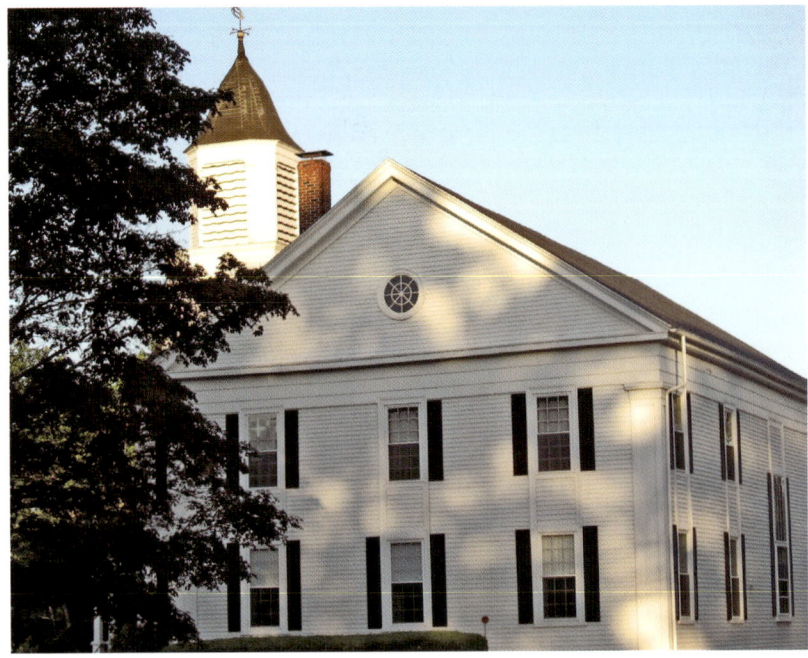

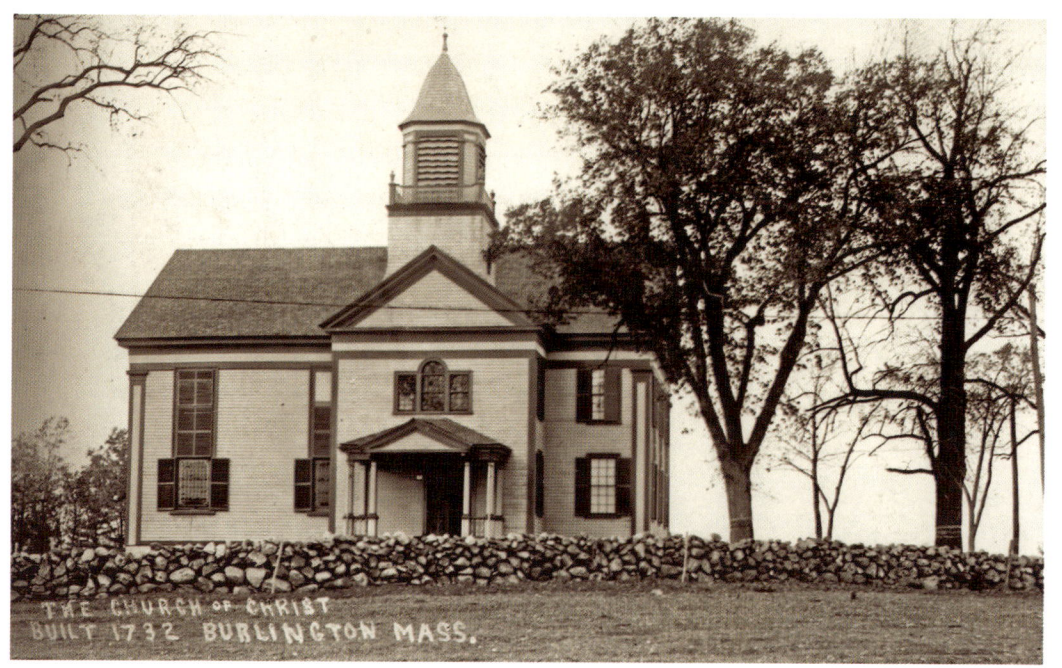

THE CHURCH OF CHRIST
BUILT 1732 BURLINGTON MASS.

**UCC 1888/Lexington Street:** The "Meeting House", today's United Church of Christ Congregation, is historically significant as a First Period (1630–1740) building with a still active congregation. In 1888, the steeple of 1846 and columns were removed, ten feet was added on the north side and the bell tower was installed. In 1990, the building was added to the National Register of Historic Places. The Second Parish Meeting House/UCC has been an enduring symbol of the heritage of the town of Burlington. (SCAN/RJC) (RJC/IMAGE)

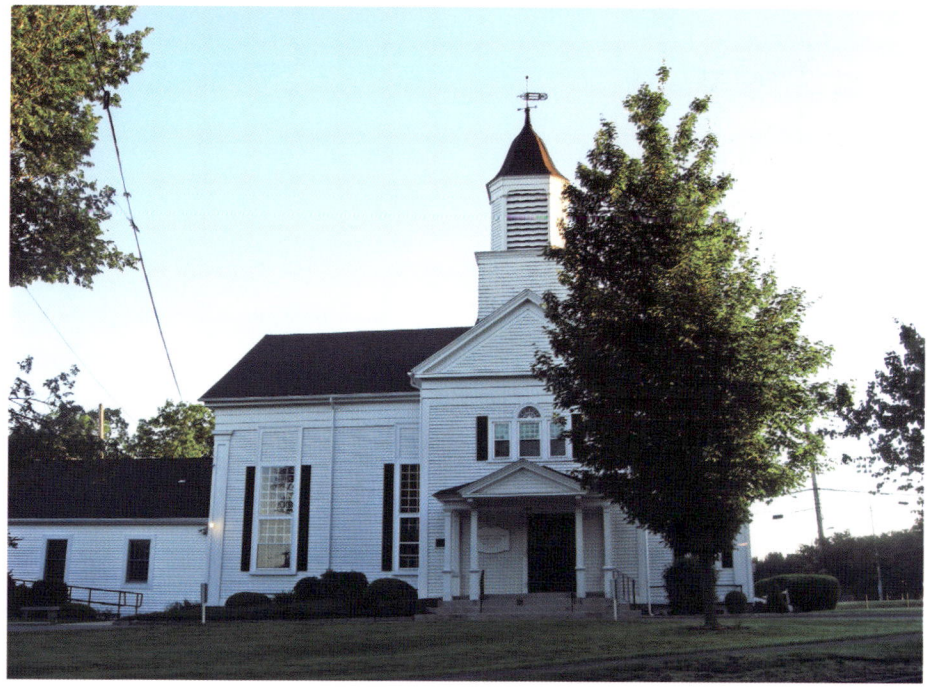

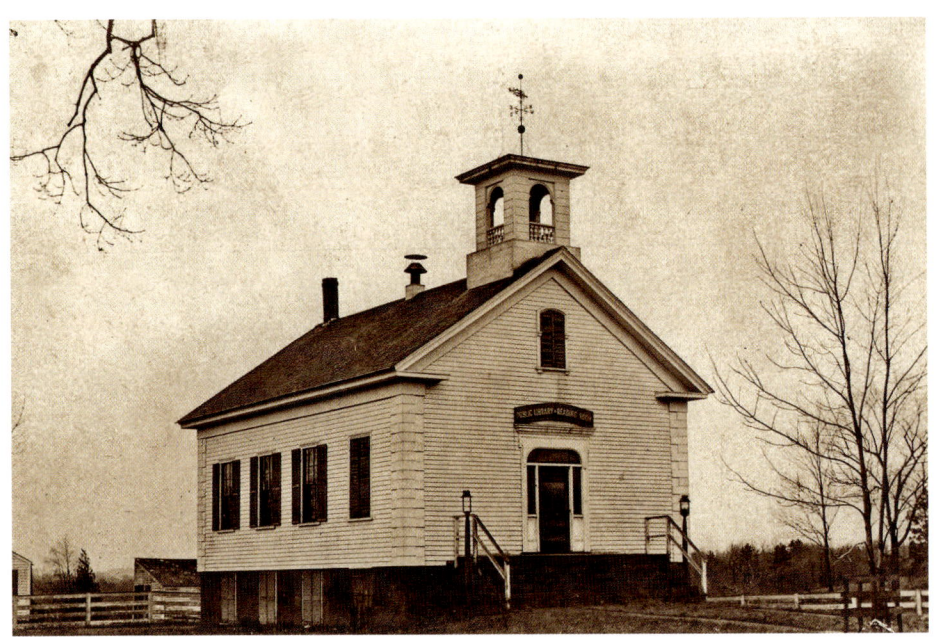

**CENTER SCHOOL 1855/MUSEUM:** School, library, temporary police station, and now the flagship of the Town Museum complex, The Center School was built in 1855 and has survived flooding and firebombing. When the Union School opened in 1898, The Center School was reborn as the town's library. On August 25, 1970, it was nearly destroyed by fire sparked by an explosive device, during its tenure as a temporary police station. The crime was never solved. (SCAN/BTA) (RJC/IMAGE)

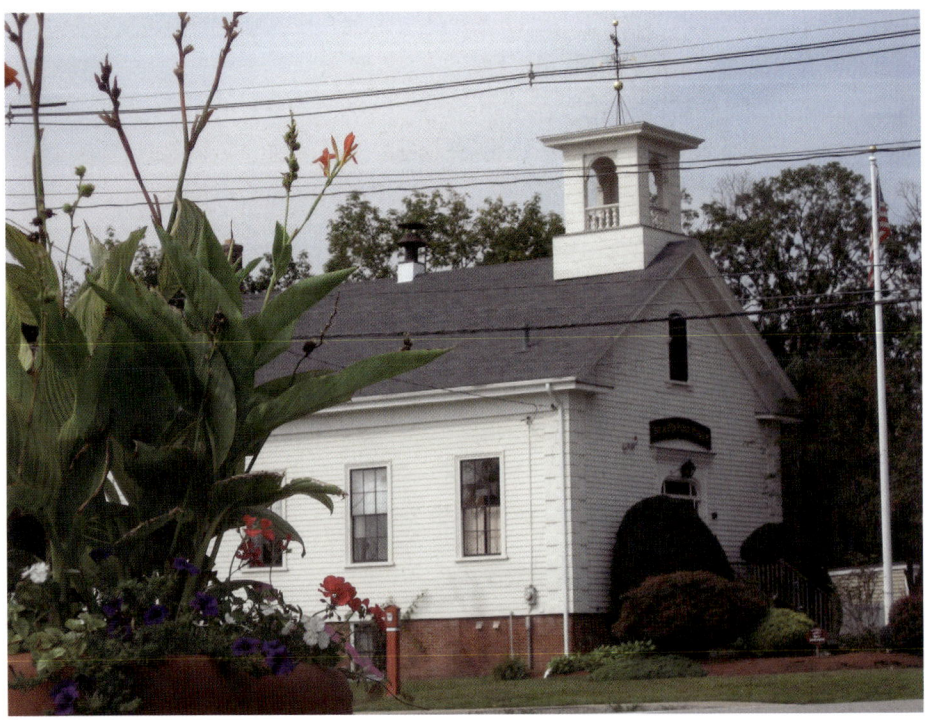

## Rev. James Walker/Walker House:

Rev. Dr. James Walker was born in 1794, in Woburn's Second Parish in the homestead that still stands today. The Walker house was built by his grandfather Captain Joshua and father John in 1780. Educated in Burlington, James attended Harvard College, graduating in 1814. Walker was an ordained minister and a founder of the American Unitarian Association. Dr. James Walker taught at Harvard from 1839–1853 and became President of Harvard College in 1853. (SCAN/BTA) (RJC/IMAGE)

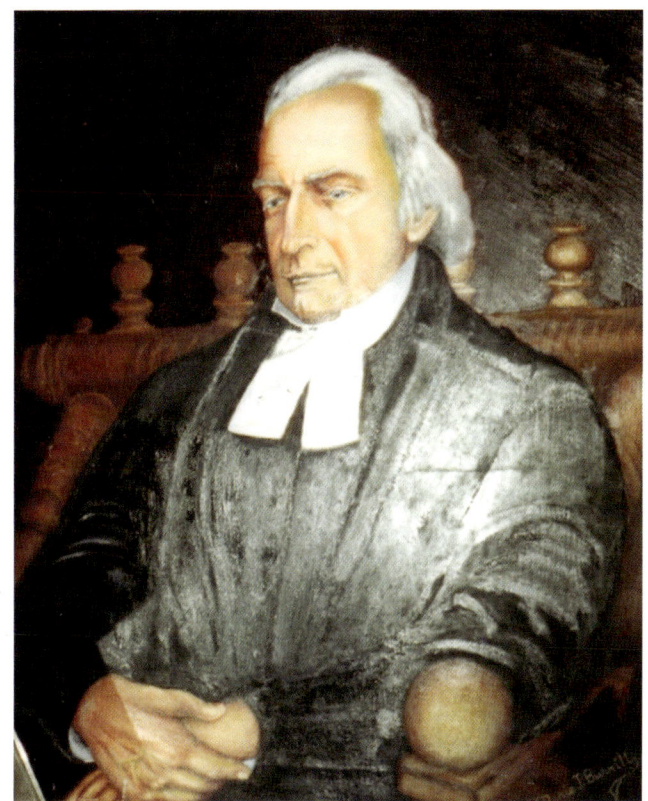

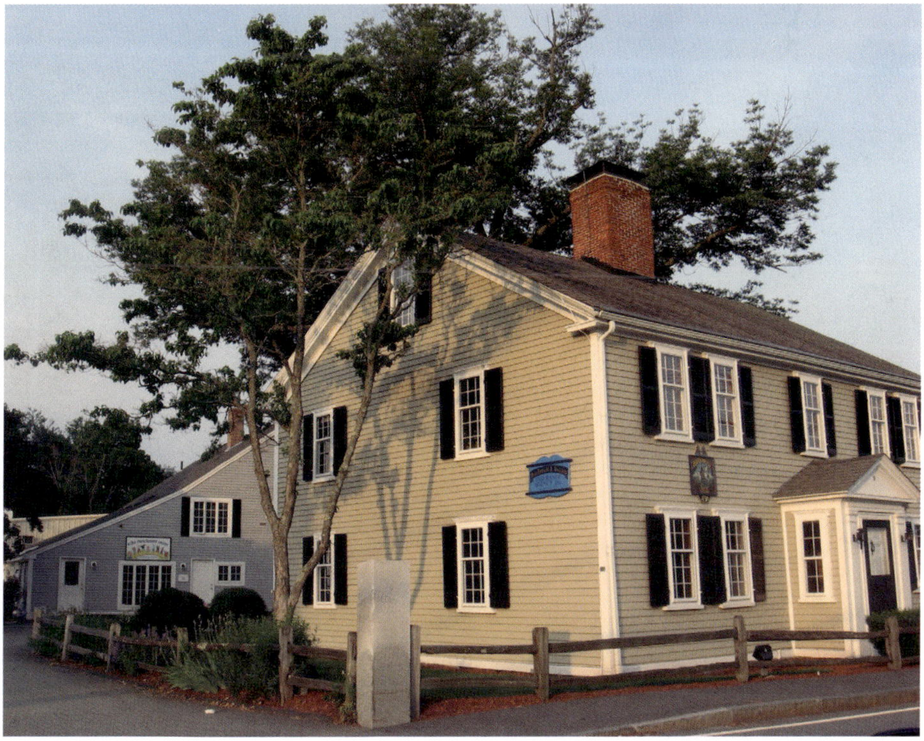

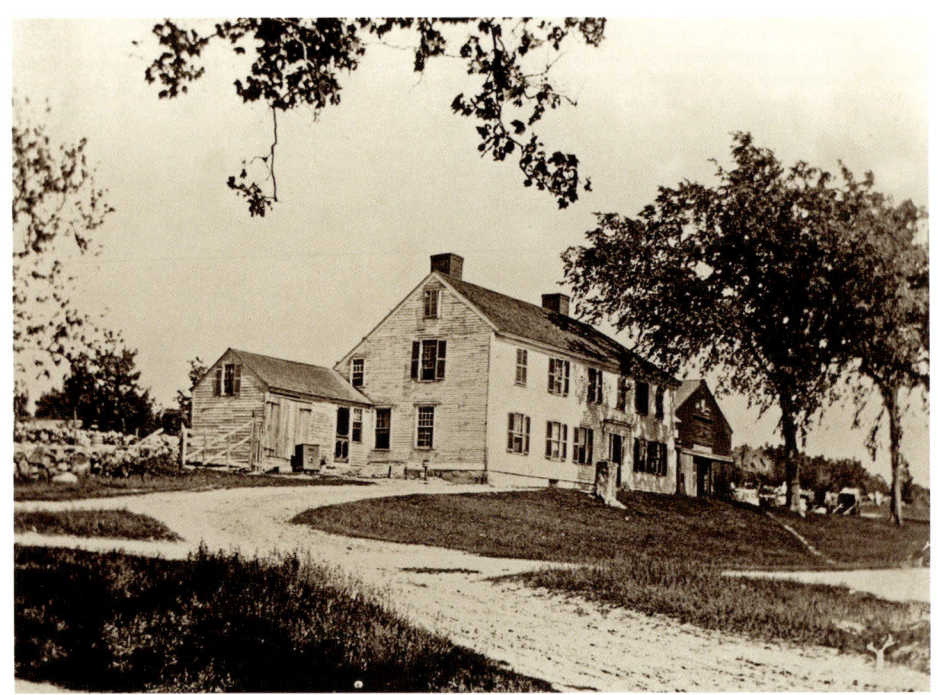

**GRANDVIEW FARM/MARION TAVERN:** Grandview Farm (also known as the McIntire Farm or Marion Tavern) was a significant architectural landmark as an outstanding example of a nineteenth century connected farmhouse complex. The structure, long a recognizable site to townspeople, was in poor condition by the end of the twentieth century. It was acquired by the town and is being completely modernized. The complex was known as the Marion Tavern for a time in the mid-nineteenth century, a stagecoach stop on the Boston-Lowell Route. (SCAN/BTA) (RJC/IMAGE)

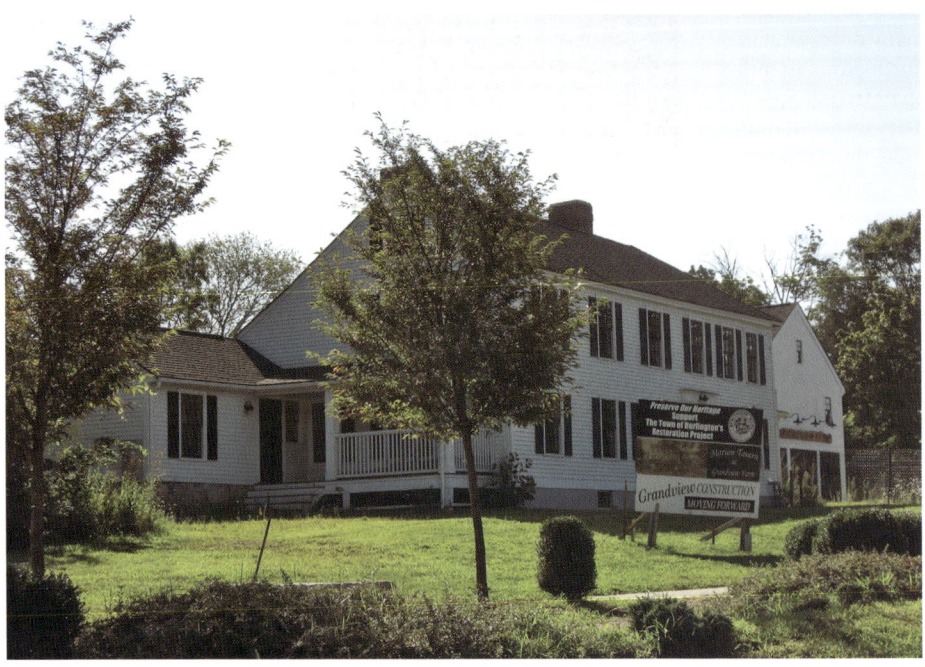

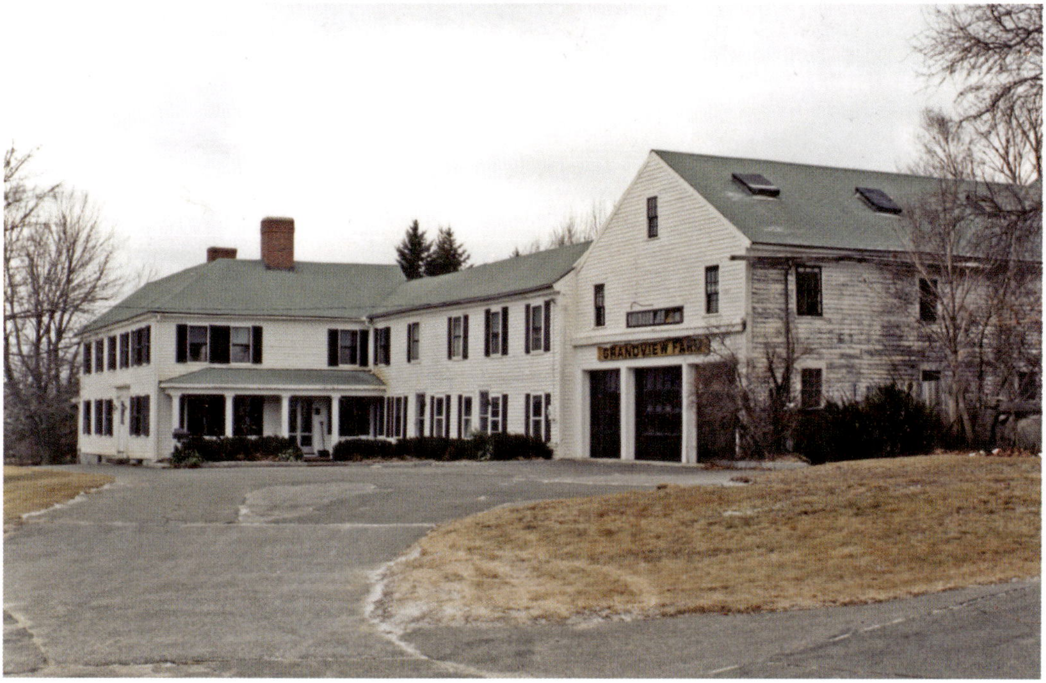

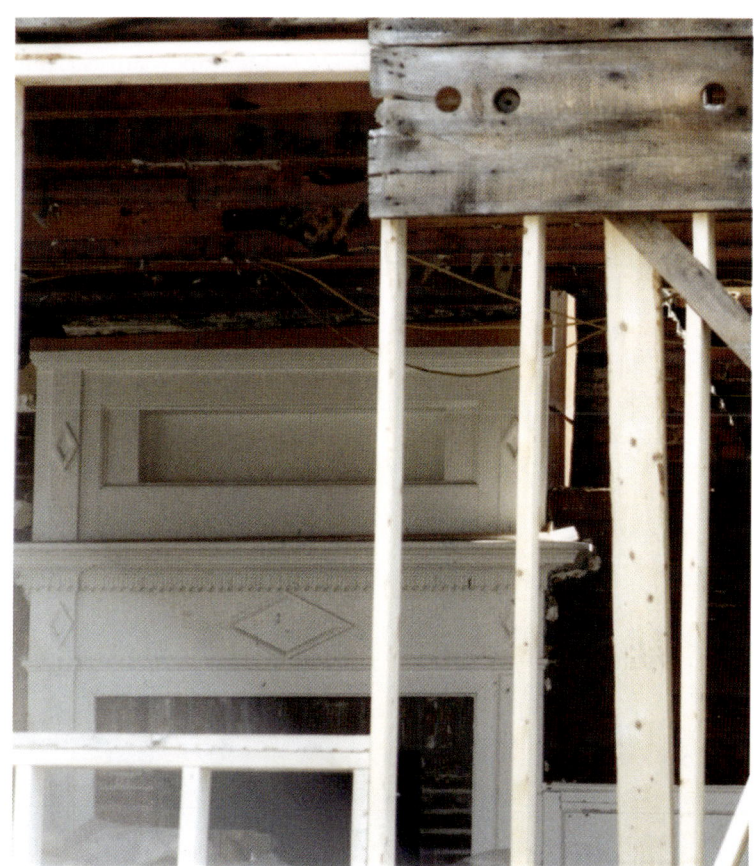

**GRANDVIEW FARM/MANTEL:**
The "grand view" that Charles McIntire saw when he purchased the property in 1870, was of Mt. Wachusett many miles west of Burlington. McIntire operated a large dairy farm and milk route for many years. He was related to the well known Federal Era architect Samuel McIntire. It is said that the mantel you see in the renovation image was Samuel's work. The view from the farm today is of an apartment complex. (SCAN/RJC) (RJC/IMAGE)

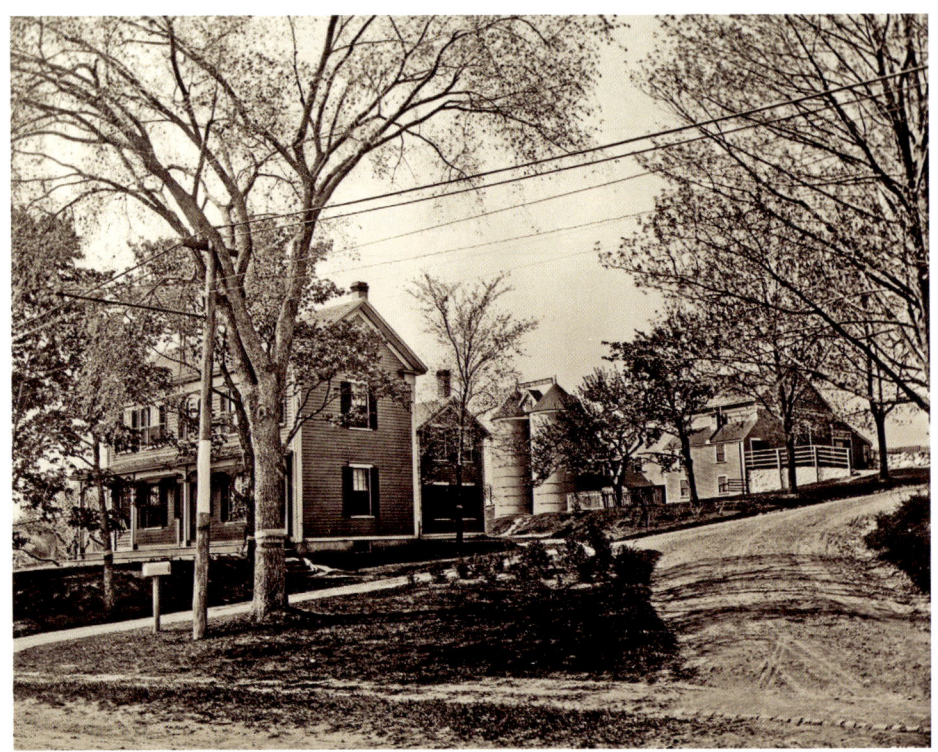

F. WALKER FARM: The Fred Freeland Walker Farm was located where the St. Margaret's Church complex and the Memorial School are located today. Walker also owned the farmhouse and land near the Middle School, known as the Walker Annex or Kerrigan Farmhouse. The Walker Farm, at its zenith *c.* 1910 had several barns, silos and even windmills. The farm was destroyed by another tragic Burlington fire, in 1930. (SCAN/BTA) (RJC/IMAGE)

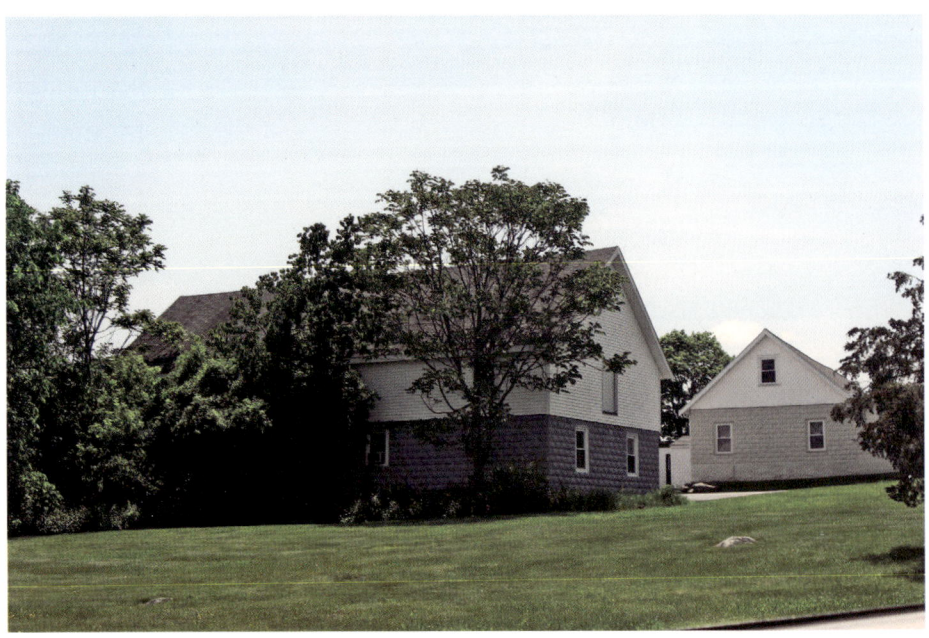

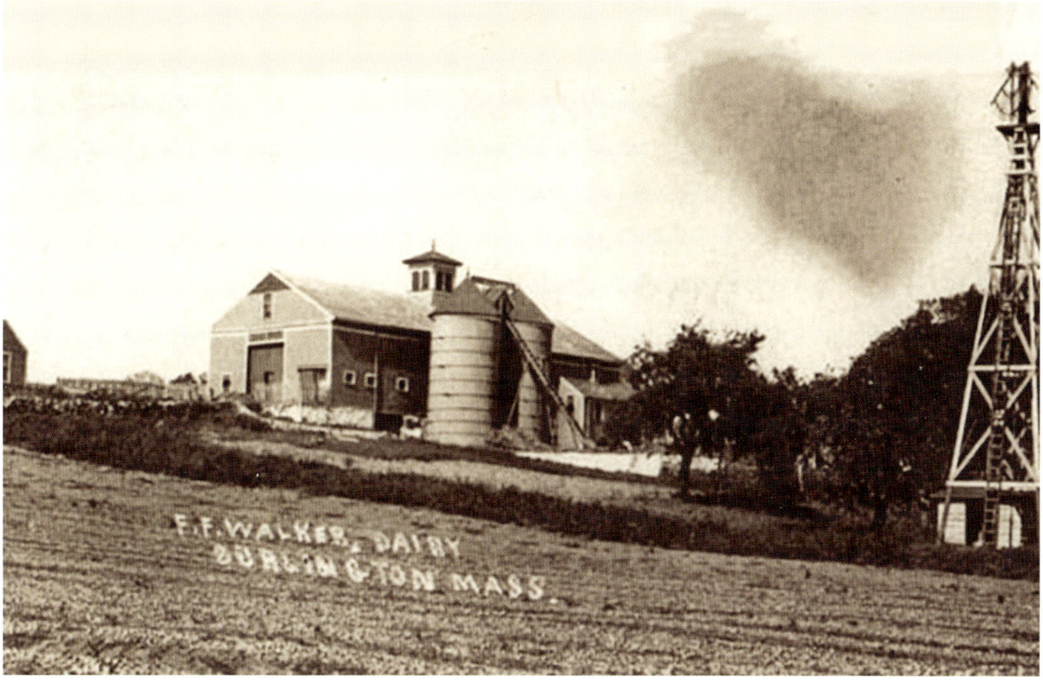

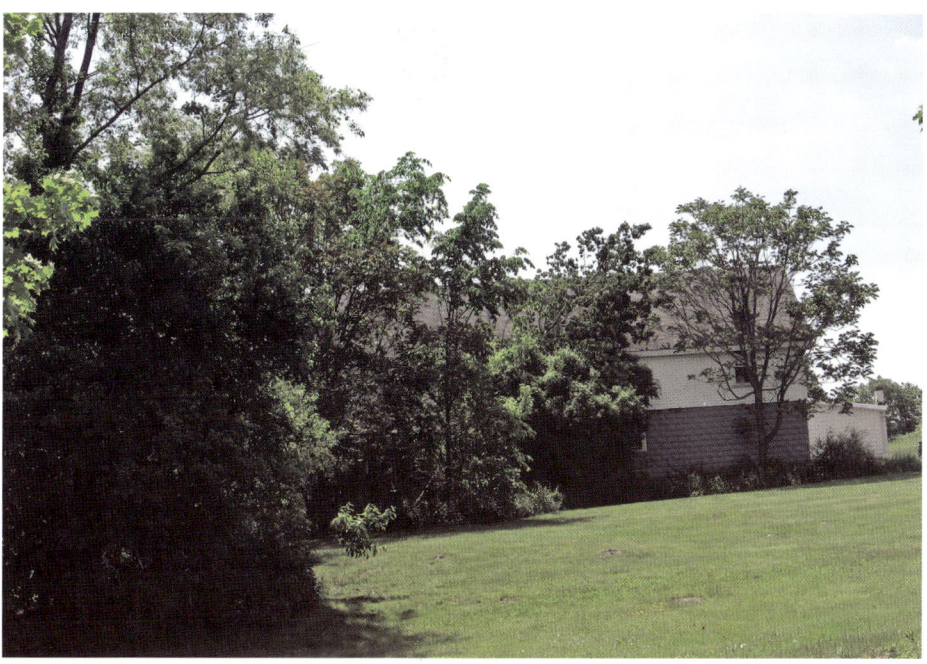

**WALKER FARM SILO:**  The *c.* 1910 pastoral image shows the F. F. Walker dairy farm in fine form, with barns, silos and windmill in place. The Walker family in America dates to early colonial times. The cannon, located on the north end of the Town Common, belonged to Samuel Walker who lived in the farmhouse still standing across Winn Street. The farm and most buildings were gone by the 1950s. The Memorial School, newly remodeled, stands on part of the site today. (SCAN/BTA) (RJC/IMAGE)

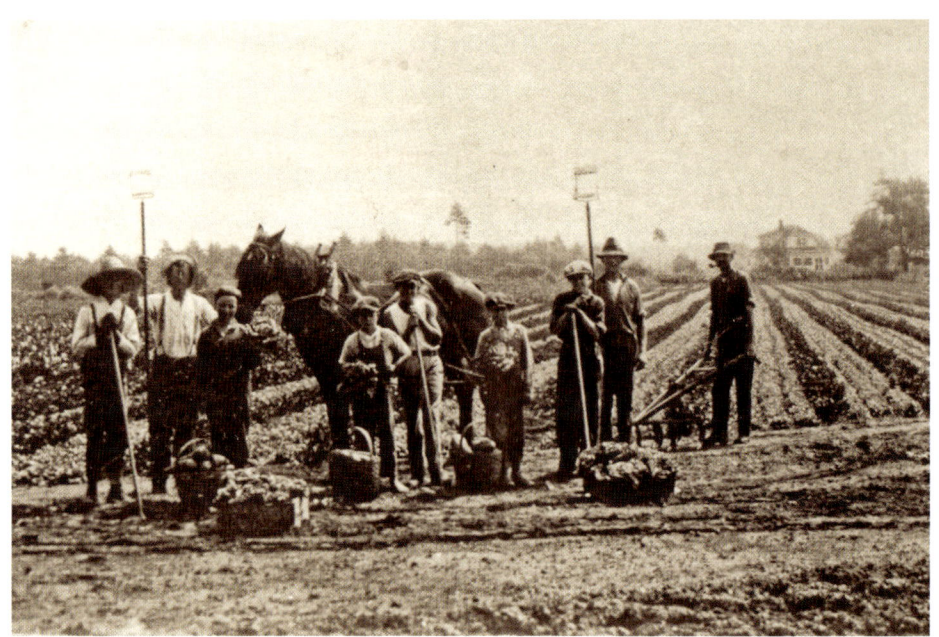

CRAWFORD FARM/ROUTE 128: Farmhands pose before the vast fields of the Crawford Farm, today located between Beacon Street and Newbridge Ave. The building of Route 128 in the 1950s split the farm in two, requiring a detour down Newbridge Avenue. Prior to the Crawford family ownership in the mid-twentieth century the land was farmed by generations of the Winn, Walker and Marion families. In colonial times the area was known as the Swamp Road. In 2013, it is the Winn Street exit to Interstate Route 95 (128). (SCAN/BTA) (RJC/IMAGE)

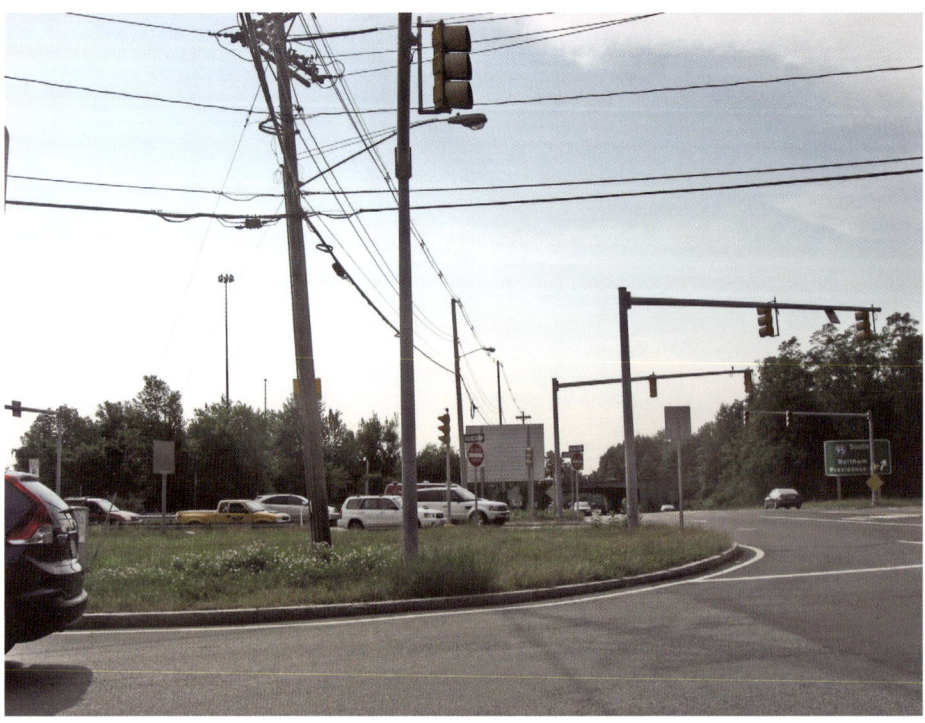

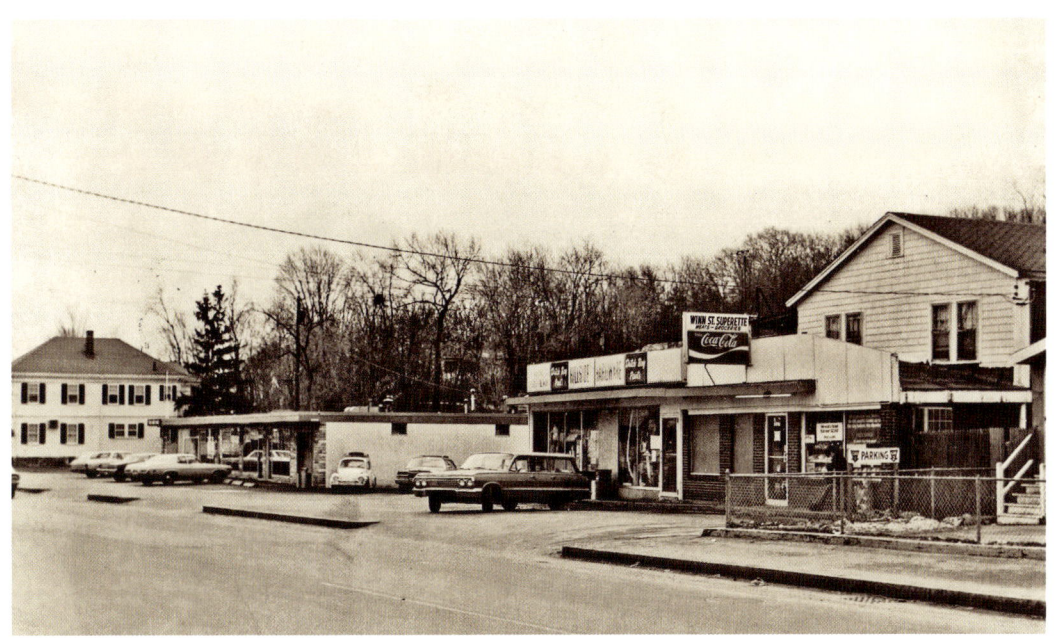

"WINNMERE": Settled very early in the town's history (1640s), the region of Woburn sometimes called 'Winnmere' has been a prosperous area. One of the founders of the town of Woburn (1642), Edward Winn and family built the first house (1642) in what is today the town of Burlington, on the corner of Winn Street and Wyman Street. Winnmere, Mt. Playnum, Copper Mtn. are all early names for this section of Burlington. As in its colonial past, small businesses still thrive in the "Winnmere" district of Burlington. (SCAN /BTA) (RJC/IMAGE)

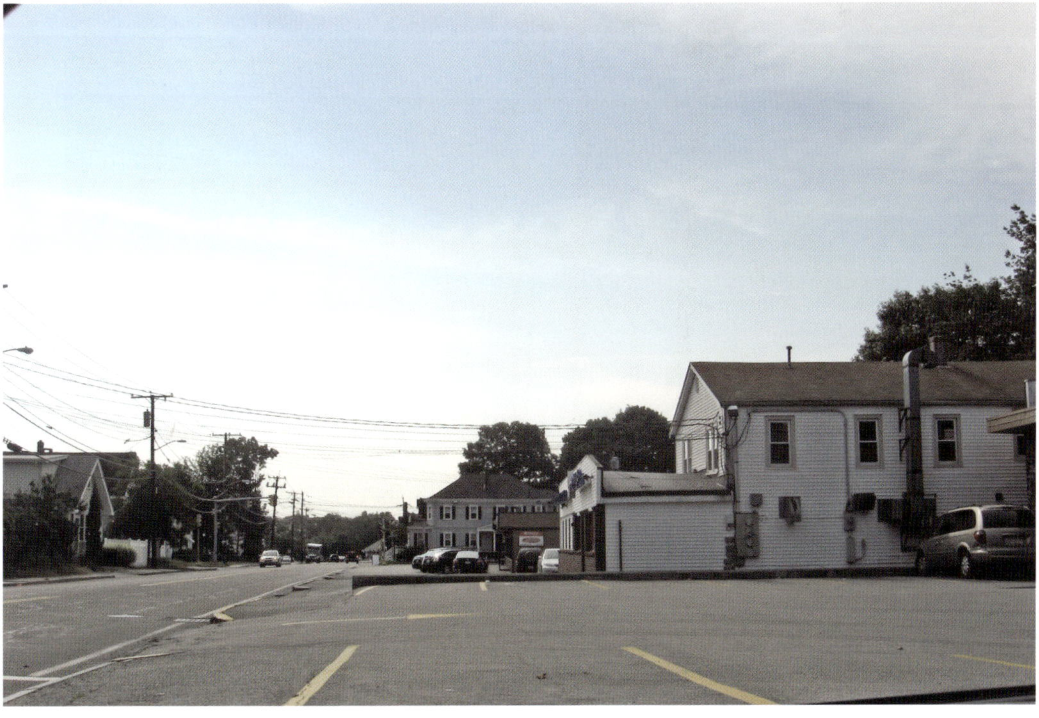

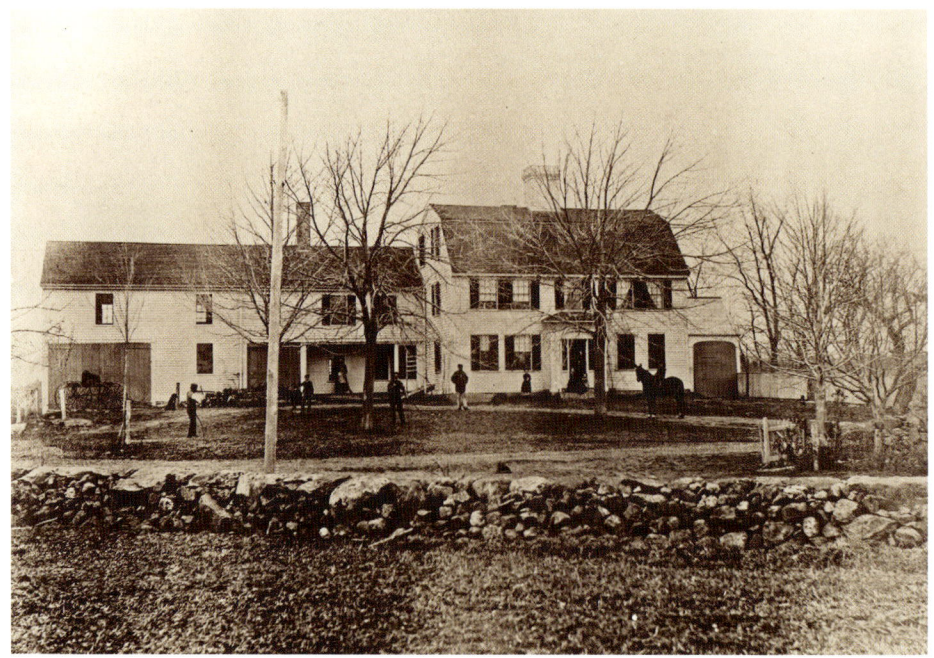

"THE HENS AND CHICKENS TAVERN": In 1642, Increase Winn was the first child born in what today is the town of Burlington. He was the son of Edward Winn, who had emigrated from England to Woburn in 1640. Increase Winn was born on the site where the John Winn House (or "Hens and Chickens Tavern") stands today. This fine example of an early Georgian gambrel mansion and colonial tavern was built in 1734. Lt. Joseph Winn operated a tavern on the site upon his return from duty in the American Revolution. (SCAN/BTA) (RJC/IMAGE)

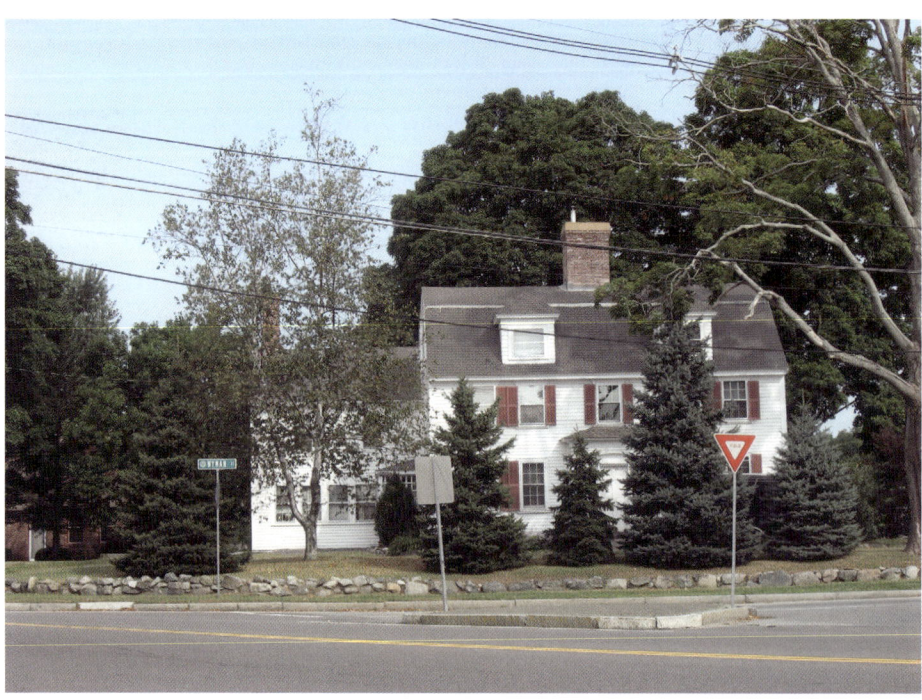

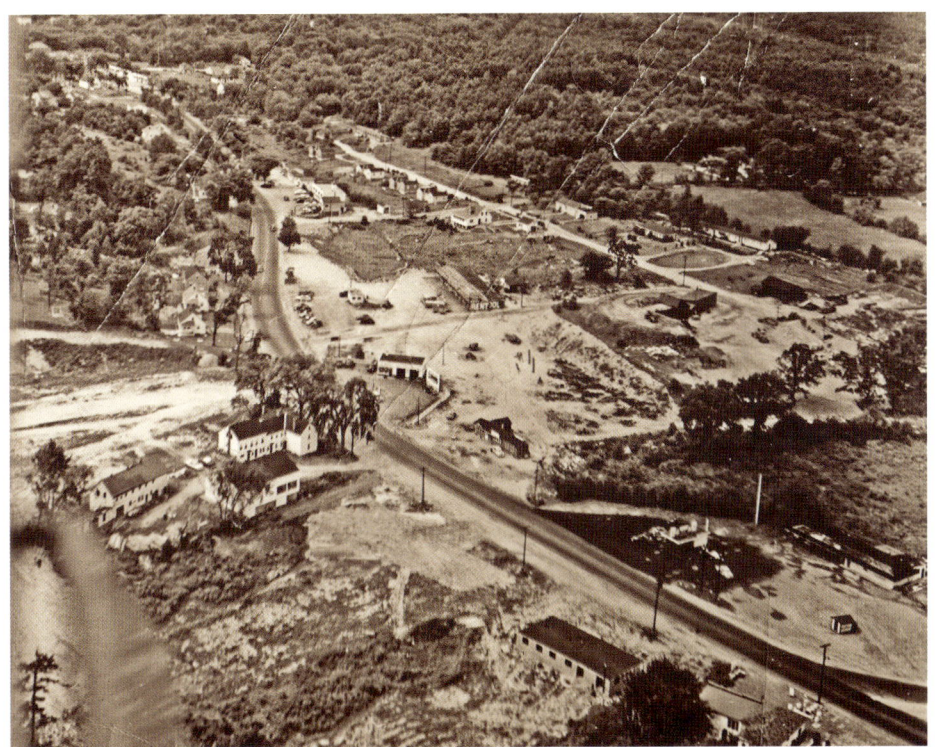

"THE CENTER":  "The Center", seen from the air, was developed as a retail and service road beginning in the 1950s. Today it is one of the most traveled and developed areas in Burlington. The centerpiece of the aerial view is the Butters Farmhouse on the corner of what would become Terry Avenue (left). A popular drive-in restaurant called the "Flying Saucer" is seen in the lower right. The Center in 2013 is clustered with small businesses and residential units. (SCAN/BTA) (RJC/IMAGE)

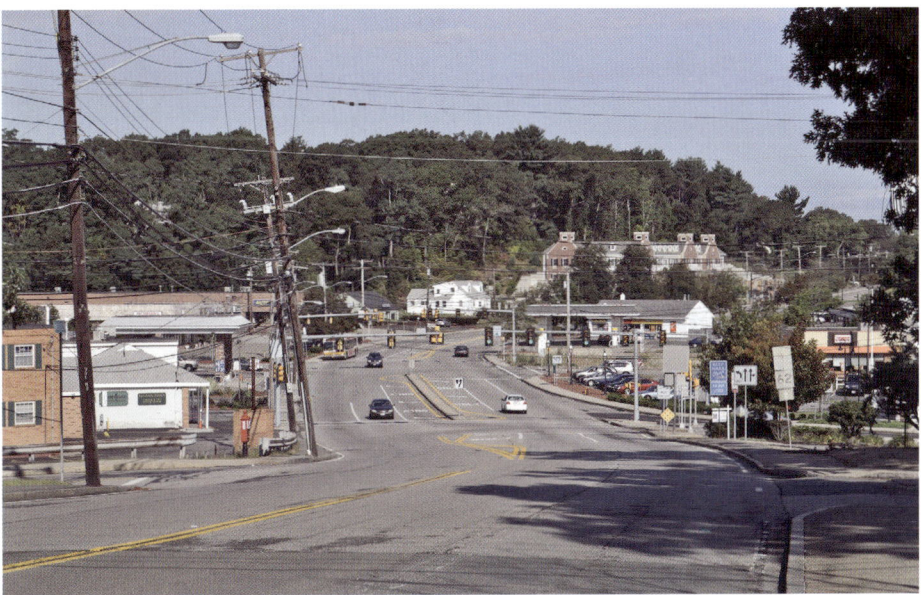

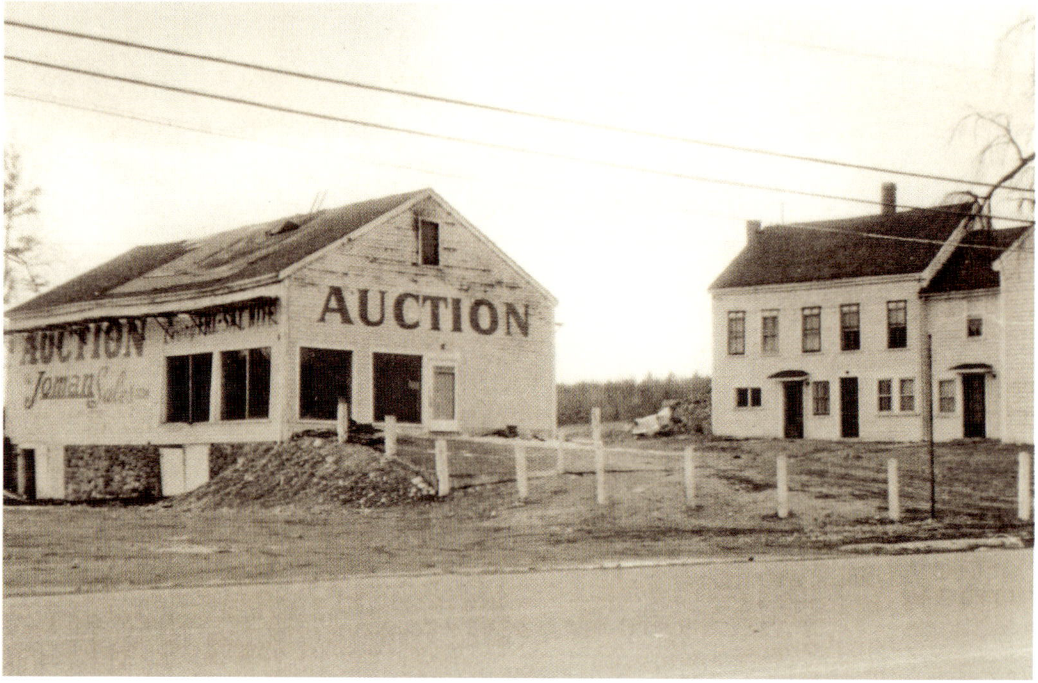

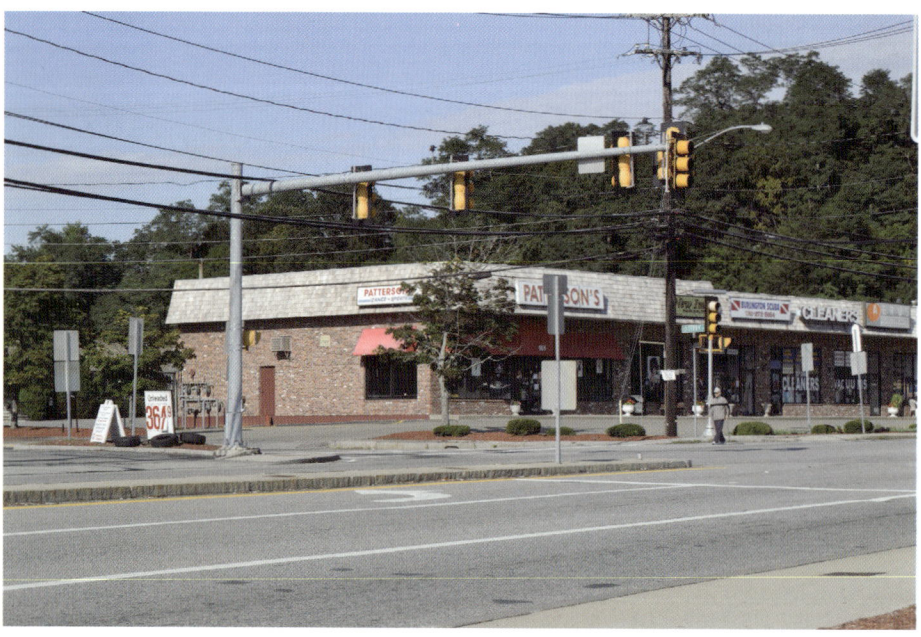

**BUTTERS FARM/AUCTION HOUSE:** This historic farmhouse and barn awaited demolition in the late 1950s to make way for the construction of Terry Avenue. For a time the barn was utilized as an auction house called the Nu-Joman Auction and Discount Center. Two large elm trees flanked the farmhouse, which was purchased by Joseph Butters in 1812. The complex has a long history, serving as a home, farm, auction house and gas station. The area today has been developed into a mixed-use residential, retail and service sector. (SCAN/BTA) (RJC/IMAGE)

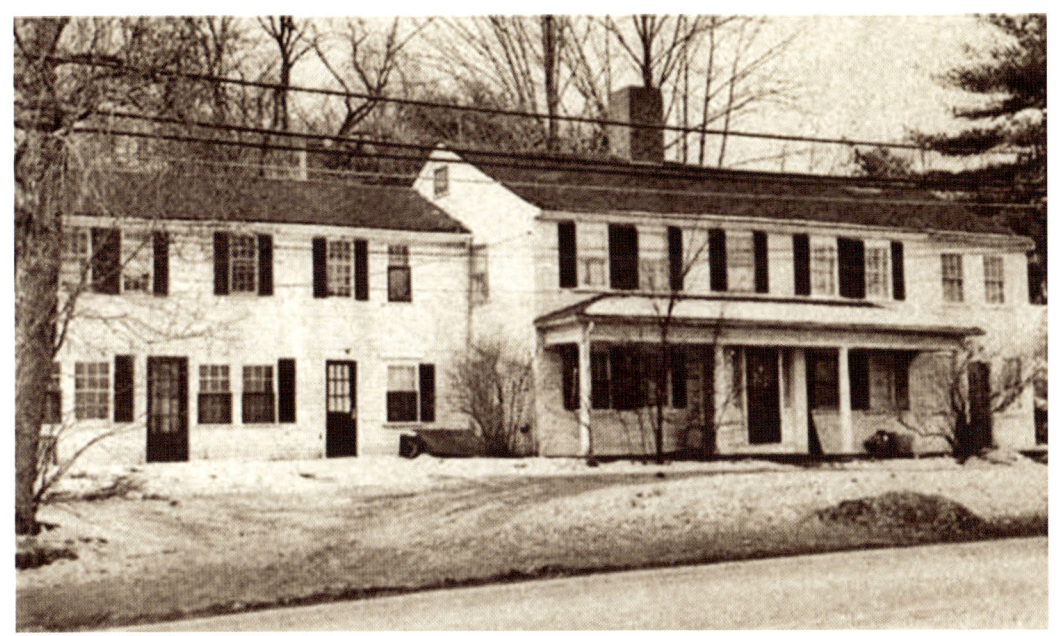

**SYLVANUS WOOD HOUSE/SITE:** Eyewitness to the Battle of Lexington, Sylvanus Wood is credited with capturing one of the first British soldiers later that day, April 19, 1775. In 1810 he acquired this house and an extensive farm that covered both sides of Cambridge Street across from Skilton Lane, and the hill behind the house (today's Arthur Woods Avenue). The house was destroyed by fire and razed by the town in 1985. The town readies for new residential construction in 2013. (SCAN/BTA) (RJC/IMAGE)

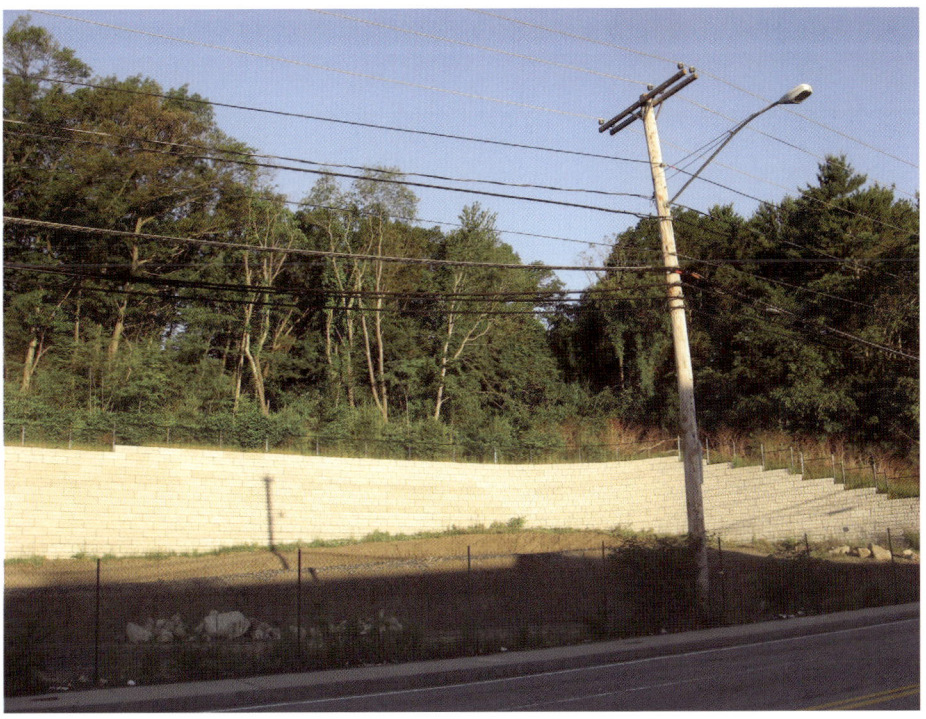

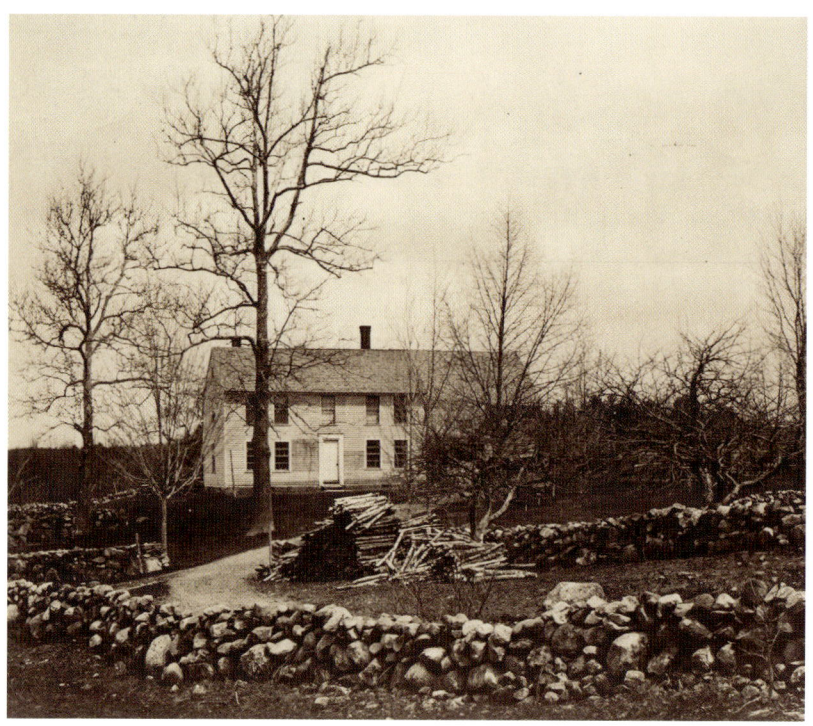

LT. NATHANIEL CUTLER HOUSE: One of the oldest houses in Burlington is located in the area once called "Wood Hill". Known as the Lt. Nathaniel Cutler house, it was built sometime in the 1720s and a Samuel Snow is on record as the first owner. Snow sold the parcel to Nathaniel Cutler in 1724. In that year the property consisted of a house, a barn and thirty-four acres of land. The private residence sits at the corner of Mill and Chandler Road. (SCAN/RJC) (RJC/IMAGE)

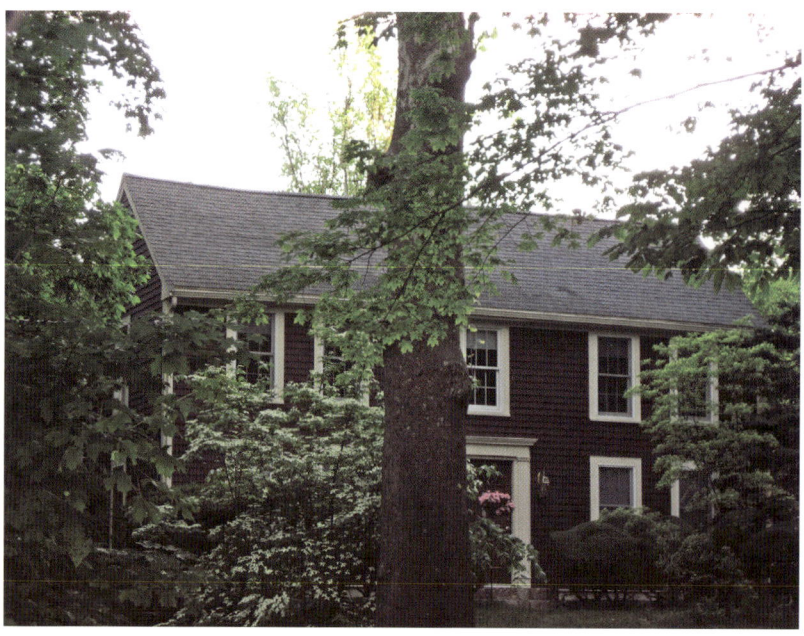

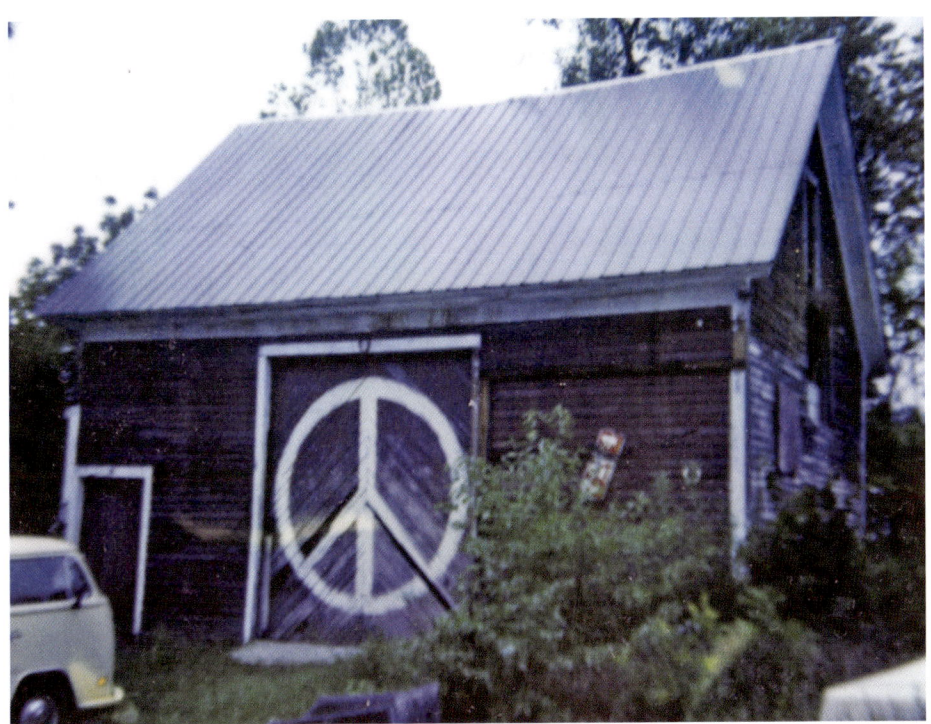

"PEACE BARN": Considered a local landmark, the "Peace Barn" was located in the Wood Hill region of Burlington, on the historic Cutler House property, until recently. It exemplifies a fine center-entrance, side–gabled, Greek-Revival style barn. The peace symbol was painted sometime in the 1970s; legends surround the reason. It stood as a beacon of hope but deteriorated over the years and was demolished in the early twenty-first century. (SCAN/RJC) (RJC/IMAGE)

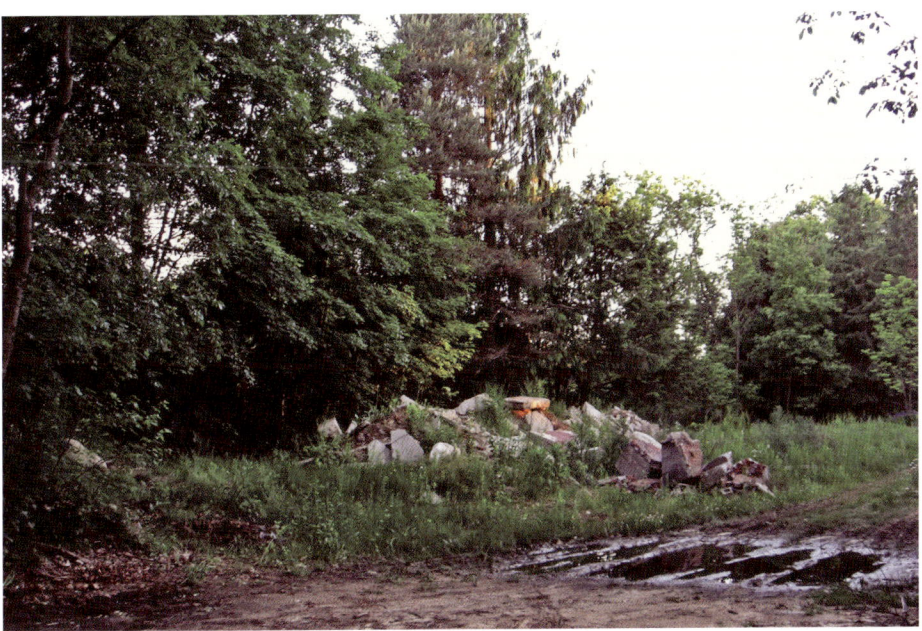

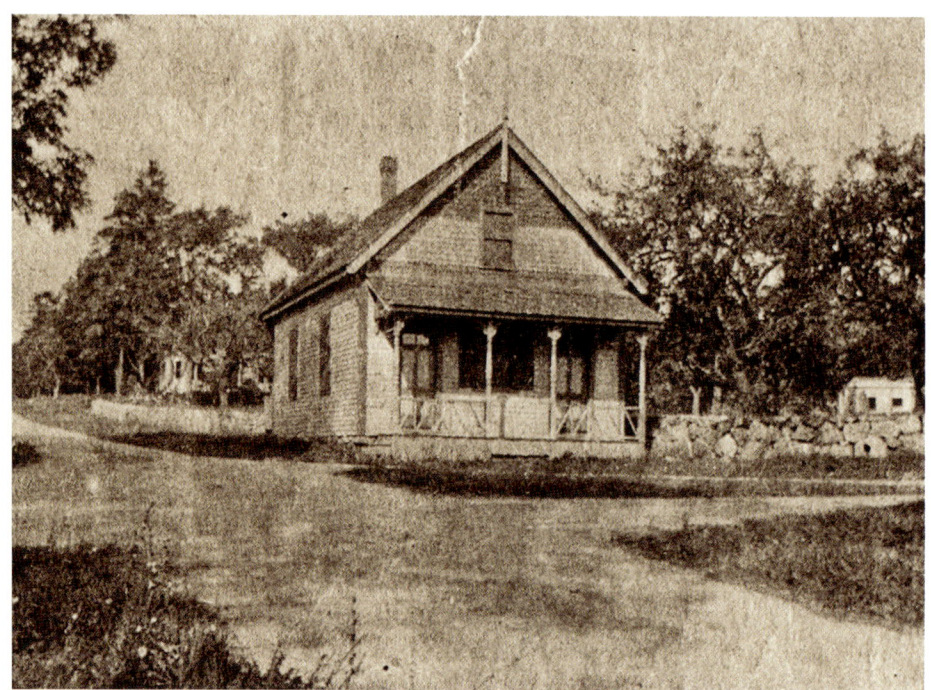

NORTH SCHOOL: Driving north on the road to Billerica, Mass, several little known, historic structures are hidden off the busy highway. Settled by the Reed family in the 1740s, the area grew and that necessitated the building of a one-room, district school in 1794. The schoolhouse was one of four that were constructed that year in the four regions of Burlington. Moved because of a land dispute, the Lt. Jesse Dean or North District school stands at the corner of Wilmington Road and Chestnut Avenue as a private home. (SCAN /BTA) (RJC/IMAGES)

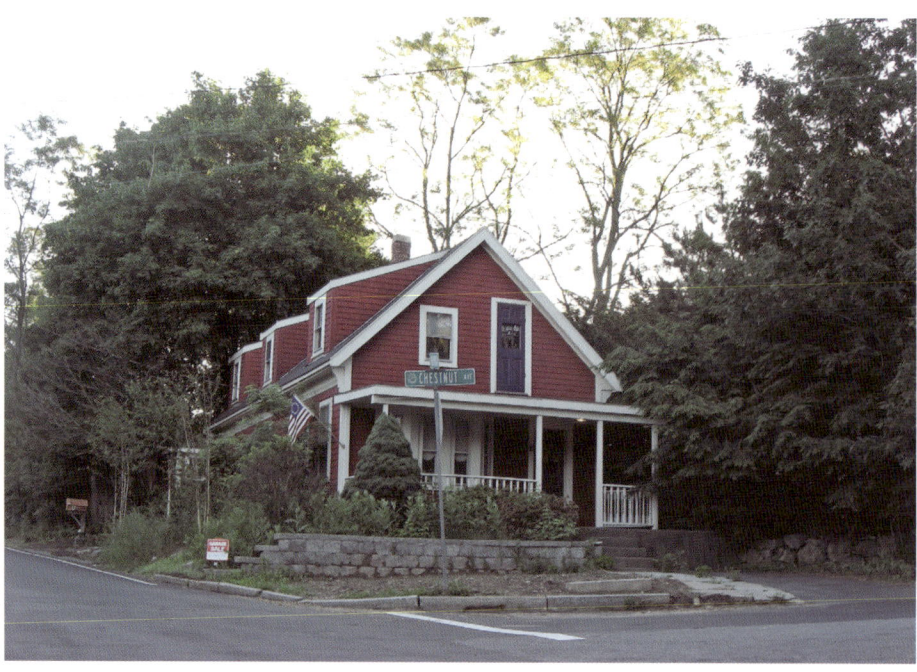

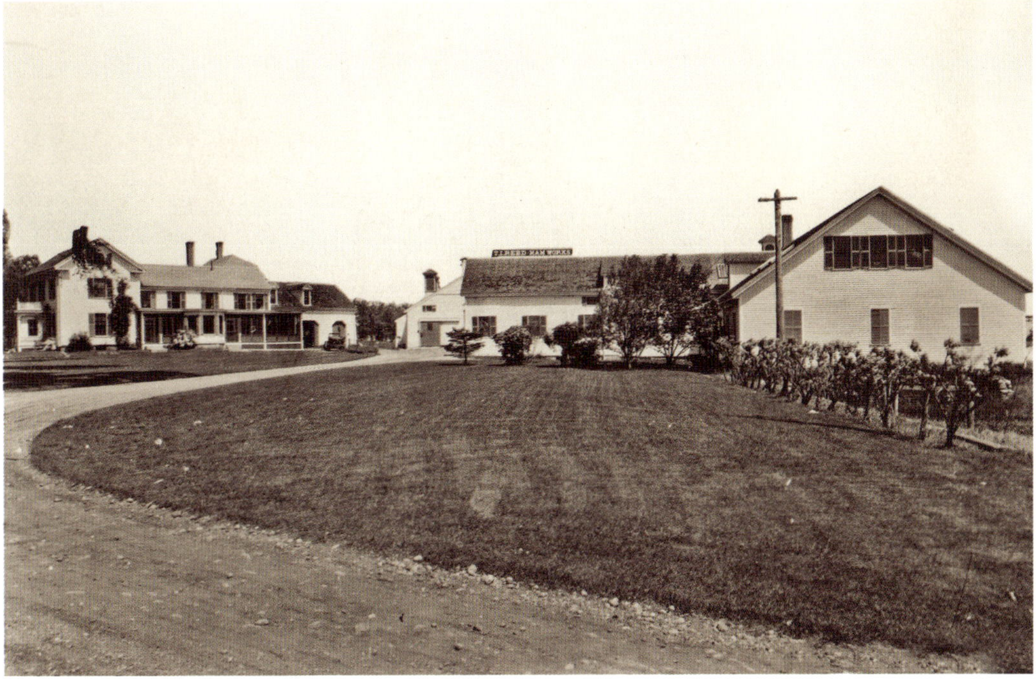

REED "HAM WORKS": T. I. Reed's "Ham Works" was a successful, well known pig farm that shipped prized smoked hams to many parts of the world in the late nineteenth century. Pig farms or 'piggeries' were a thriving business in Burlington at that time. Isaiah Reed built the house and started the ham curing business *c.* 1846. Business declined during the Great Depression and the ham works ended. The T. I. Reed house and ham works barn still stand as private businesses. (SCAN/BTA) (RJC/IMAGE)

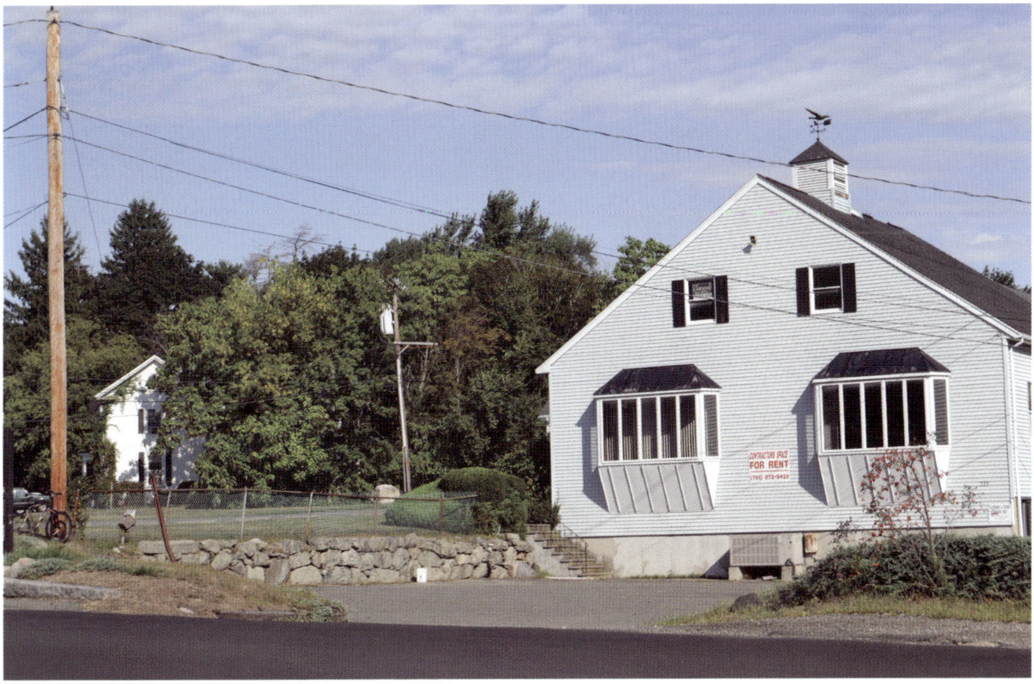

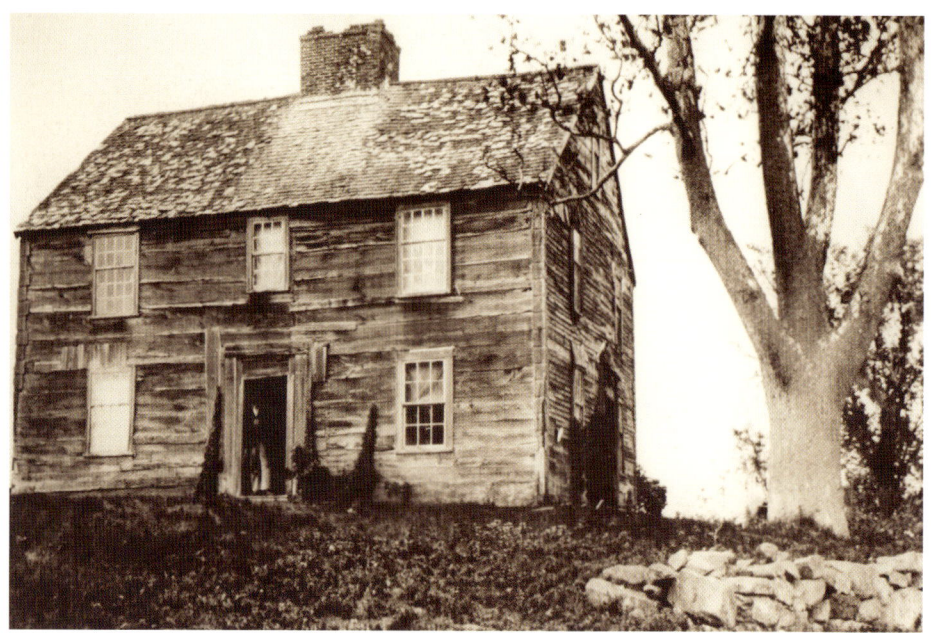

THE FRANCIS WYMAN HOUSE: A Joshua Reed family member stands in the doorway of Burlington's iconic historic structure, the Francis Wyman House in 1899. Built in 1666, remodeled in the 1740s and burned in a destructive fire in 1996, it is a survivor of three centuries. The homestead of the Wyman Association (1899) in America, it has been restored and will be part of Burlington's museum complex. It has been named in the National Register of Historic Places. (SCAN/BTA) (RJC/IMAGE)

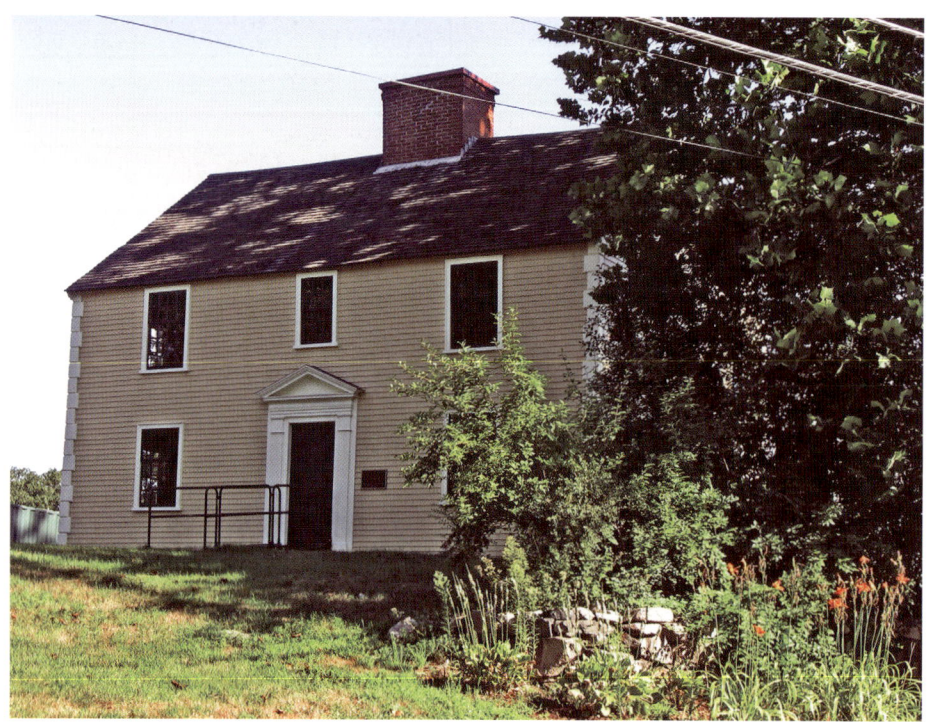

## THE HIDING PLACE:

"The secret hiding place" is an intriguing feature of this early Georgian farmhouse. The original house was built by Francis and John Wyman *c.* 1666, and was remodeled in the 1740s. Much of the original paneling and other early features were destroyed in the fire of 1996. The legend is that the enclosure was to be used to conceal small children in the event of hostilities with Native Americans, who had lived in the region for centuries and called it Shawshin. (SCAN/RJC) (RJC/IMAGE)

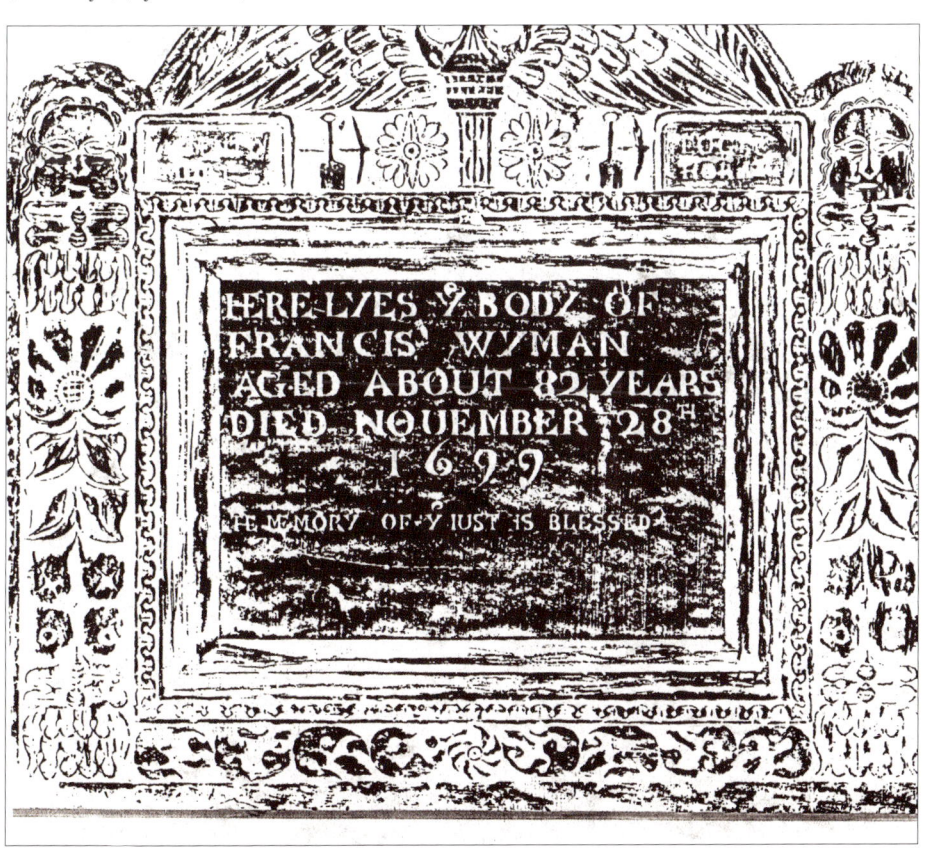

HERE LYES Y BODZ OF FRANCIS WYMAN AGED ABOUT 82 YEARS DIED NOUEMBER 28 1699 Y MEMORY OF Y IUST IS BLESSED

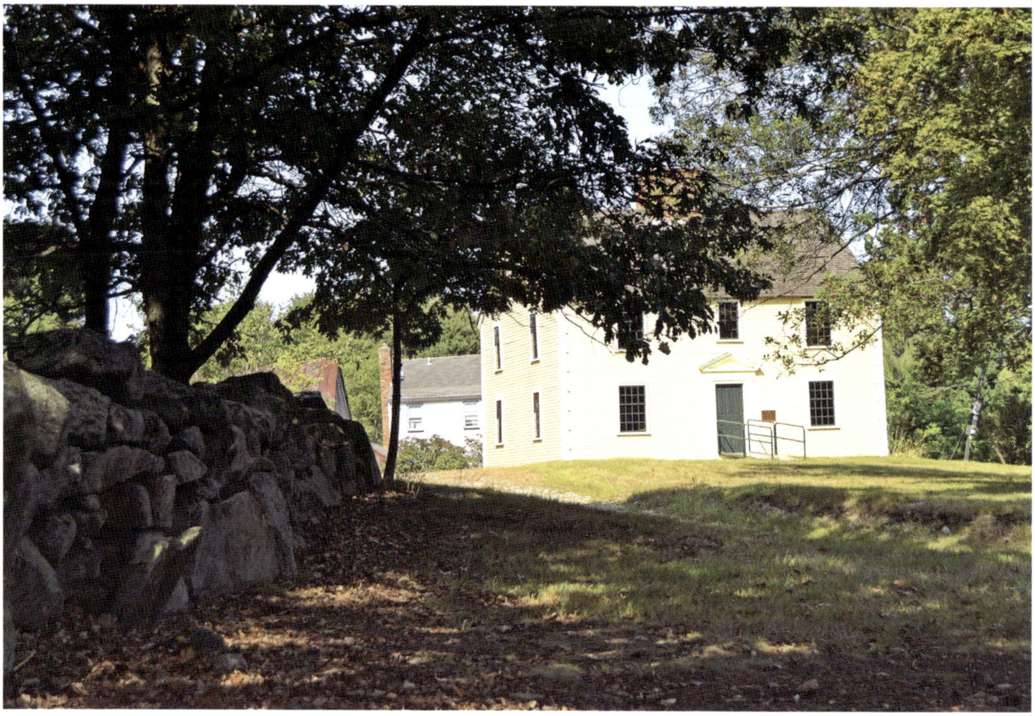

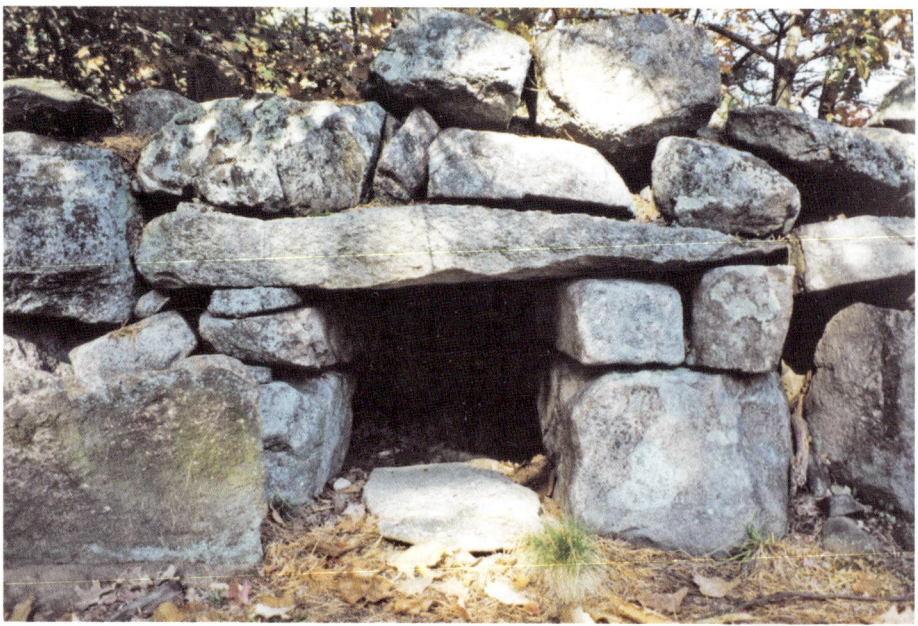

THE "SHEEP COTE":  Neolithic remnant, Native American artifact, or colonial livestock enclosure, this curious feature is part of the massive stone fence surrounding the last of the Wyman family land holdings. Most agree it is a seventeenth-or early eighteenth-century "sheep cote", modeled after English styles, to house stray livestock. Built of large fieldstones it is capped with an enormous stone slab that forms the roof of the enclosure. Several such stone pens are shown on a 1799 map of Burlington. (SCAN/HISTORIC PRESERVATION STUDY) (RJC/IMAGE)

### THE WYMAN FAMILY:

The coat of arms of the historic Wyman Family features a rooster atop a sheaf of wheat, and three fireballs with the motto "Bold and Vigilant." Francis and his brother, John Wyman, emigrated from West Mill, England, to America in 1640. Founders of Woburn in 1642, they both raised large families and hundreds of descendents claim their lineage today. Members of the Wyman Family in America surround the gravestone of their common ancestor during one of their recent annual reunions. (SCAN/RJC) (RJC/IMAGE)

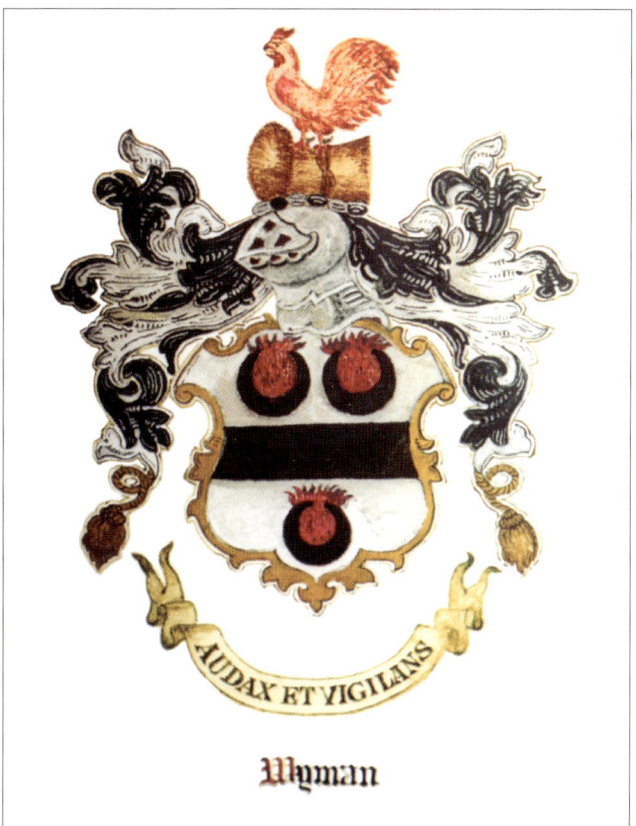

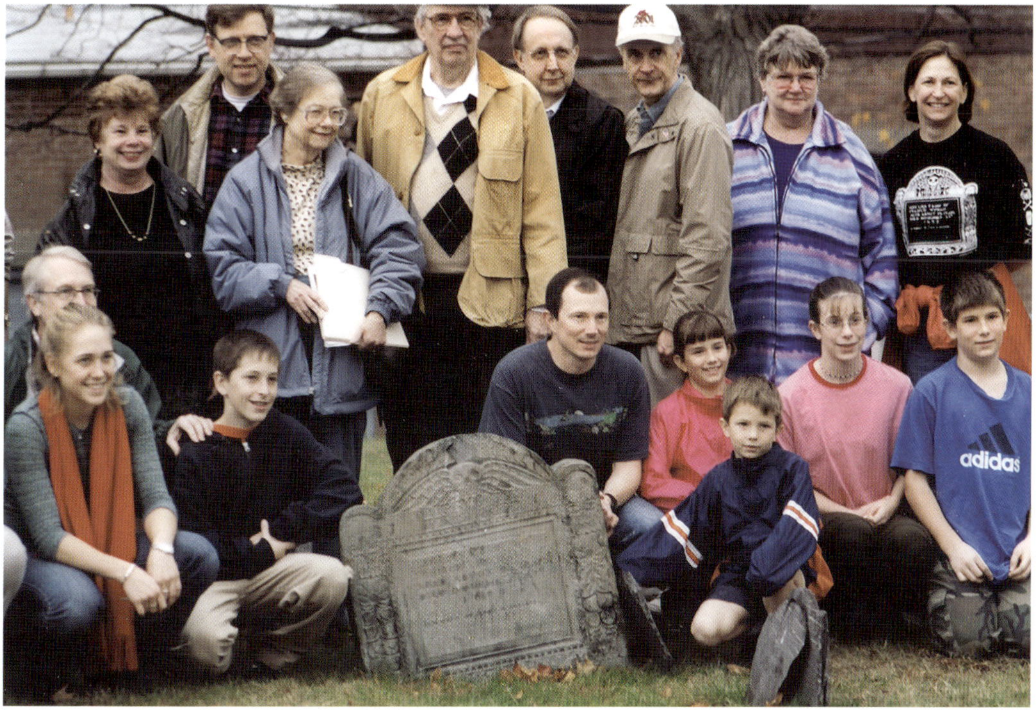

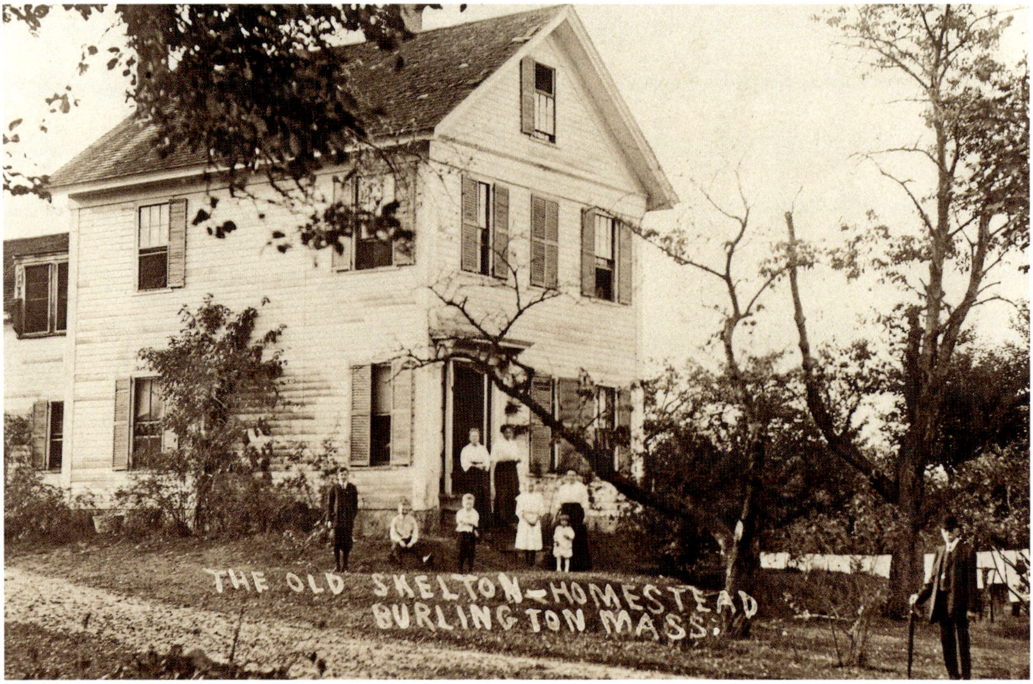

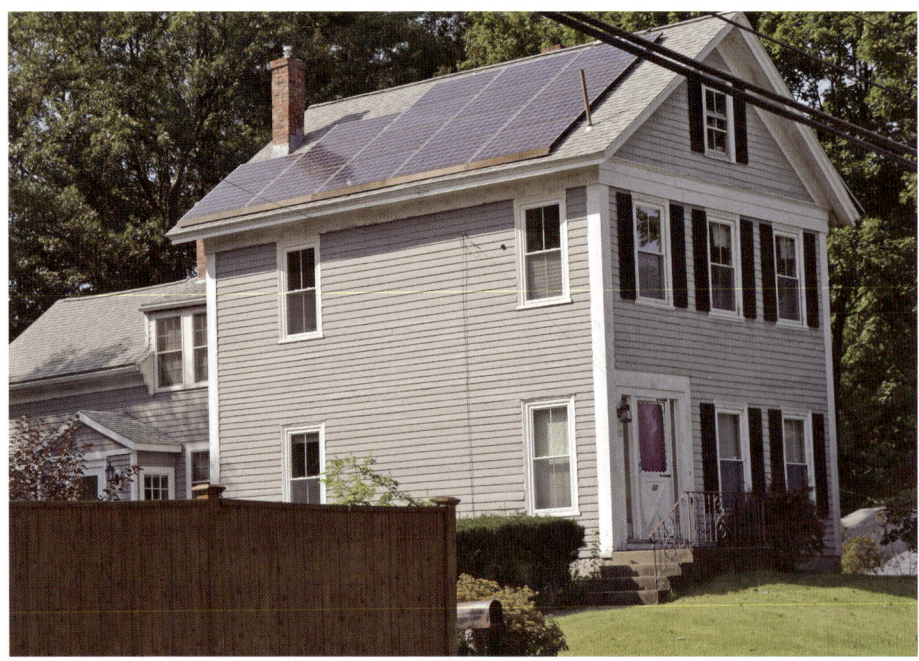

**BRADFORD SKELTON HOUSE:** Bradford Skelton built this house, still standing on Francis Wyman Road, in 1864, shortly after returning from the California "gold fields". Skelton was twenty-one when he left Burlington to find his fortune in the California Gold Rush. He spent several years searching in vain, but sent many colorful letters home describing his adventures. Bradford and his wife, Alma Shedd, raised four sons who were all prominent in town affairs. (SCAN/BTA) (RJC/IMAGE)

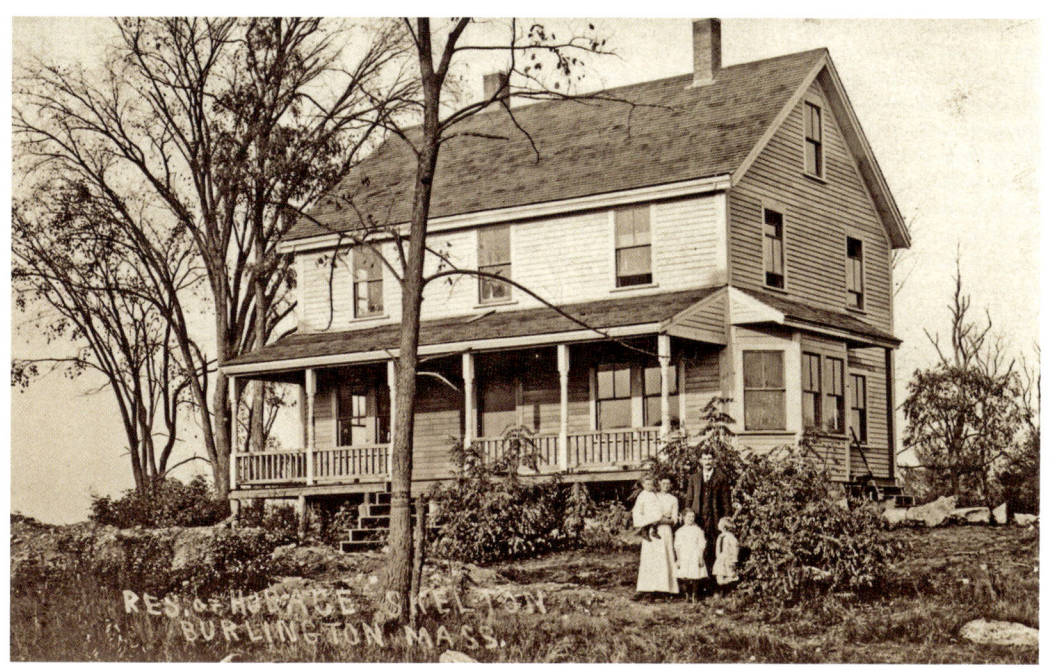

**HORACE SKELTON HOUSE:** Horace Bradford Skelton born in Burlington in 1879, was one of the four sons of Bradford and Alma Skelton. The Skelton family in America can be traced to 1630. Horace acquired this family property, the deed of which is said to date to colonial times. He operated a large chicken farm on the property but was also a very involved town leader. He served as selectman, moderator and member of the Board of Health. (SCAN/RJC) (RJC/IMAGE)

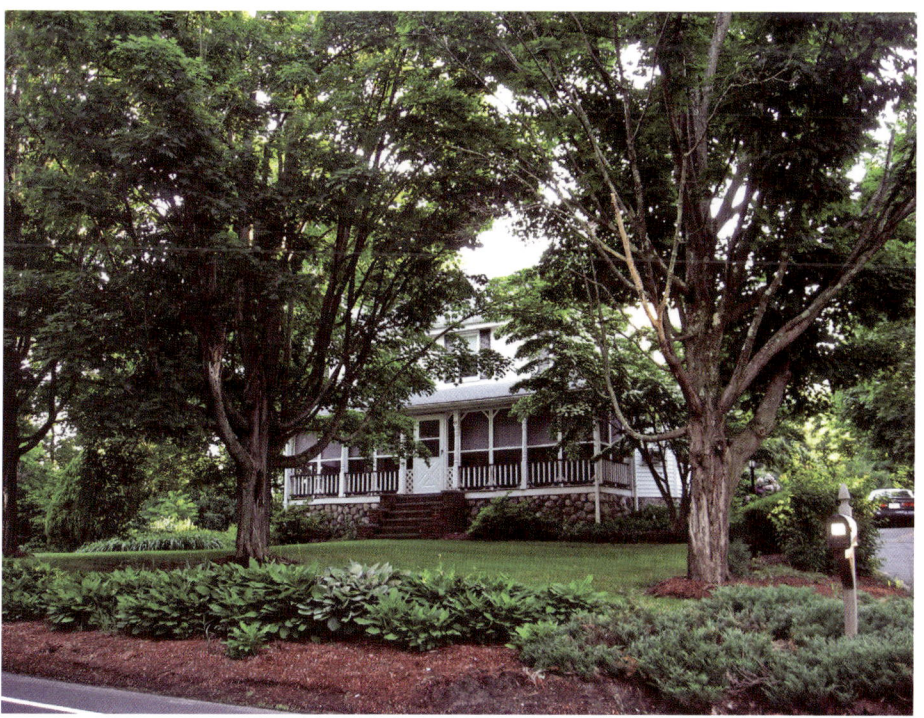

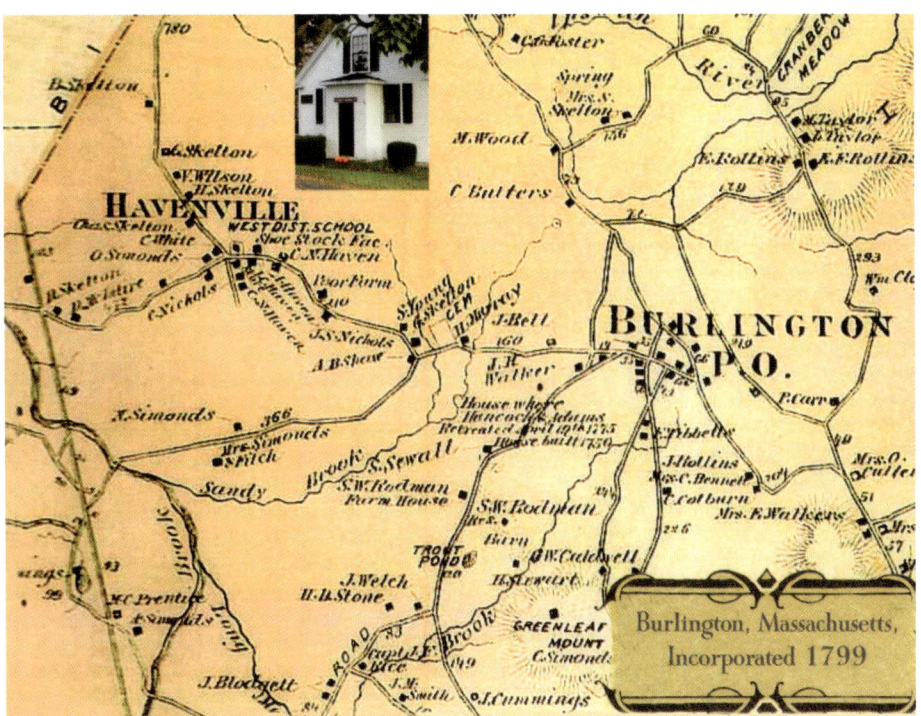

Burlington, Massachusetts,
Incorporated 1799

HAVENVILLE:  The Village of Havenville existed for a time in the late nineteenth century at this very busy intersection of Francis Wyman Road and Bedford Street as depicted on an early map. It appears to be a residential area today but *c.* 1900 it was a bustling region consisting of the West District School, several small leather shops and many small residences. Today the West School stands guardian over a part of "Lost Burlington". (SCAN/MARY LOPRESTI) (RJC/IMAGE)

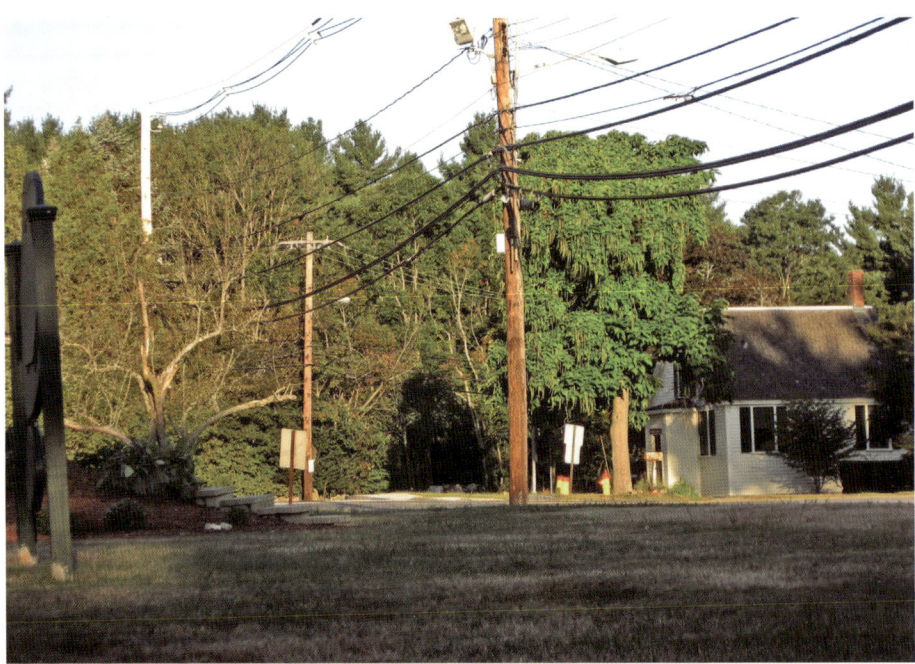

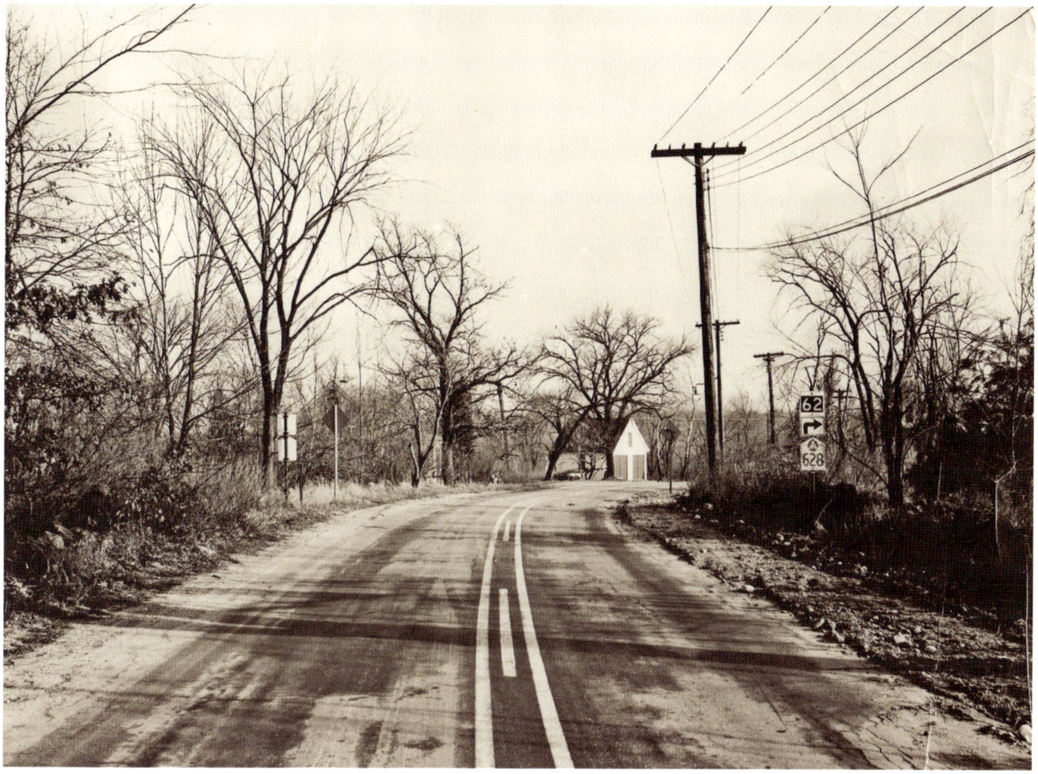

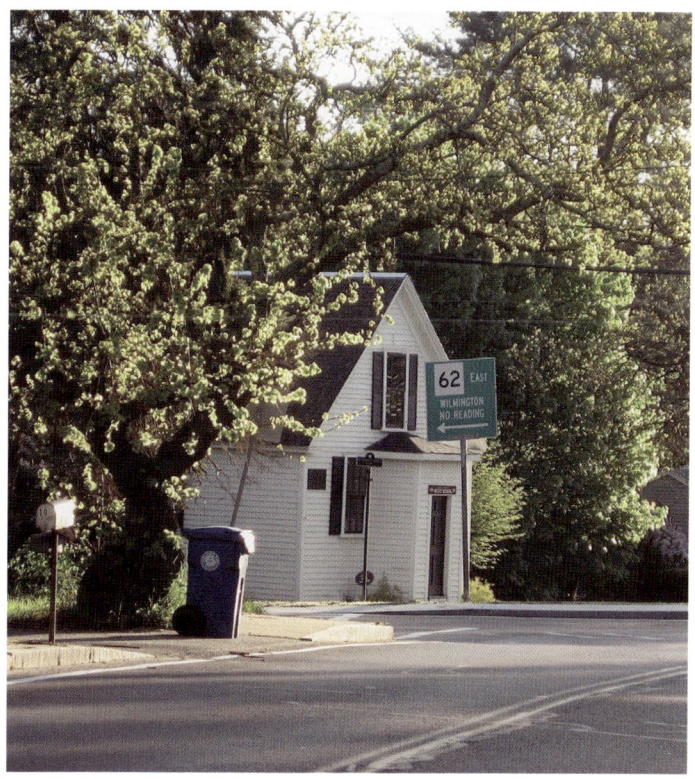

**THE WEST SCHOOL:**
Originally built on the hill in Simonds Park in 1794, this very recognizable Burlington landmark was called the Center School. Sometime between 1830–1840, the building was moved down the hill to the Havenville section, and became the West District School. The creation of the Burlington Historical Society developed over the struggle to preserve this structure in 1964. History and heritage won this struggle and today it is a proud part of the town's museum complex, run by the Burlington Historical Commission. (SCAN /RJC) (IMAGE/RJC)

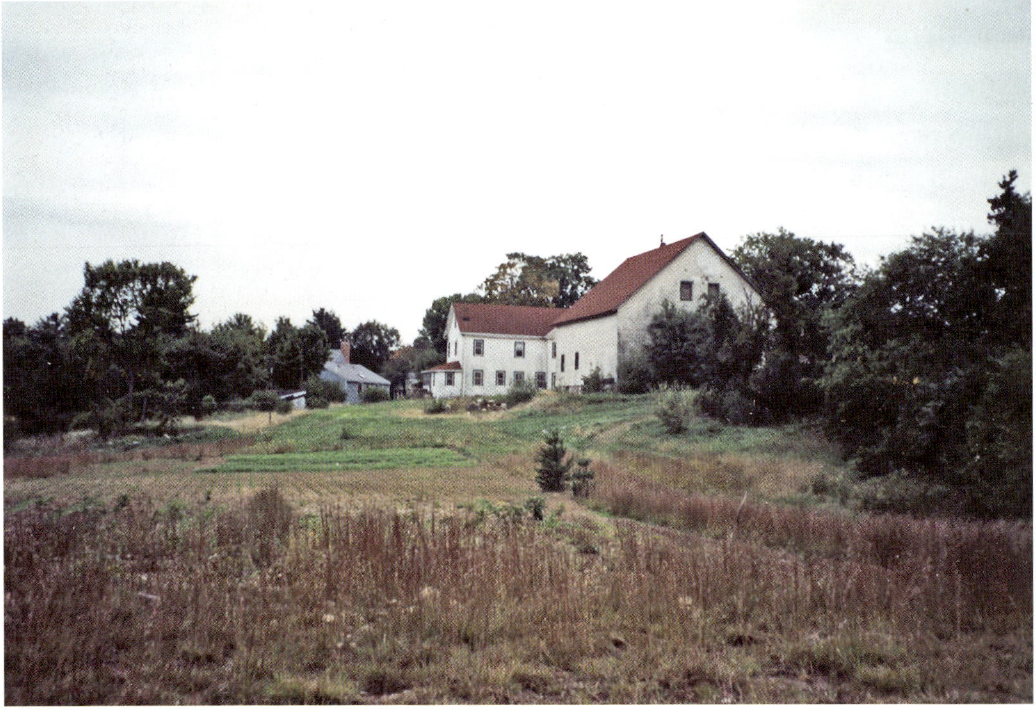

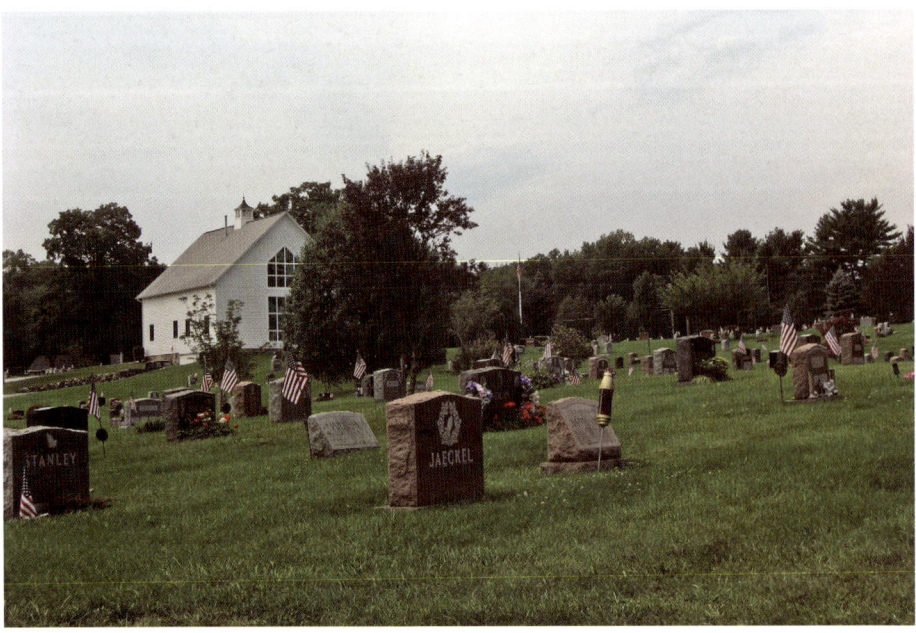

THE "POOR FARM":   The "almshouse" or "Poor Farm" was located on one the earliest Burlington farms, and one of the last small farms to be developed for modern use. Daniel McIntire and family had a house or barn on the site since the 1750s. The town acquired the property after the Civil War and used it as an "almshouse"—a working farm that housed the town's homeless, until it closed in 1906. It serves the town today as the third cemetery. (SCAN/RJC) (RJC/IMAGE)

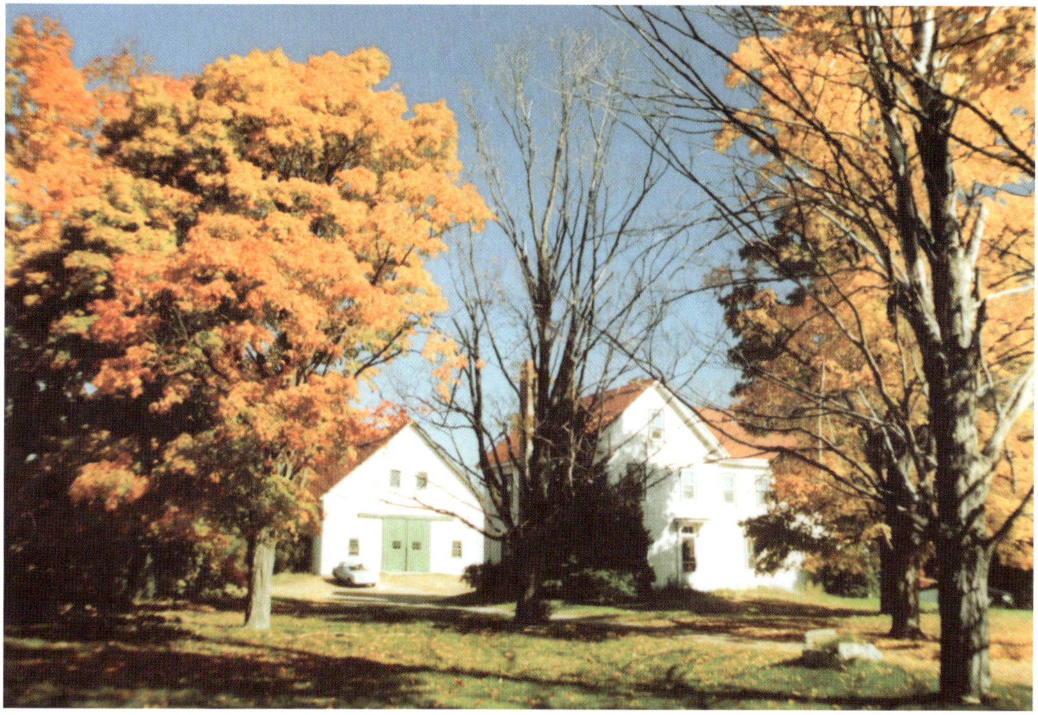

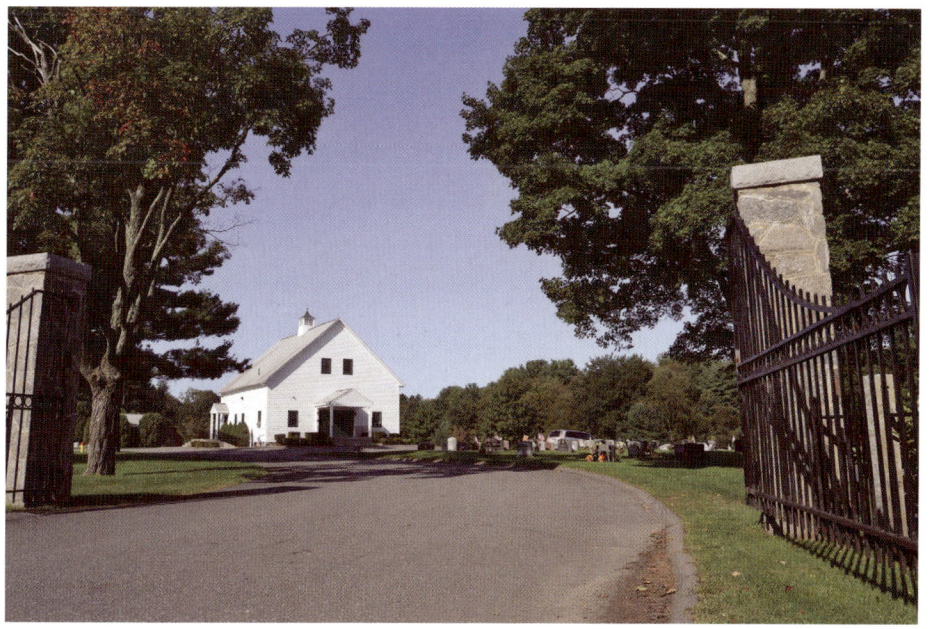

THE "POOR FARM" BARN: Burlington barns, once so prevalent, are now rare. The town has renovated some, like this fine example of a *c.* 1847, Greek Revival style, structure. It has been remodeled to serve as a muti-denominational chapel. Once considered part of Havenville, the farmland was converted into Pine Haven Cemetery and is reaching capacity as of 2013. Before the town acquired the land, it was a small farm owned by a local barber and politician Gerald Seminatore. (SCAN/RJC) (RJC/IMAGE)

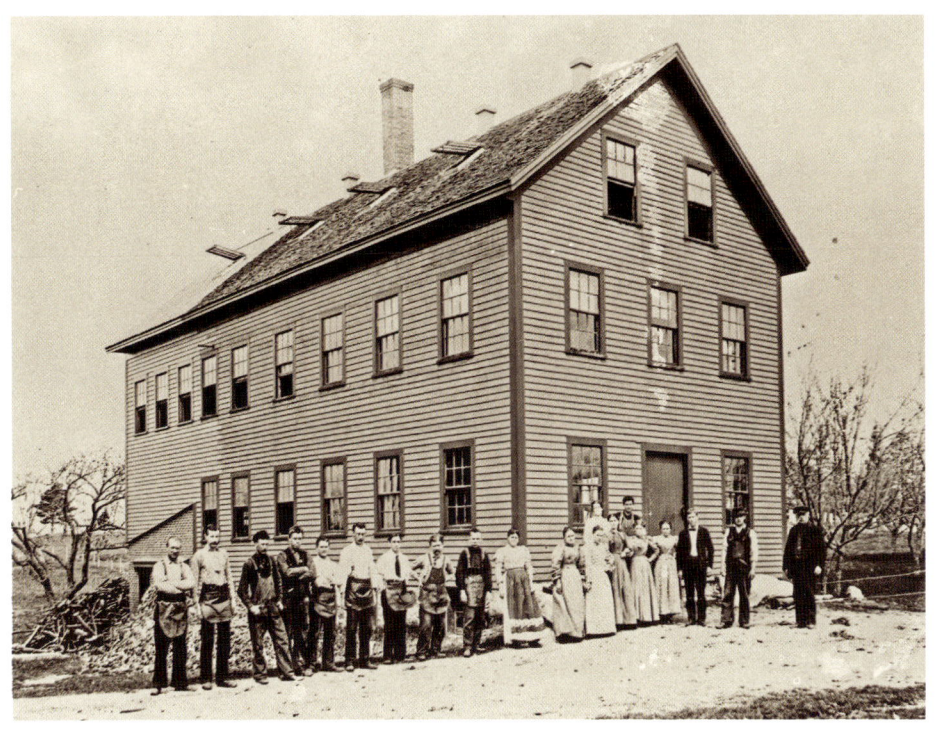

**W. E. CARTER SHOE STOCK FACTORY:** Standing very near Cambridge Street workers from W. E.Carter shoe stock factory line up to face the camera in this *c.* 1900 image. Carter owned the heel shop or shoe stock business from 1880–1904. The heel shop employees were from Burlington and Woburn; the Woburn girls boarded with the Burlington families. The heels were made from scrap leather trimmings from the Woburn tanneries. The finished product was sent to a shoe shop in Brockton. Today part of the complex still exists and is used by small businesses. (SCAN BTA) (RJC/IMAGE)

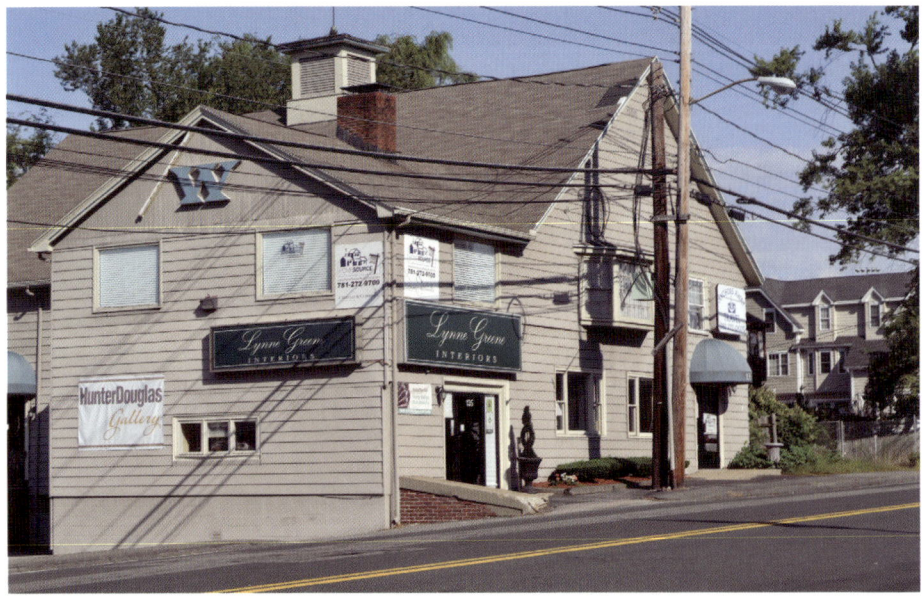

# SECTION 2

# A Walk or Ride Down Lexington Street

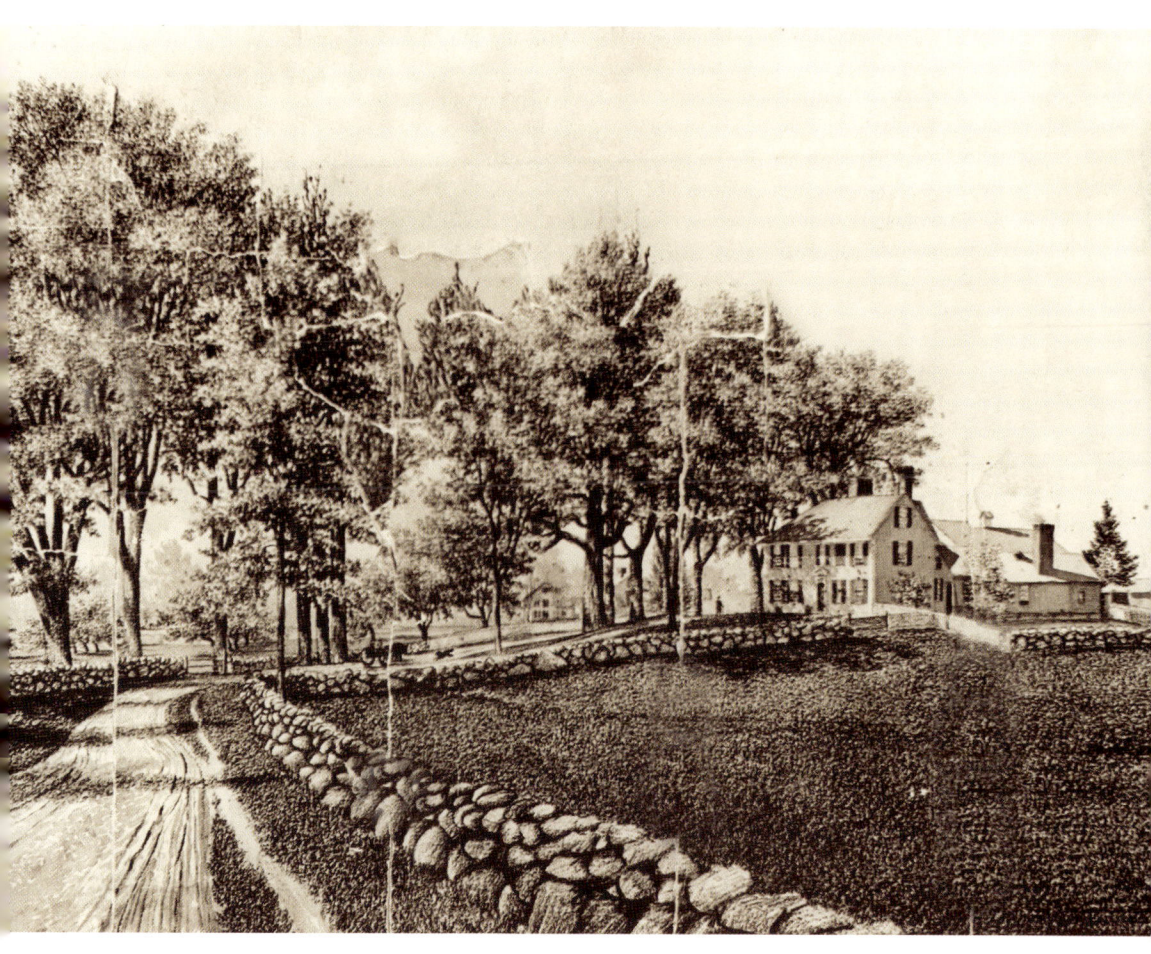

# SECTION 2

# INTRODUCTION

In 1909 Martha Elizabeth Sewall Curtis, a local historian and activist, spoke before her congregation on the occasion known as Old Home Sunday of life and history of the town in the mid-nineteenth century. It was titled, "A Walk in Old Burlington," describing the historic attractions and everyday life, throughout the town. At the turn of the twentieth century change had come to Burlington and a era was passing. In the spirit of the article and the woman, this section takes a 2013 walk or ride down Lexington Street. One of the historic and scenic roadways in Burlington, the ancient pathway to Lexington, it is also connected to the Road to the American Revolution. Several significant but little known events on April 18–19, 1775 took place on this road. Start on "Forest Field Hill", at the Second Parish Meeting House, for this magical history tour.

*Previous page:* Lexington Street seen in this late nineteenth century painting could also be known as the Pathway to the American Revolution.

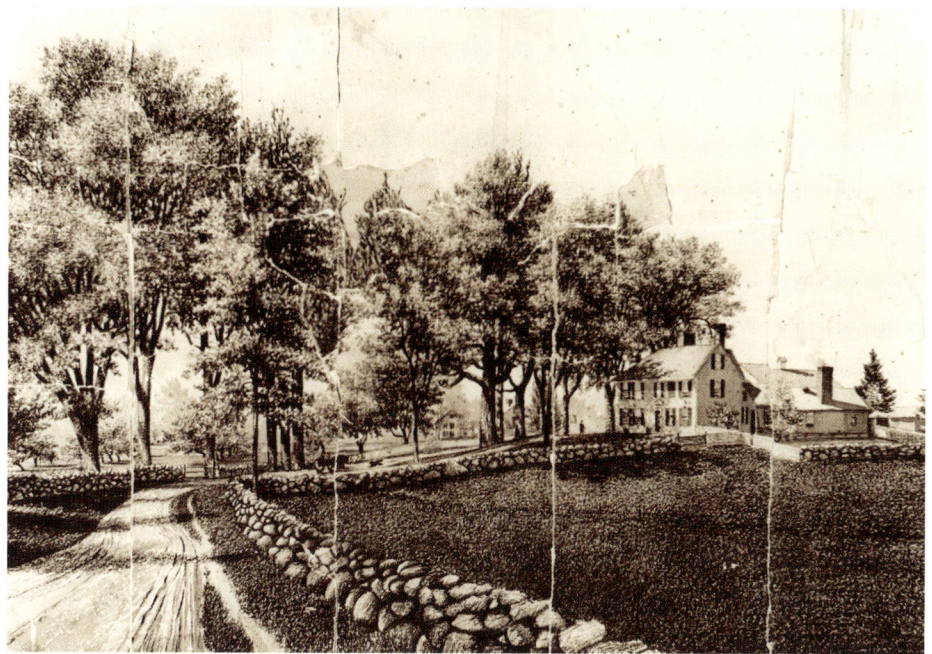

LEXINGTON STREET/THE SAMUEL SEWALL HOUSE: A roving Wilmington artist named James Franklin Gilman painted this beautiful view of Lexington Street. This sketch was signed and dated 1872 and then discarded in pieces. Local historian Elizabeth Bennett Lowther rescued it, in fragments. In both scenes, the Sewall house, historically significant, but little known, is featured. The house was built in 1732 and is depicted on the town seal. The Jotham Johnson house, also built *c.* 1732, is seen in the background. It is still standing in 2013. (SCAN/BTA) (SCAN/SPNEA

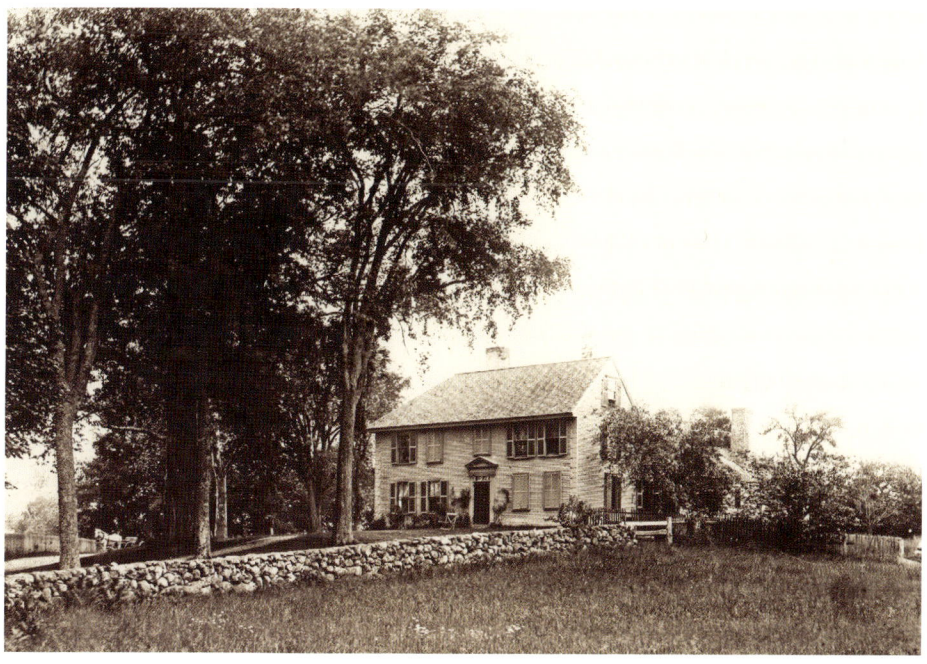

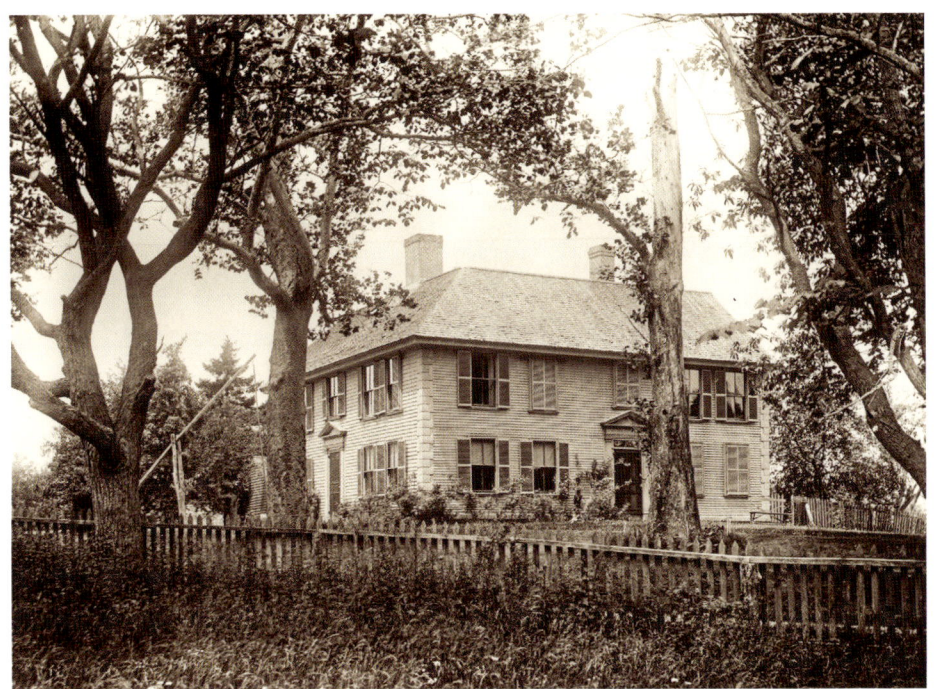

**THE SAMUEL SEWALL HOUSE:** The Samuel Sewall house was built *c.* 1732 by Benjamin Johnson. The house changed property owners several times, but by 1751, it had become the parsonage for Woburn's second parish church. It ceased to be the parsonage in 1844 and became the private residence of the famous Sewall family. In a tragic fire in 1897, it burned to the ground. A modern, private residence stands on the site today, bearing some resemblance to the historic structure. (SCAN/SPNEA) (RJC/IMAGE)

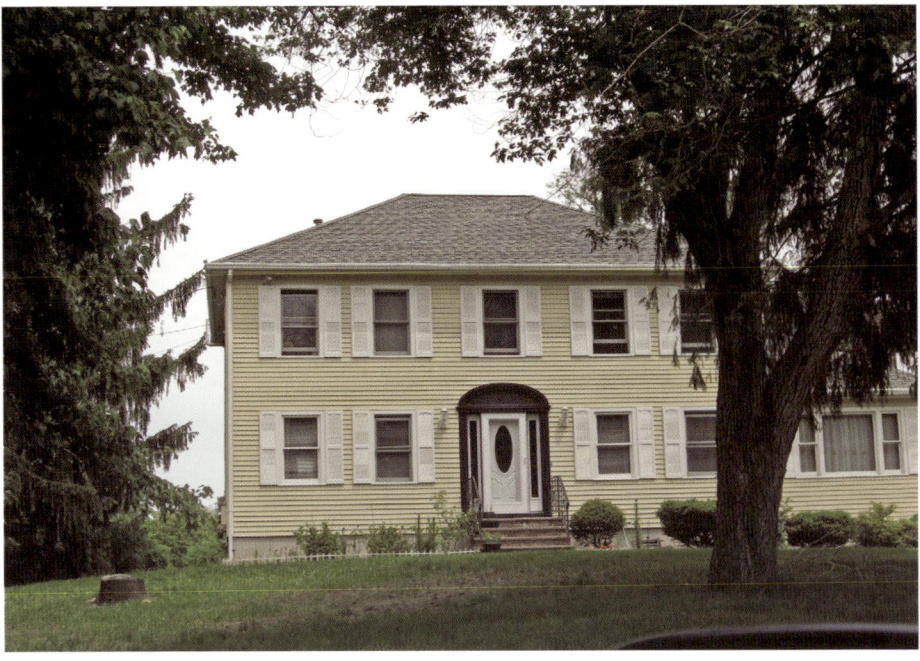

**SAMUEL SEWALL:**
Samuel Sewall was born in Marblehead, Mass. in 1785. He was a direct descendant of Judge (Justice) Samuel Sewall, a major figure in the Witch Trials of 1692. Sewall attended Harvard College from 1800–1804, then studied theology and became a minister of the Congregational Church. He and his family came to Burlington in 1814, as minister of the Burlington Congregational Church (UCC today). Rev. Samuel Sewall died in 1868 and is buried in the Chestnut Hill Cemetery. (SCAN/RJC) (RJC/IMAGE)

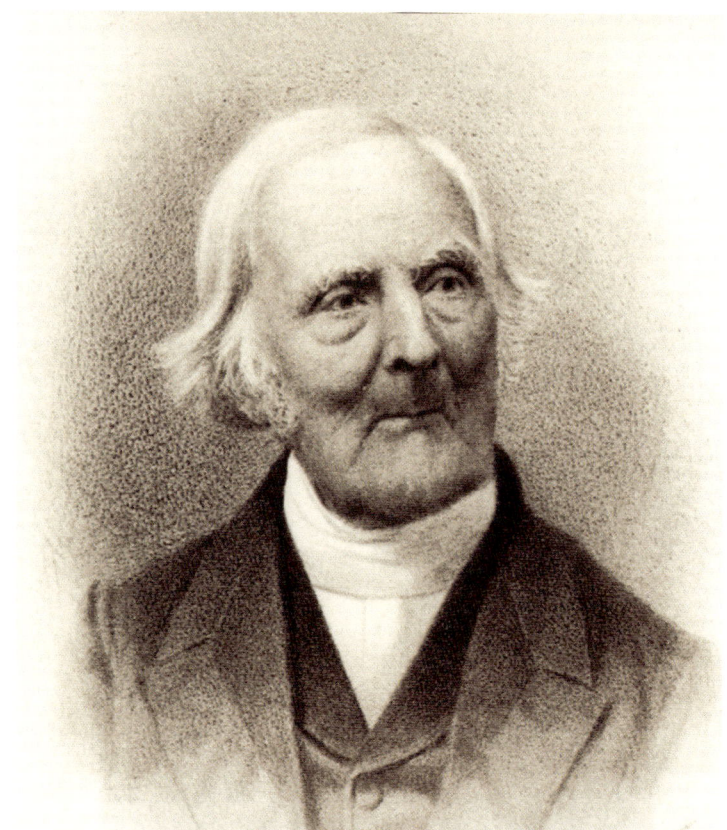

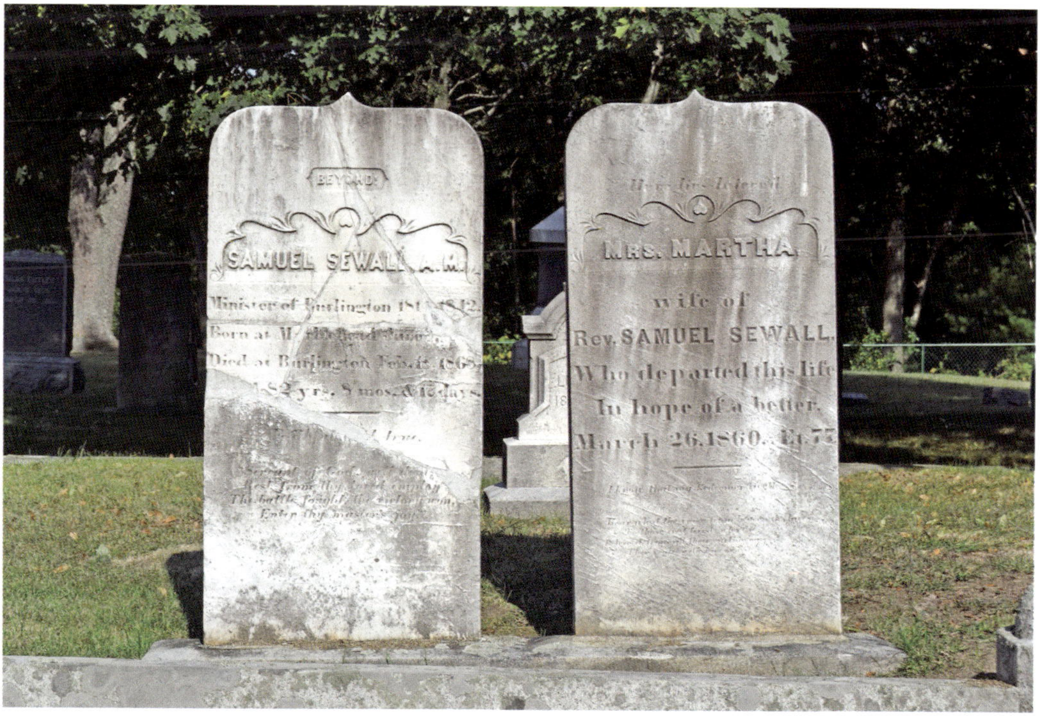

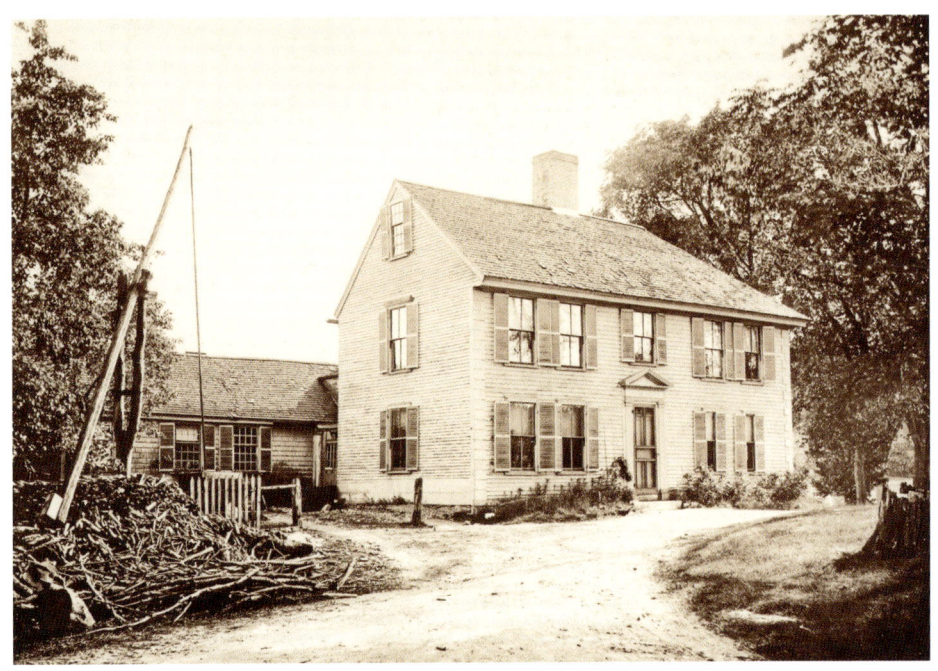

SEWALL WELL/SALMON DINNER: Revolutionary War leaders John Hancock and Samuel Adams, fleeing from British patrols stayed at this venerable sixteen-room, L-shaped, Sewall "mansion" for a short time on April 18–19, 1775. The home was owned by widow Madam Abigail Jones who lived there with her "domestic servant" Cuff. Hancock, Adams and party were about to dine on a large salmon, when a messenger warned the group of British proximity. This vivid painting by local artists Don Gorvett and Jeff Weaver portrays the possible scene. (SCAN/RJC) (RJC/IMAGE)

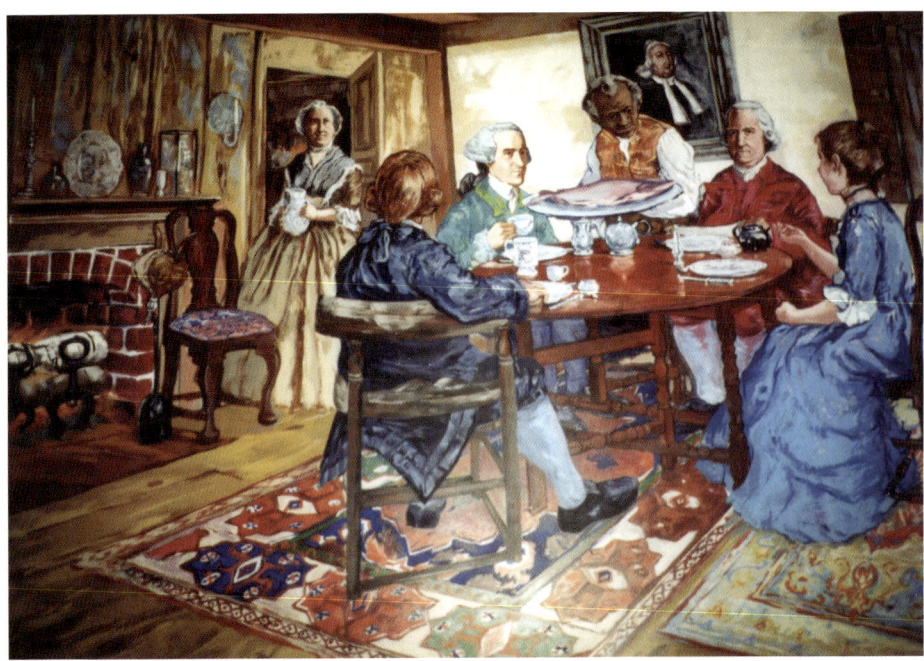

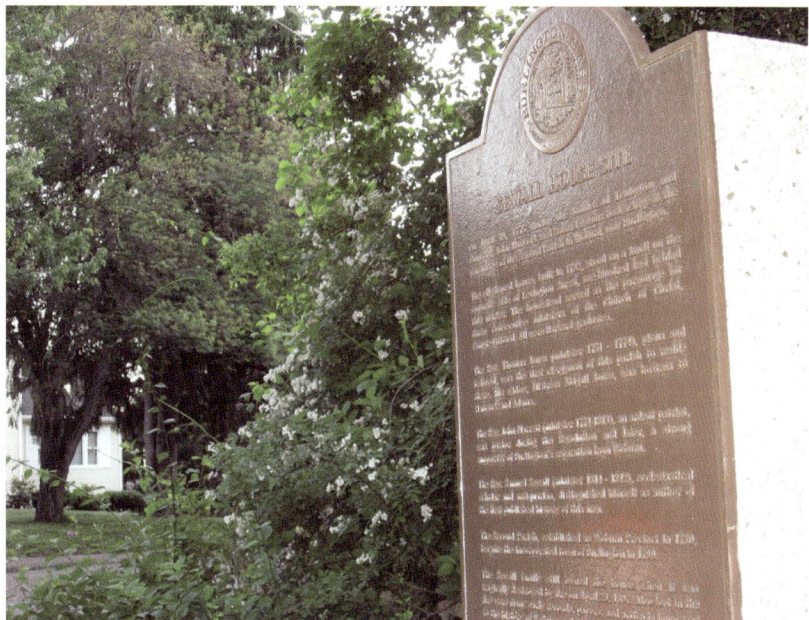

**THE SEWALL HOUSE MARKER AND SITE:** History and writing were interests shared by the Sewall family that occupied this site from the 1840s–1897. The 'mansion' became the repository for a priceless collection of documents and artifacts pertaining to the history of the area dating to the 1640s. Rev. Samuel Sewall wrote one of the first histories of what is today Burlington, in his 1868 publication, *A History of Woburn*. On April 23, 1897 the mansion was destroyed by fire, and a great amount of history was lost. The Social Studies Department of Burlington High School sponsored the fine marker that stands across from the site. (SCAN/RJC) (RJC/IMAGE)

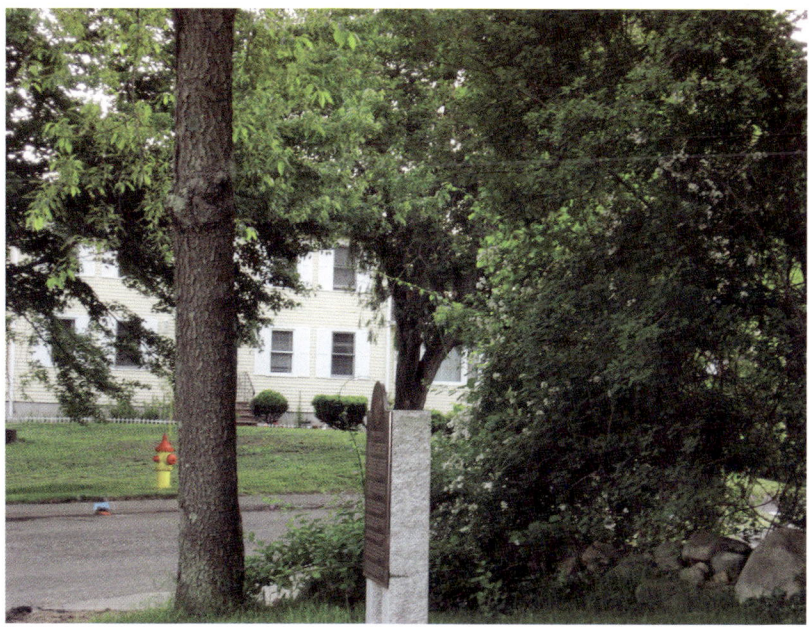

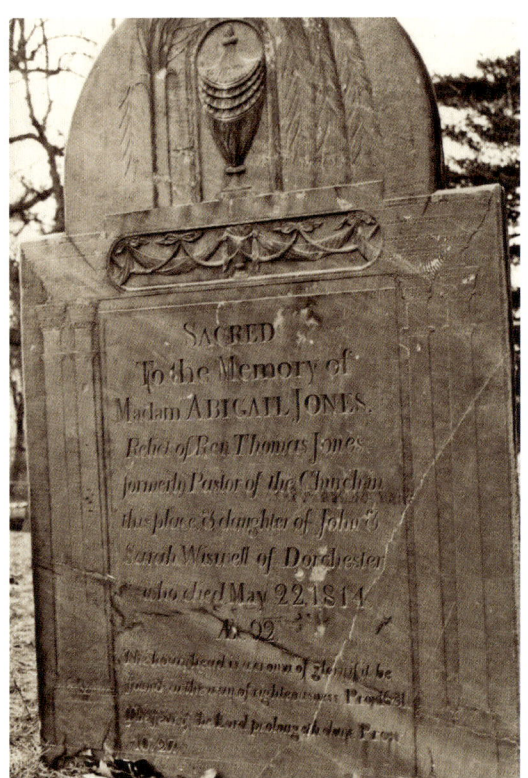

**MADAM ABIGAIL JONES/CUFF TROT:**
Abigail Wiswall Jones, came to Woburn's second parish church with her husband, Rev. Thomas Jones in 1751. At the time of the American Revolution, Abigail Jones lived in the Benjamin Johnson (Sewall) house. She was the hostess at the salmon lunch served to distinguished guests John Hancock and Samuel Adams. Cuff Trot also lived in the famous house as the "domestic servant" of the Jones family. Cuff Trot and Venus Rowe were two African Americans owned (until 1783) by families in this area. (SCAN + IMAGE/RJC)

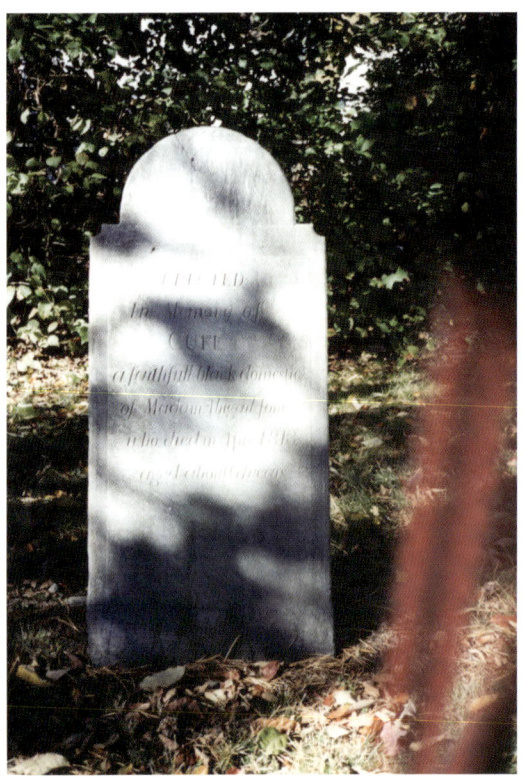

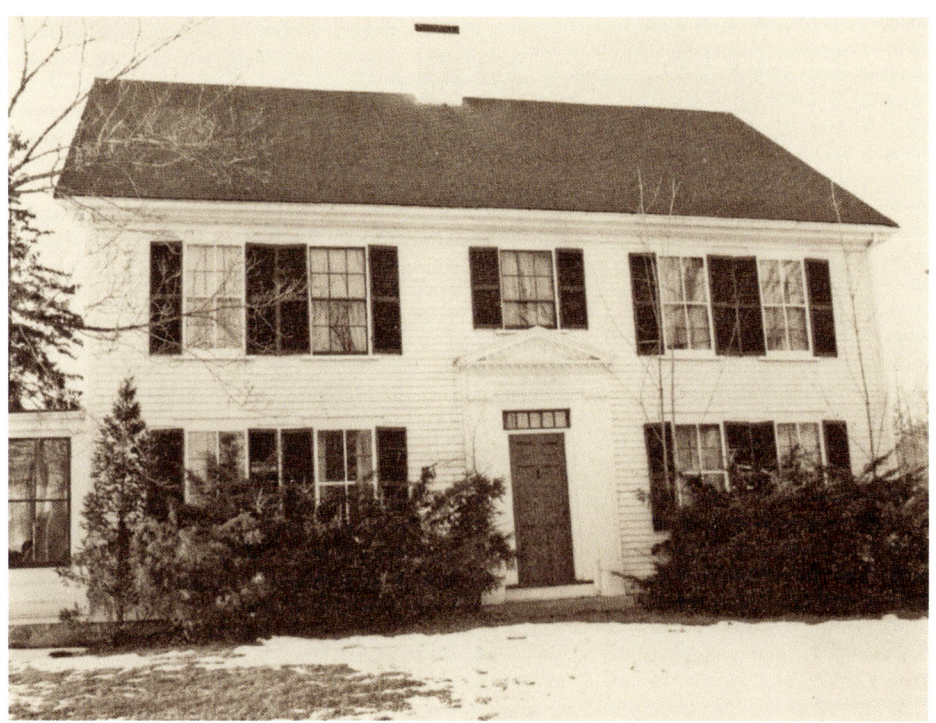

THE JOTHAM JOHNSON HOUSE: One of the finest examples of an early Georgian, center chimney, colonial structure can be found on the road to Lexington, just past the Sewall House site. Known as the Jotham Johnson house, this private residence has many early, distinctive, architectural features, such as the front door pediment. Mystery surrounds the building date of this house, which varies from 1734–1770s, according to local historians, Lotta Dunham and John Fogelberg. (SCAN + IMAGE/RJC)

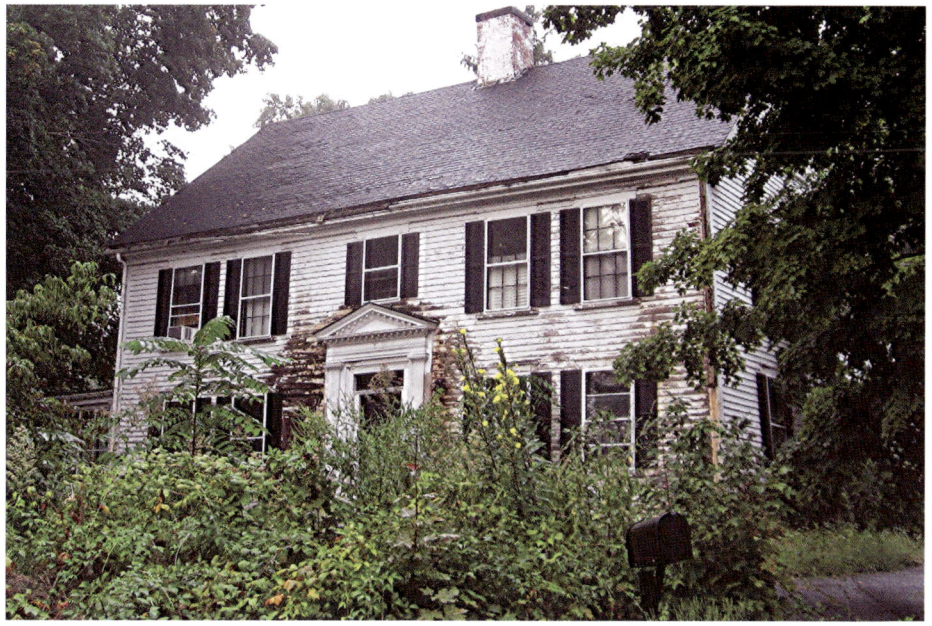

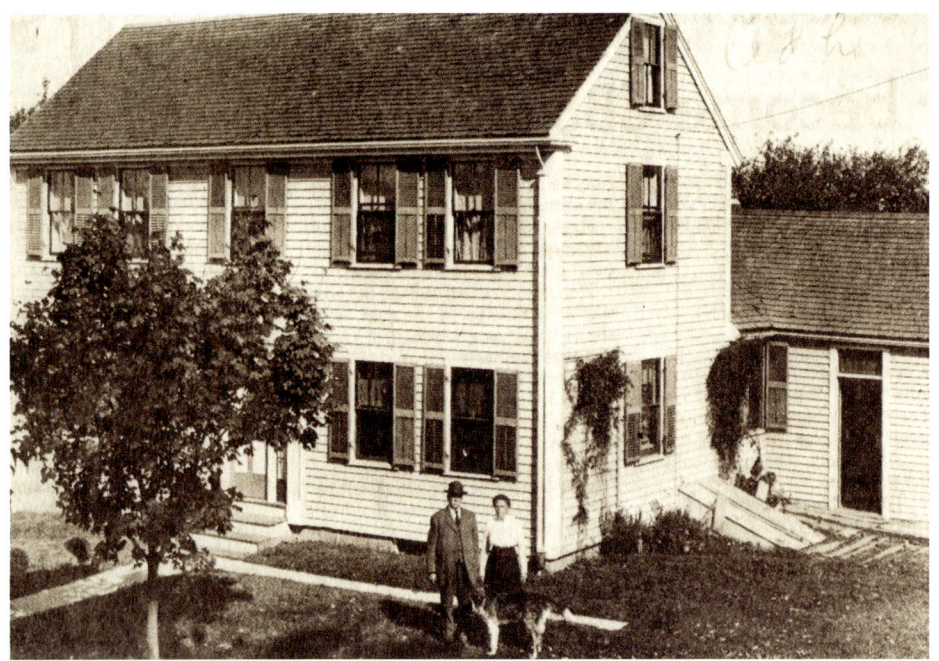

THOMAS LOCKE HOUSE: In the area of Burlington once called "Long Meadow", on Stoney Brook Road, sits a beautifully maintained Greek Revival era gem, the Thomas Locke house. Probably built "around the 1850s" (Goff), there is some dispute among historians Lotta Dunham (1950) and John Fogelberg (1975) concerning the date. It is thought that the talented local cabinetmaker and builder, William Lawrence, influenced the redesign. The land was farmed as a market garden, until the 1940s when most of the property was sold for development. (SCAN + IMAGE/RJC)

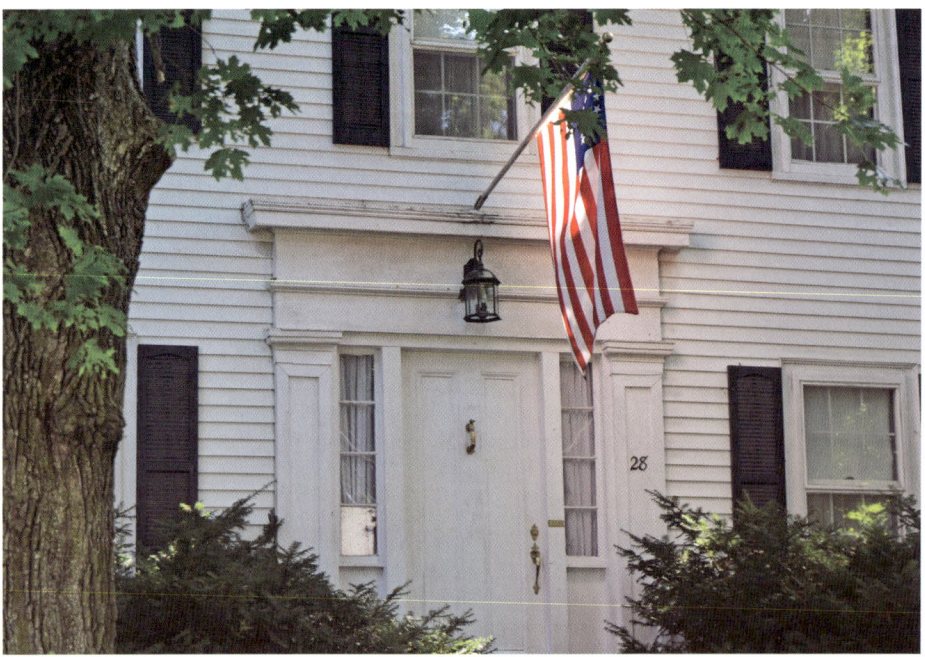

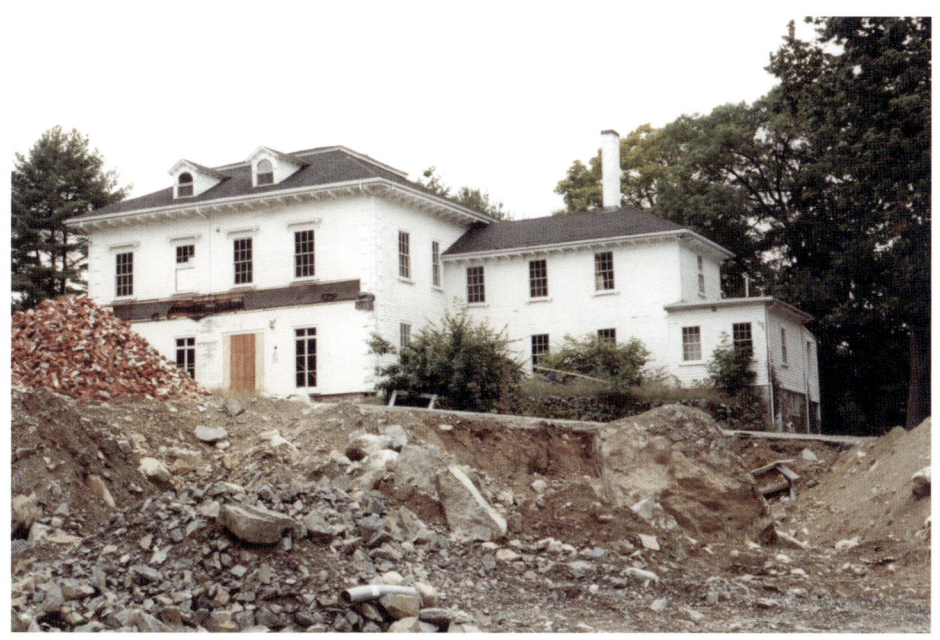

REV. DR. NATHANIEL FROTHINGHAM "MANSION": Atop Spruce Hill is located a modern reminder of our historic past. Once known as the Dr. Nathaniel Frothingham "Mansion", it was described in 1860 as the finest house in Burlington. It was built for one of Boston and Burlington's most notable citizens, Rev. Dr. Nathaniel Frothingham. Today the once extensive grounds have been developed but the "Mansion" has been nicely remodeled as a private residence. The farmland, once extensive, was developed into a cluster of large homes.

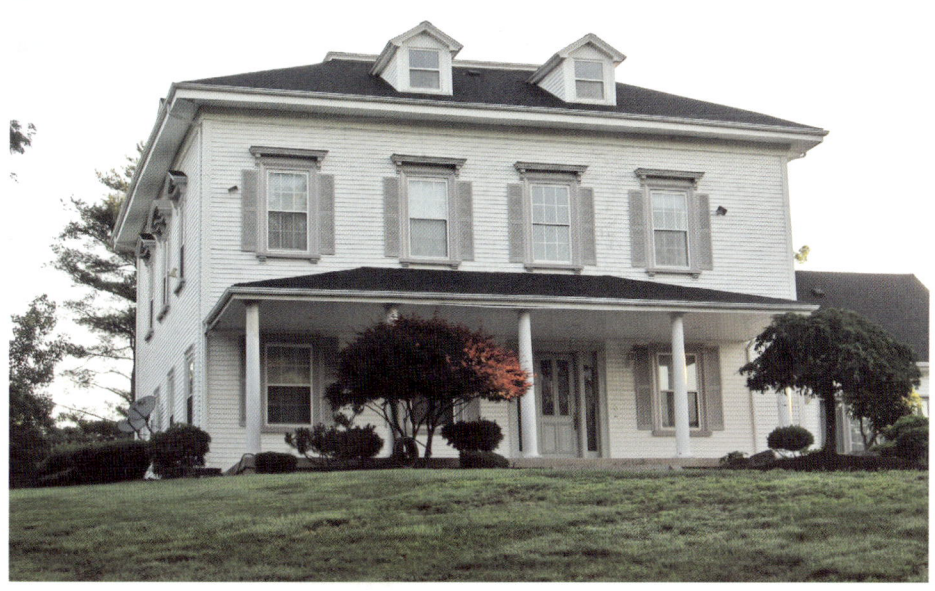

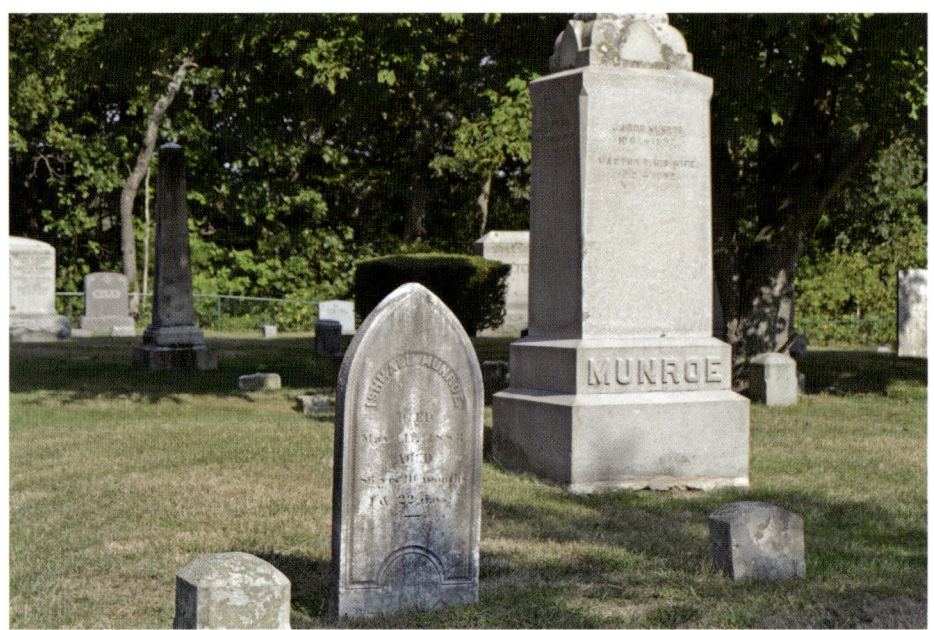

CAPTAIN ISHMAEL MONROE HOUSE:  A notable nineteenth-century landmark on the corner of South Bedford Street and Lexington is the Ishmael Munroe House, also called the Captain Joseph Rice House. A much earlier house, built by James Simonds in 1730, was incorporated in the remodeling of the present structure in *c.* 1850. Lotta Rice Dunham, a Burlington historian, who was born in the house in 1891, recorded a very detailed history of her birthplace, her family and once large farm.  (SCAN + Image/RJC)

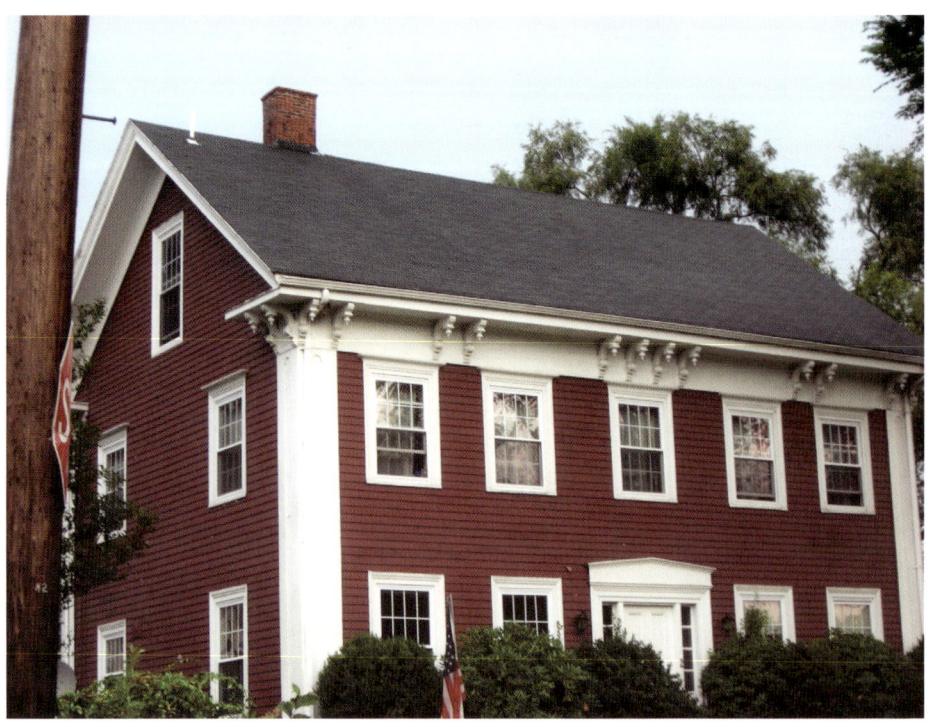

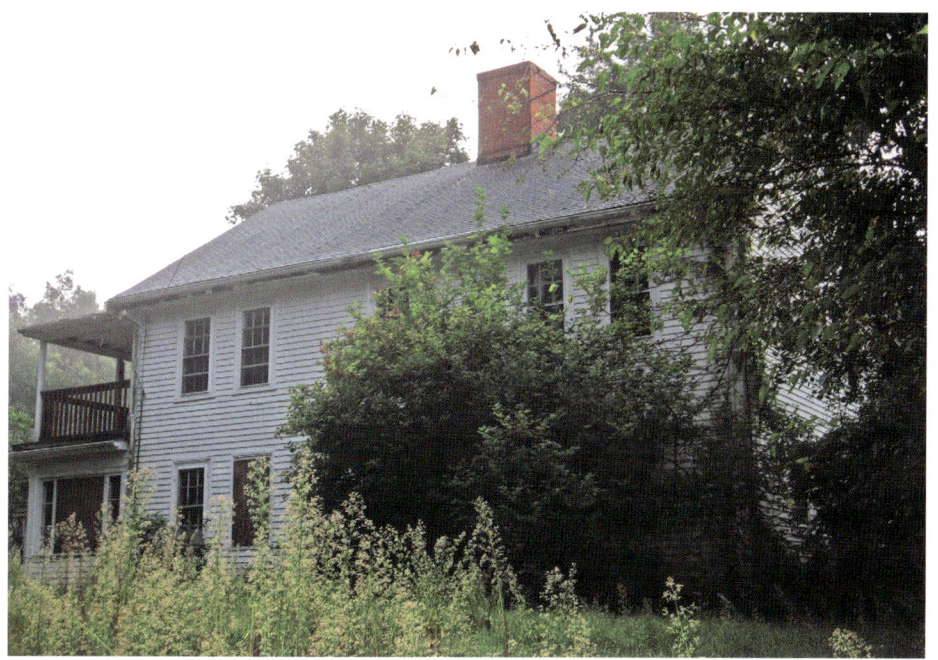

**THE DEACON JONATHAN SIMONDS HOUSE:** Soon to be lost in Burlington history, the Deacon Jonathan Simonds house was built in 1781 and remodeled in the early nineteenth century by noted housewright and neighbor Ishmael Monroe. Monroe considered it a fine example of a country Federal Style house with Greek Revival details. Jonathan Simonds, yet another Second Parish militiaman who served in Captain Joshua Walker's militia company, participated in the events on April 19, 1775. (SCAN + IMAGE /RJC)

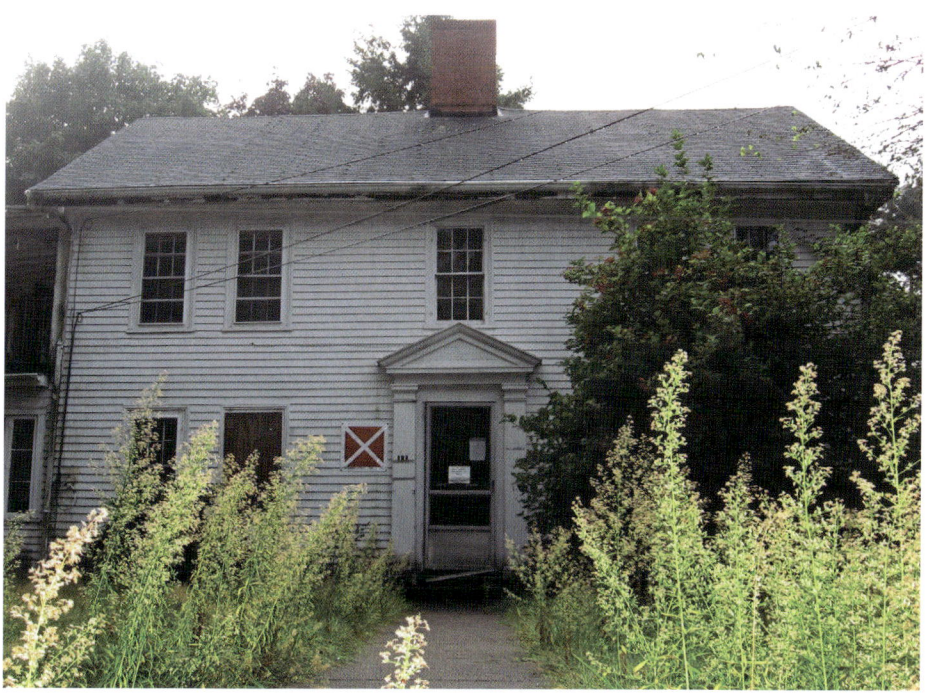

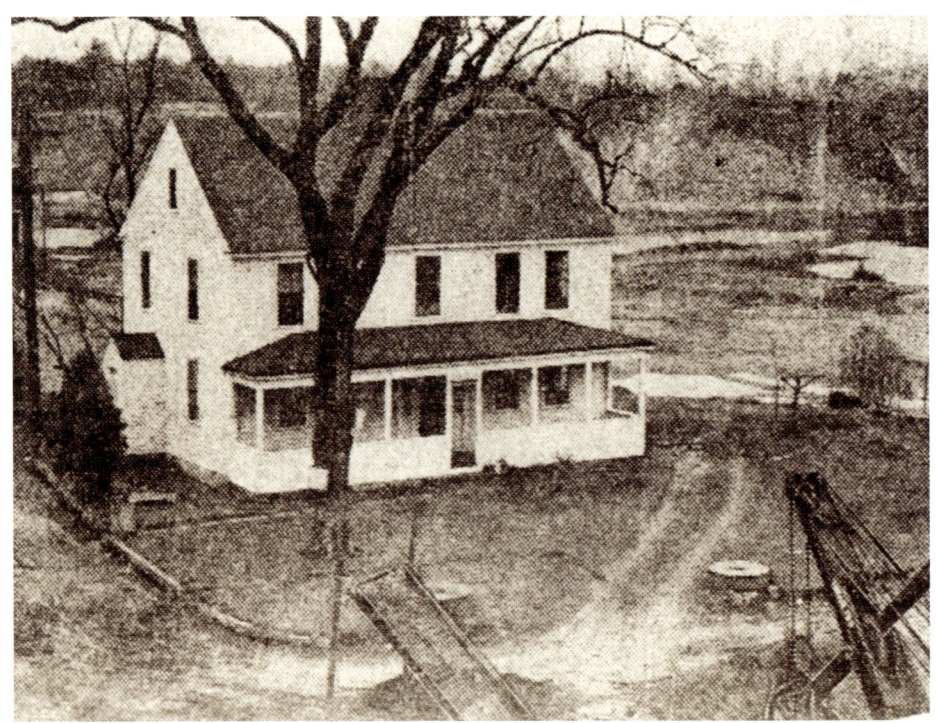

**CAPTAIN JAMES REED'S FARM SITE:** Captain James Reed was a member of the Second Parish militia unit who saw action in the opening event of the American Revolution on April 19, 1775. Reed is credited with holding British prisoners of the days fighting captive on his farm. His house and farmlands once stood on the "lost" part of Lexington Street where Route 128 and the Route 3 interchange are located in 2013. The house was moved in 1955 to make way for Route 128, was abandoned and later burned. (SCAN + IMAGE/RJC)

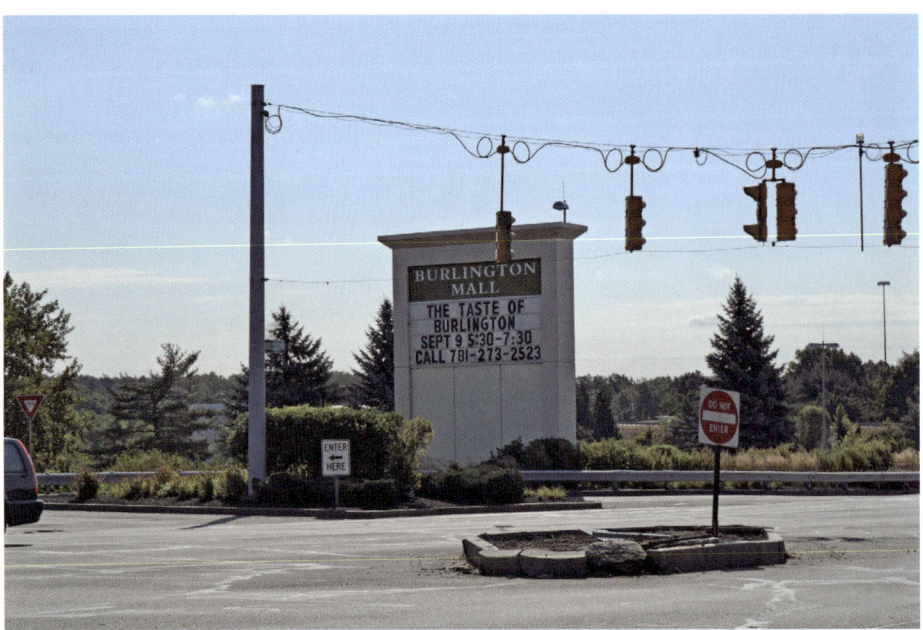

# SECTION 3

# THE DISTRICT SCHOOLHOUSE

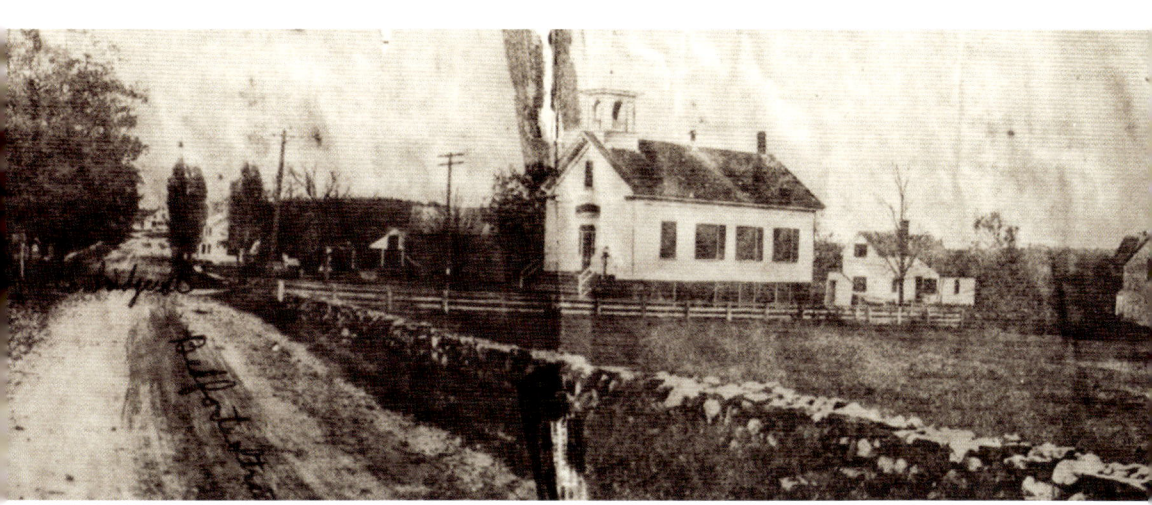

# SECTION 3

# INTRODUCTION

After graduation from the University of Massachusetts, Amherst, with a B.A. in History, the author began teaching at Burlington High School in 1974. The town of Burlington, and Woburn before it, valued the concept of public education. Since 1794, with the law that required the building of four one-room, district schoolhouses, the town has provided quality structures for the education of their children. Burlington has been resourceful in creating, renovating and maintaining its houses of learning. Historical structures have been saved and reutilized. The impressive work on the Memorial and Marshall Simonds Middle School in 2012 illustrates this assertion.

*Previous page:* The Center School of 1855 when it housed the Town Library *c.* 1900, now the Burlington Public Museum.

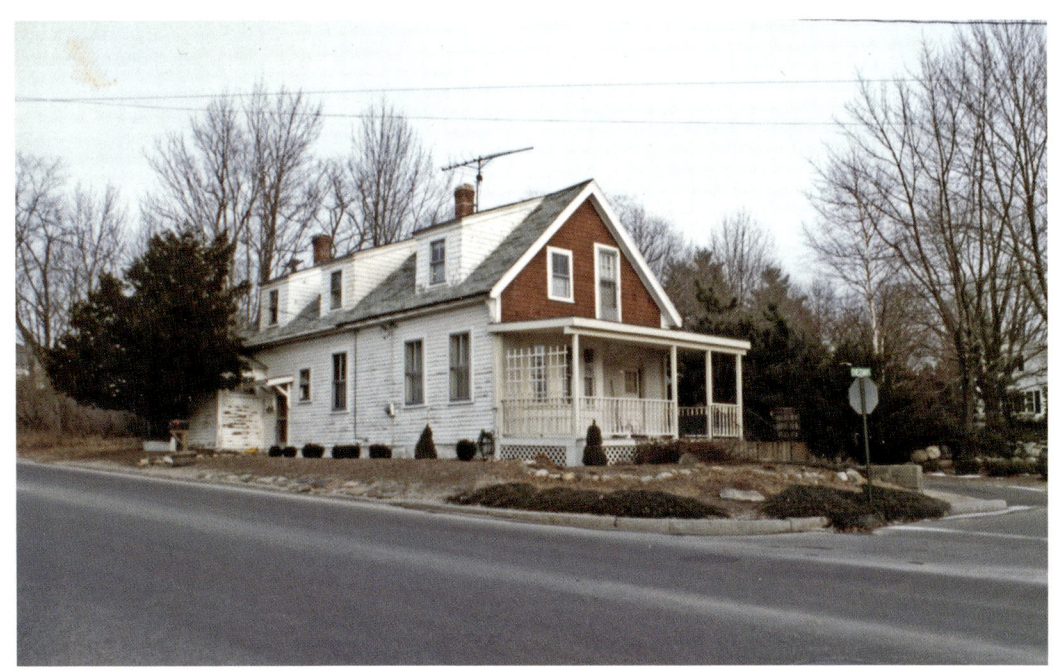

NORTH SCHOOL:  In 1794 the town of Woburn authorized the building of four one-room schoolhouses in the Second Parish, today the town of Burlington. The North School or Lt. Jesse Dean's District School was moved from its original location on Chesnut Ave. over a land dispute. All district schools were closed by 1898 when the Union School opened. It is now a private residence. (SCAN/RJC) (RJC/IMAGE)

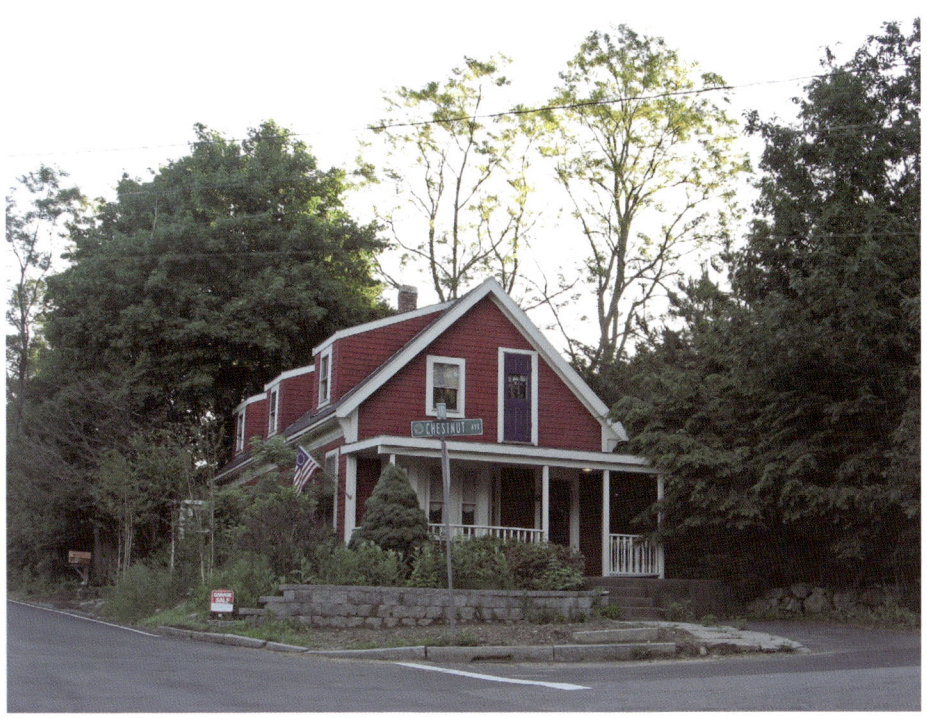

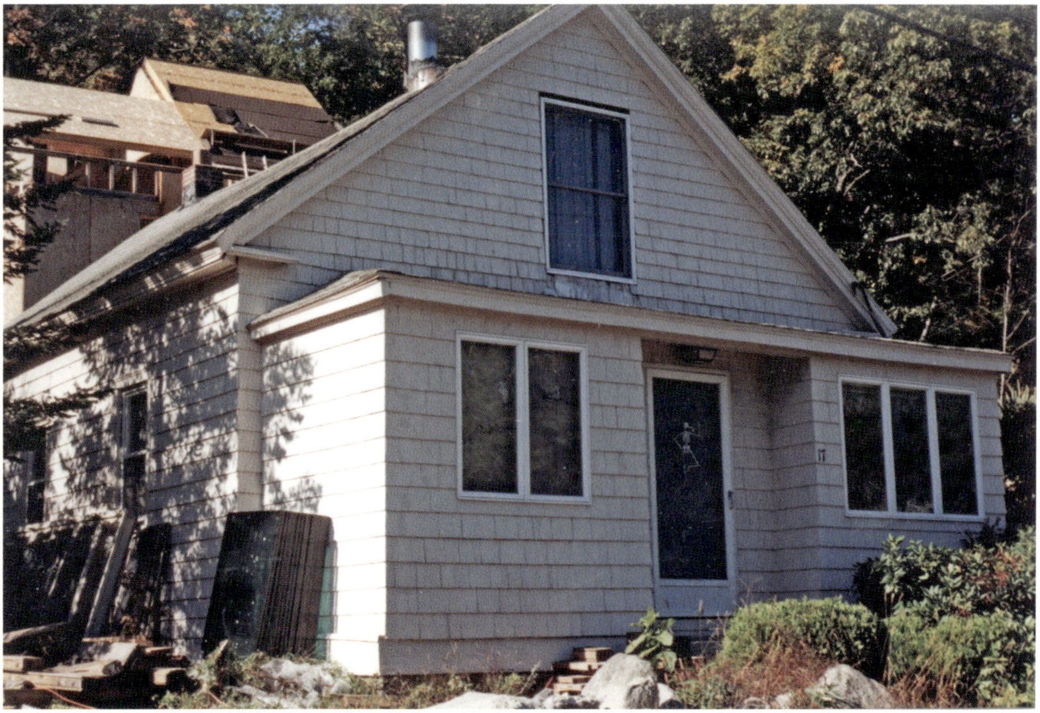

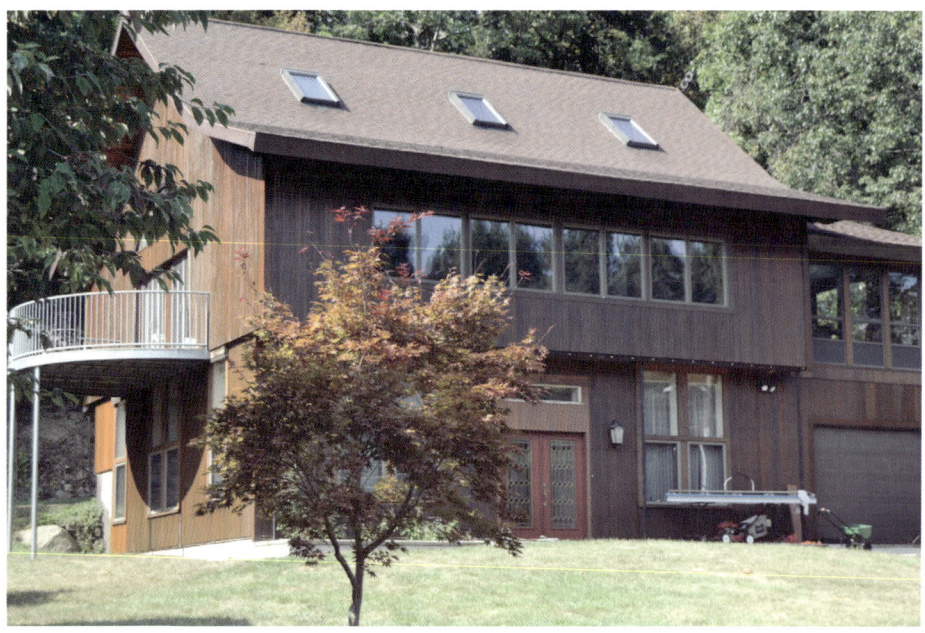

**THE EAST SCHOOL:** The East School or Lt. Joseph Winn District School was a recent loss for Burlington's rich past. Built on Mountain Rd. in 1794, it had been a private home until *c.* 2000, when a modern, much larger structure was built and the East School destroyed. The Winn family, led by Edward Winn, settled in this region in 1642. Lt. Joseph Winn, a descendant of Edward Winn, was a militiaman in the American Revolution and opened the Hens and Chickens Tavern. (SCAN/BTA) (RJC/IMAGE)

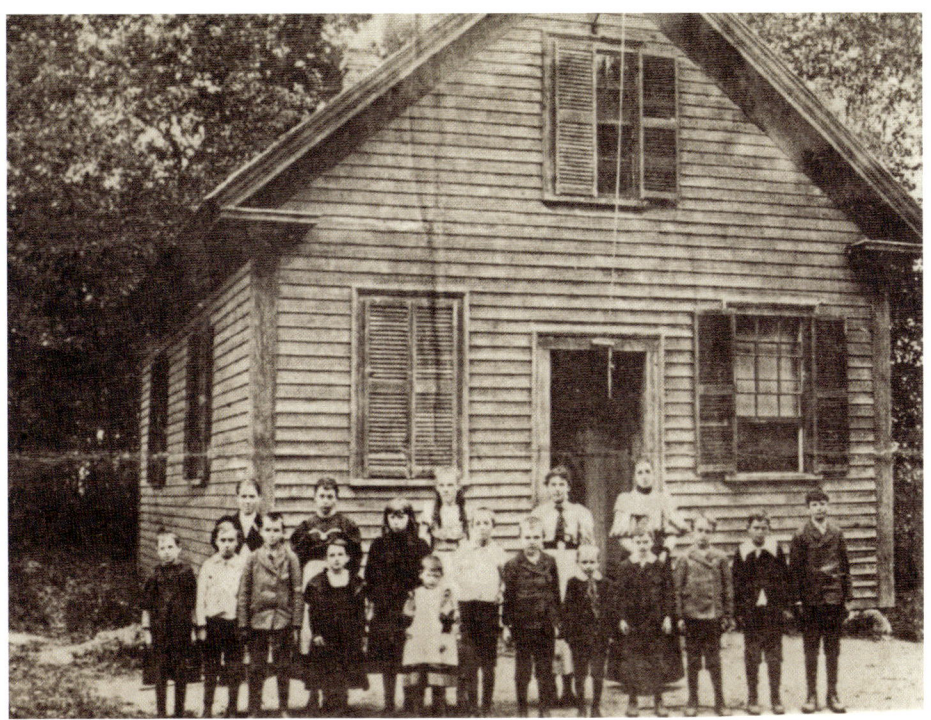

THE SOUTH SCHOOL: In the lost section of Lexington Street, where the Burlington Mall is now, the South School or Captain James Reed's District School was erected in 1794. Lexington Street extended through the mall area to eventually connect with the road to the town of Lexington. After it ceased use as a school 1898, the South School was used as a private home, and later moved further down Blanchard Rd. (its original location). By the 1950s it had fallen into disrepair and was demolished.(SCAN/BTA) (RJC/IMAGE)

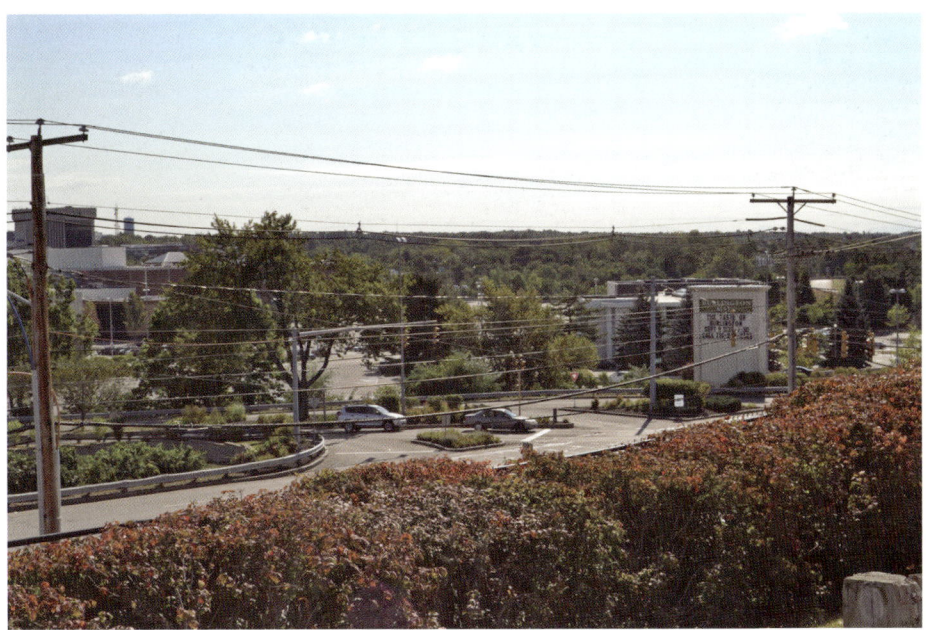

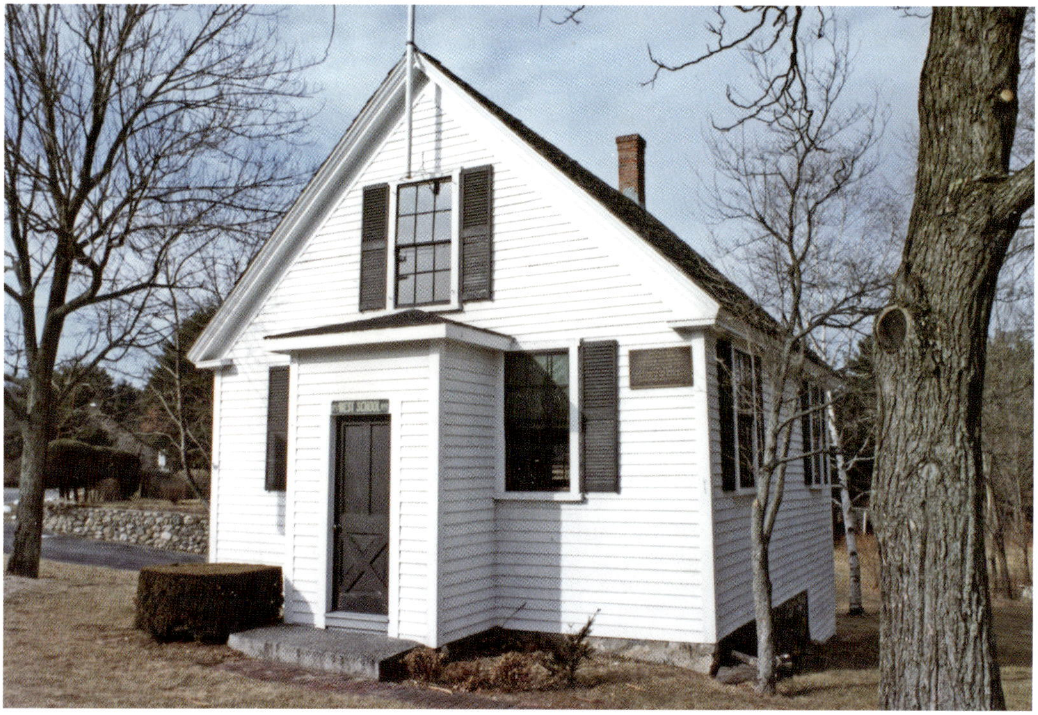

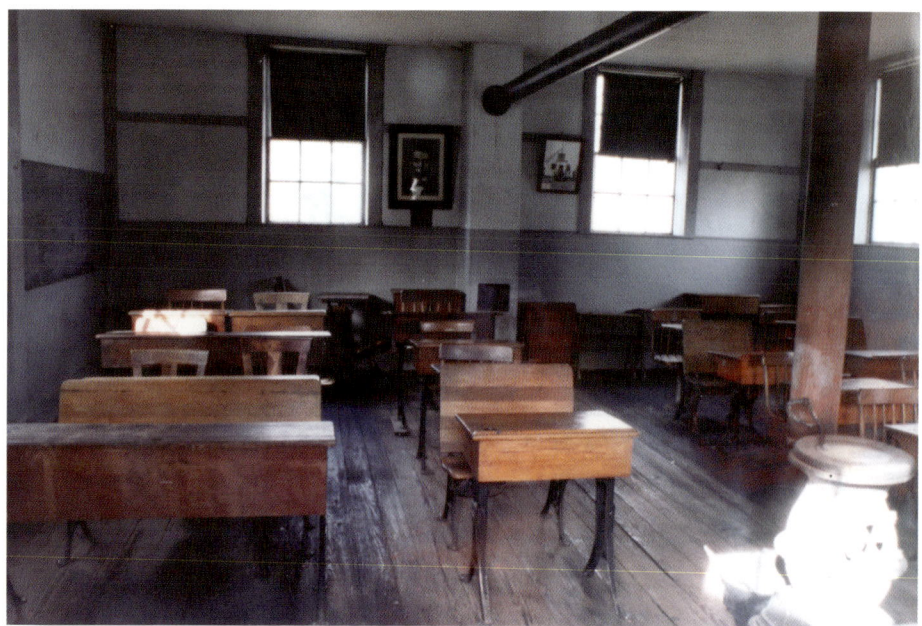

WEST SCHOOL:   Another iconic Burlington landmark, one that has been placed on the National Register of Historic Places—is the West School. Originally built on the hill in today's Simond Park in 1794, it was moved to Havenville in 1839. The West School was spared from destruction in 1964, when it was used as an auto shop and slated for destruction. The Burlington Historical Society was organized and worked to save and renovate today's West School Historical Museum. (SCAN + IMAGE/RJC)

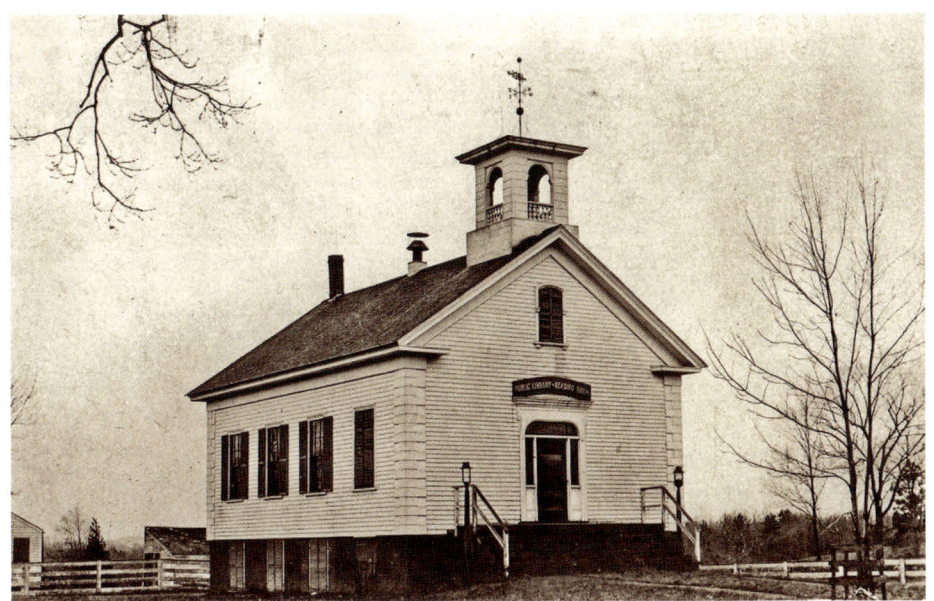

CENTER SCHOOL 1855: A most recognizable sight near the Burlington Town Common is the historic 1855 Center School. This sturdy building has seen use as a school, library, temporary Police Station and is now the Burlington Town Museum. When the Union School opened in 1898, it became obsolete but was reborn and has served the town to this day. Run by the town's Historical Commission, it contains an interesting collection of local artifacts and is often open to visits from today's schoolchildren. (SCAN/BTA) (RJC/IMAGE)

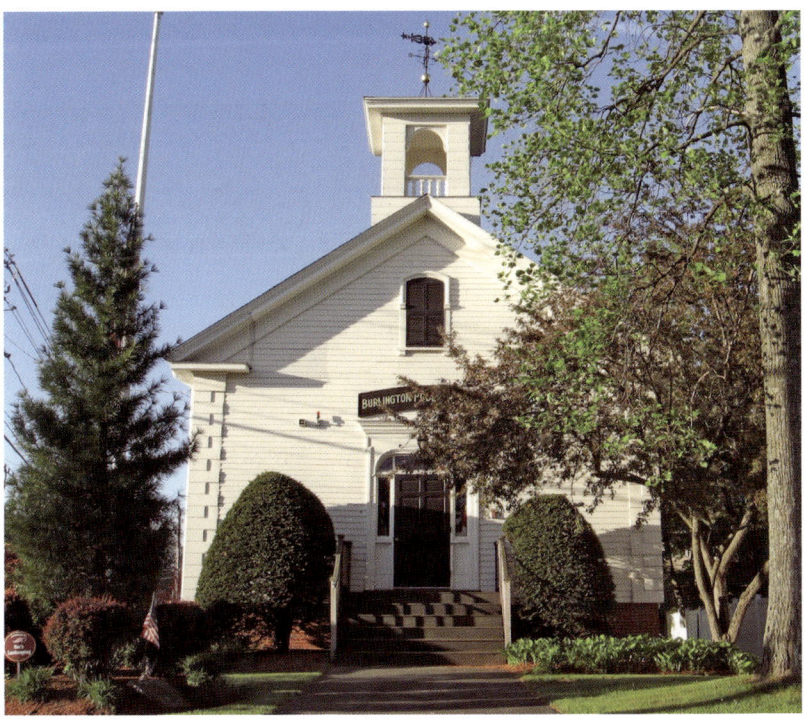

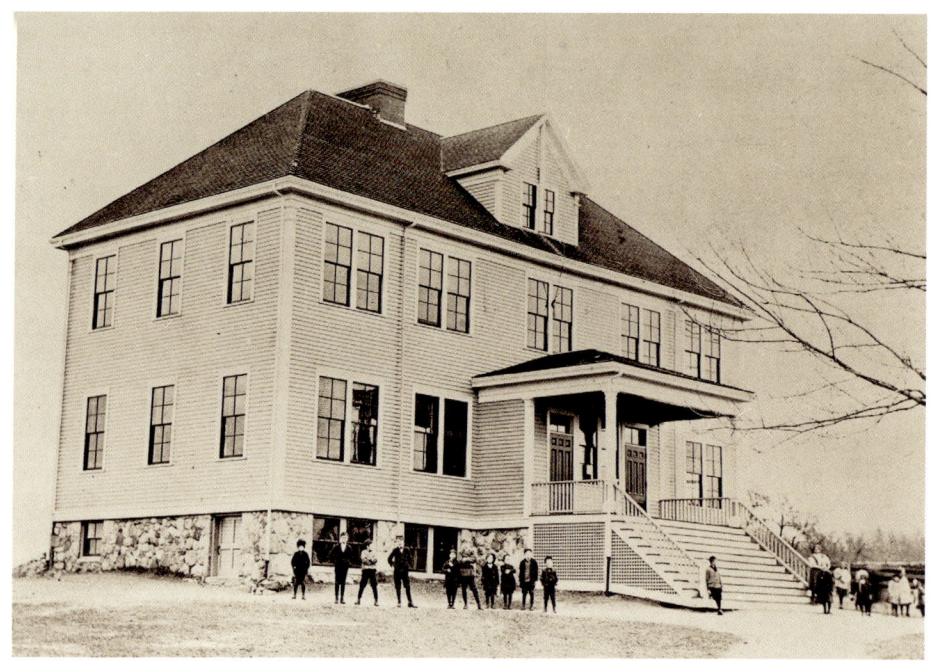

UNION SCHOOL/BPD: The Union School was built in 1898 with the intent to consolidate the town's school population. At the turn of the twentieth century the trend in public education was for a centralized school district. The original structure had two rooms upstairs and two rooms down. In 1972 the school was closed but the building continued to serve the town as a senior center, coffee house, and bank. Today a modernized Union School is home to the Burlington Police Department. (SCAN/BTA) (RJC/IMAGE)

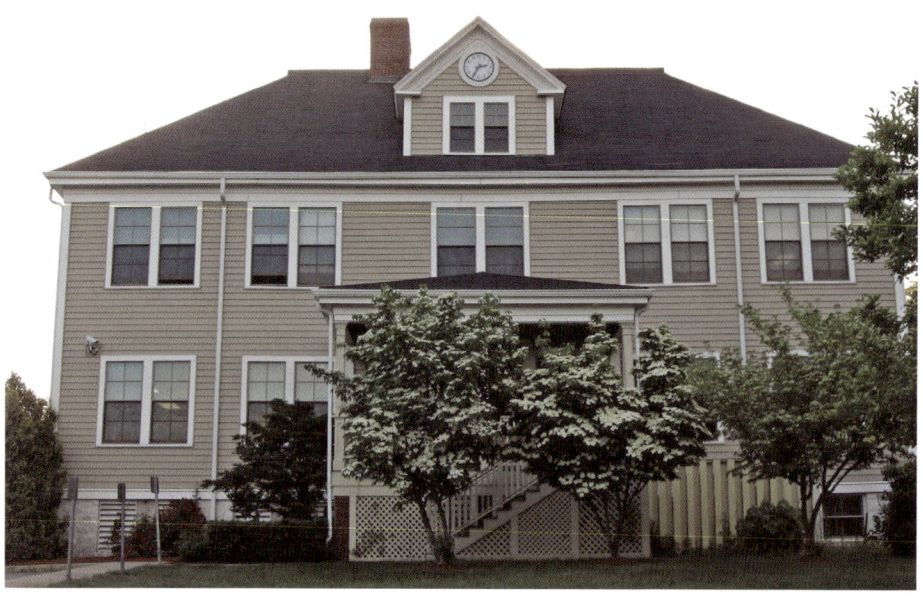

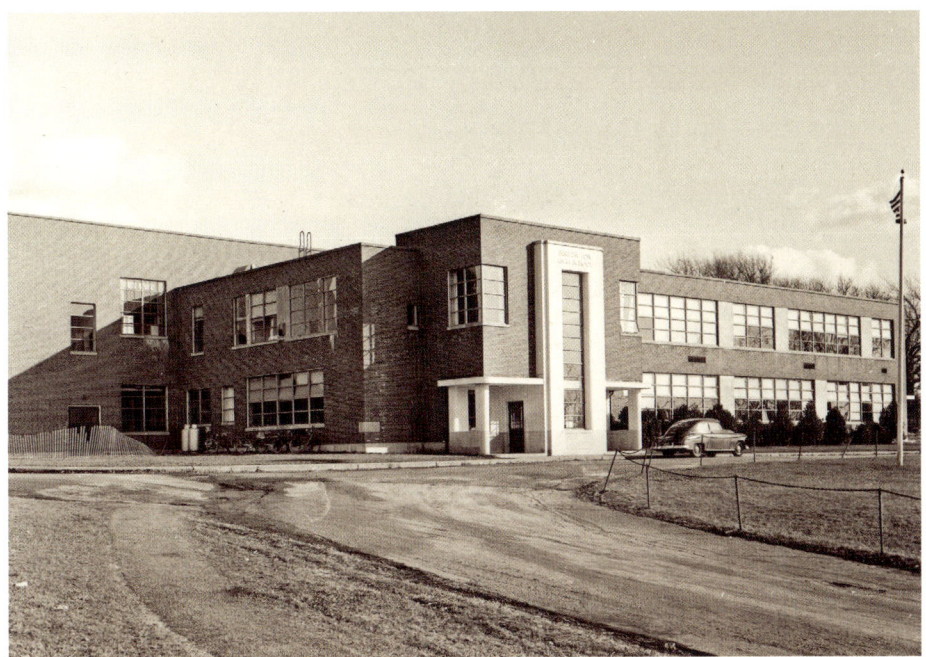

BURLINGTON HIGH SCHOOL I/REC:  By 1939 Burlington needed its own High School. Prior to this time, town school children were sent to Woburn and Lexington's High Schools. During the end of the Great Depression work began on the first Burlington High School by the Works Progress Administration, a New Deal agency. The work was completed by 1939 and it remained a school facility until the 1970s. Burlington's Senior Center, the Recreation Department, and other town agencies occupy the Center School today. (SCAN/BTA) (RJC/IMAGE)

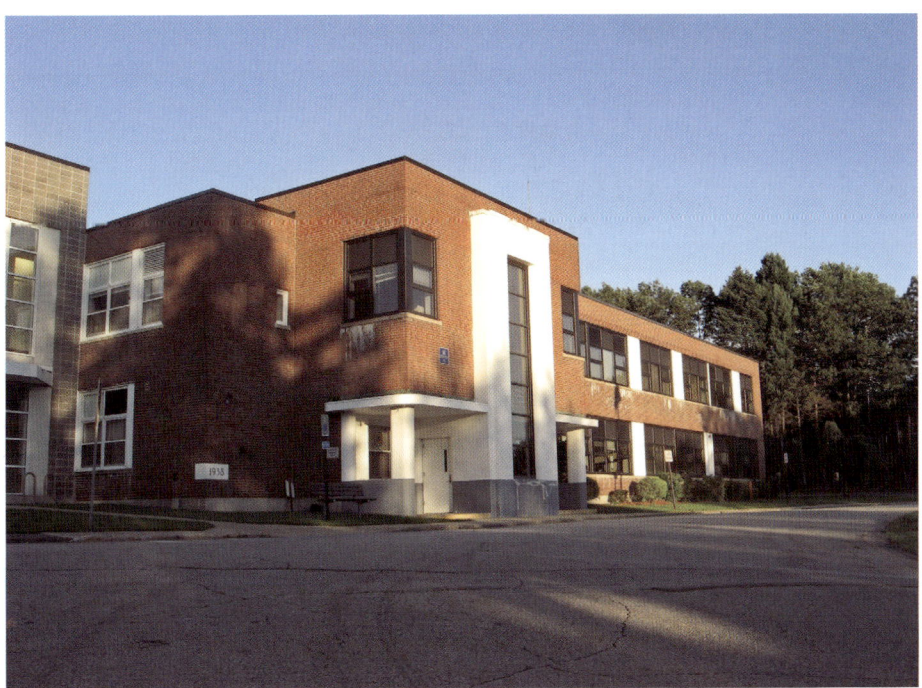

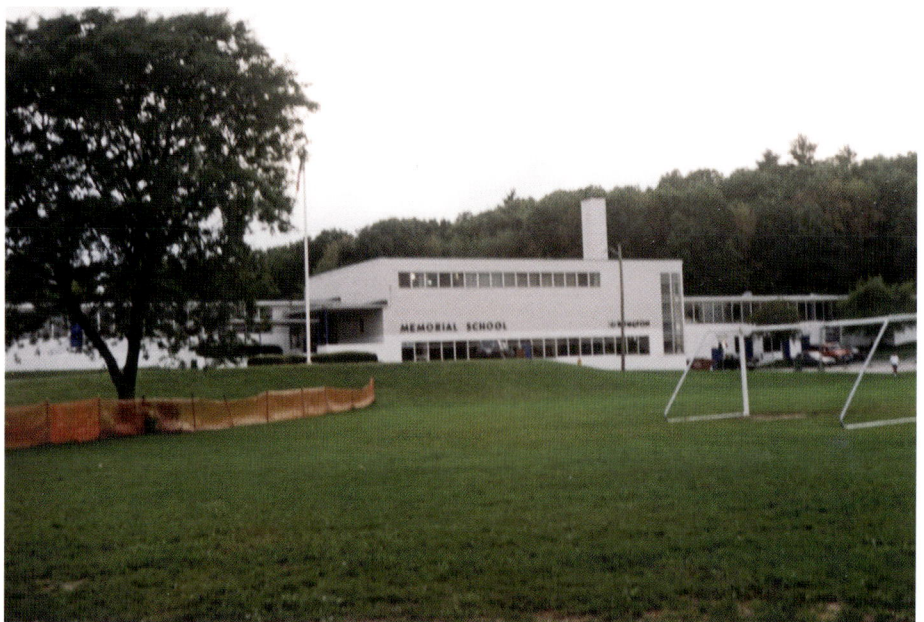

THE MEMORIAL SCHOOL: Burlington's population spiked in the years following the Second World War through the early 1960s. Urban dwellers, eager to leave the city for country life, aided by the new Route 128, discovered the pastoral splendor that was Burlington. After the Korean War, the town opened its first elementary school and in honor of the veterans of the "conflict", named it Memorial. That building was replaced with the very new (2012) Memorial School, today occupying the former playing fields of Burlington's first real elementary school. (SCAN + IMAGE/RJC)

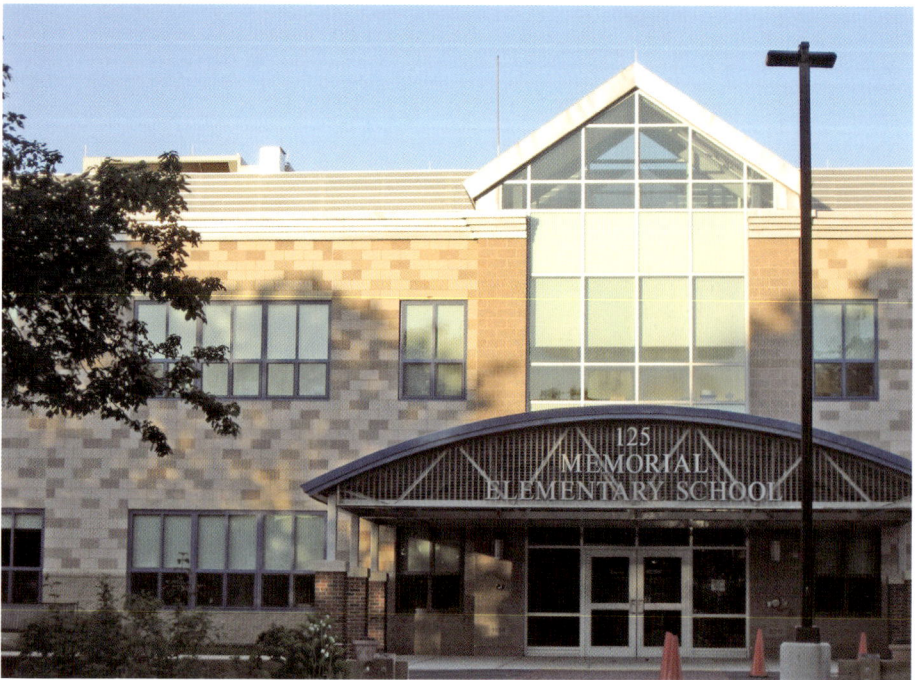

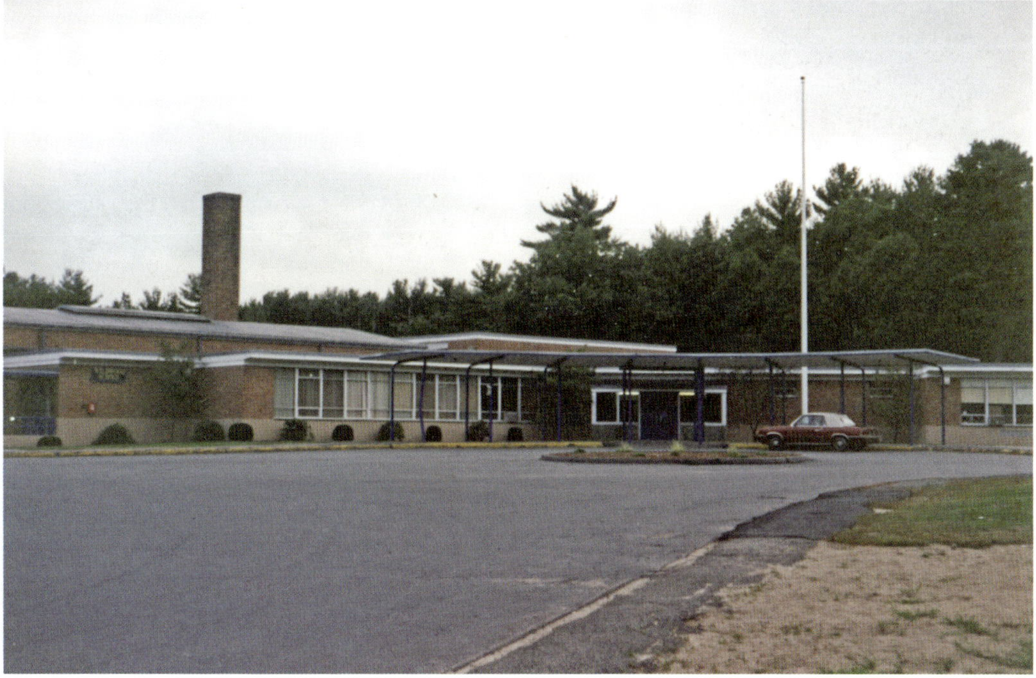

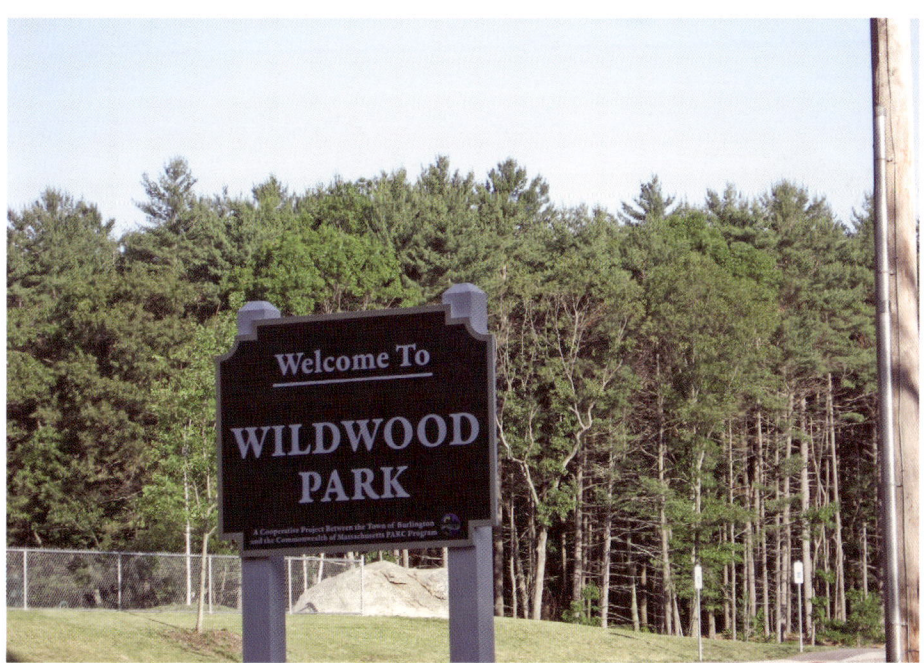

THE WILDWOOD SCHOOL:   Burlington continued to expand its population through the 1950s and in 1957 built another elementary school named Wildwood. It was located on land that was owned by the Simonds Family, in the section of Burlington called Havenville. By the turn of the twenty-first century it was vacant and had deteriorated. The building was razed and after debate about utilization of the site, the town wisely decided to create a new park for the community. It is named Wildwood. (SCAN + IMAGE/RJC)

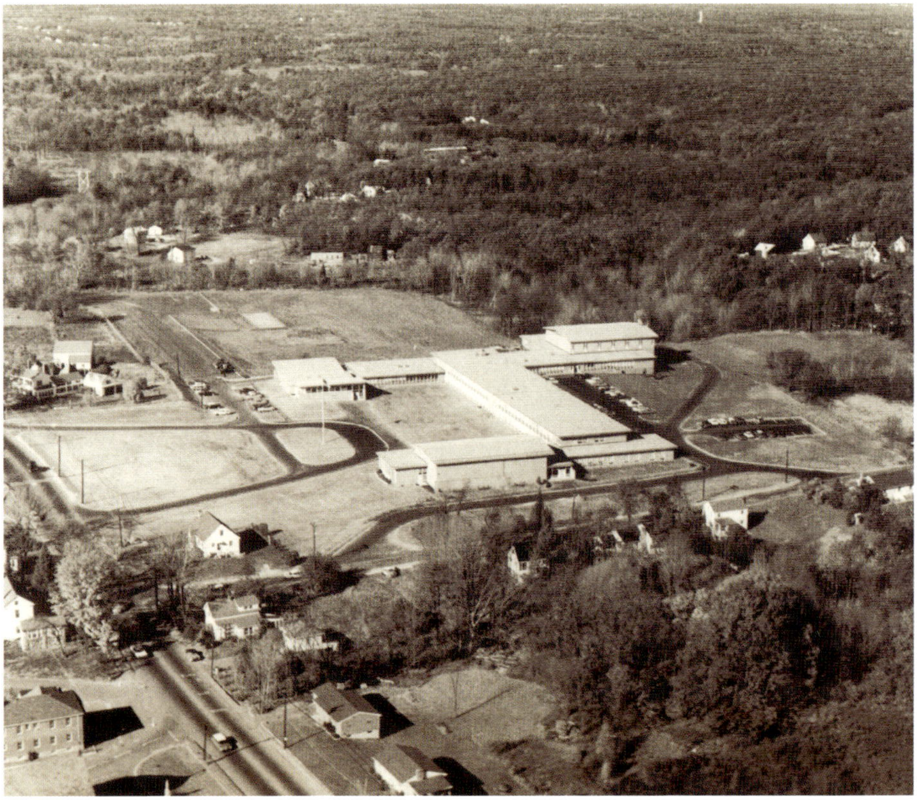

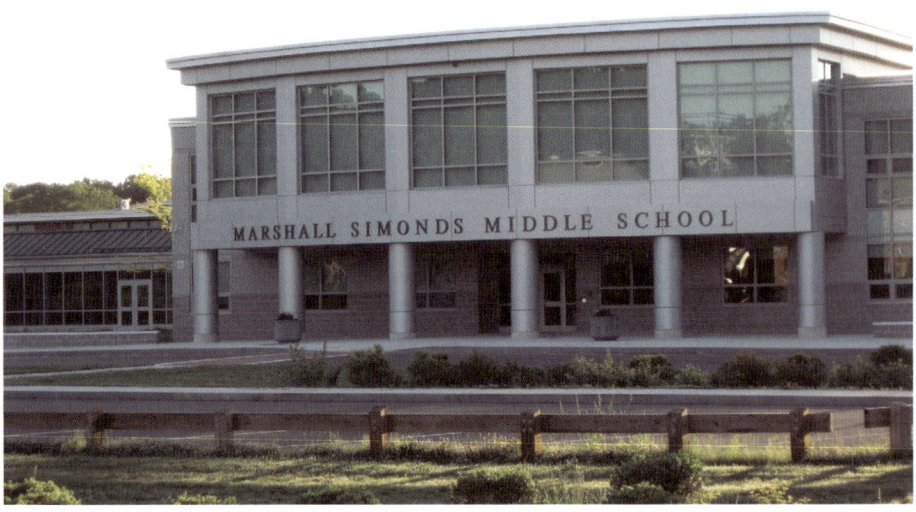

**BHS II/MSMS:** The bold new Marshall Simonds Middle School, greatly expanded, sits proudly on the former farmlands of the Walker family. Burlington's second high school opened in 1961 and once held grades 8–12. The school population had increased dramatically from the late 1950s to the early 1970s, and more space was needed. This was the Burlington High School the author attended. By 1972 there was such overcrowding, a new High School was built and the site eventually became the Marshall Simonds Middle School. (SCAN + IMAGE/RJC)

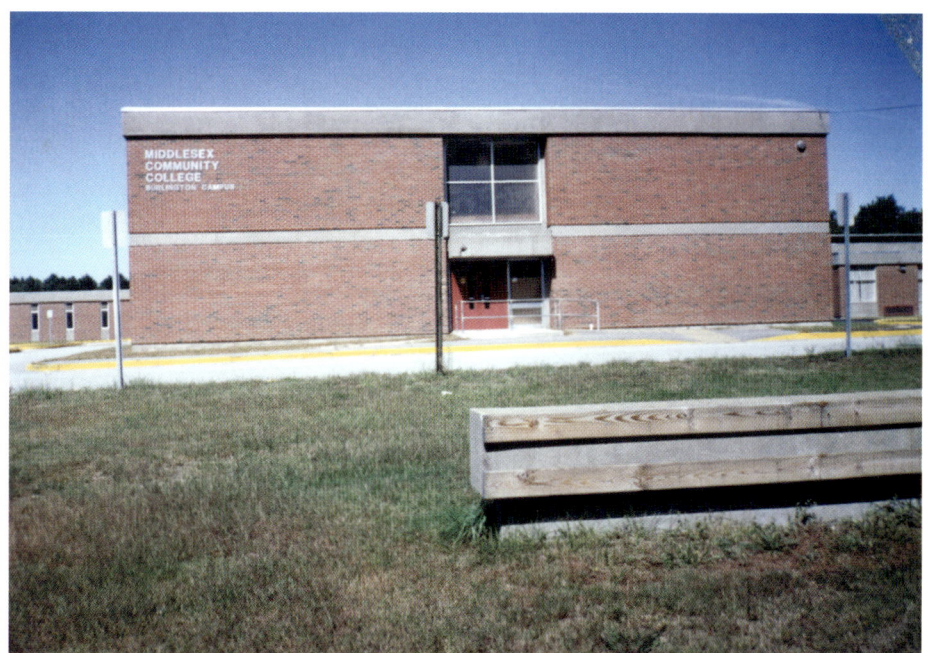

FRANCIS WYMAN ELEMENTARY SCHOOL:    Named after one of the earliest settlers of the region, the Francis Wyman School was completed in 1968, and opened as a Junior High School. When the third and current Burlington High School opened in 1973, the system was reorganized and it became a Middle School for a time. After its use as a middle school, the town rented the building to various groups including a Police Academy and Middlesex Community College. It has returned to its original use as an elementary school, expanded and modernized. (SCAN + IMAGE/RJC)

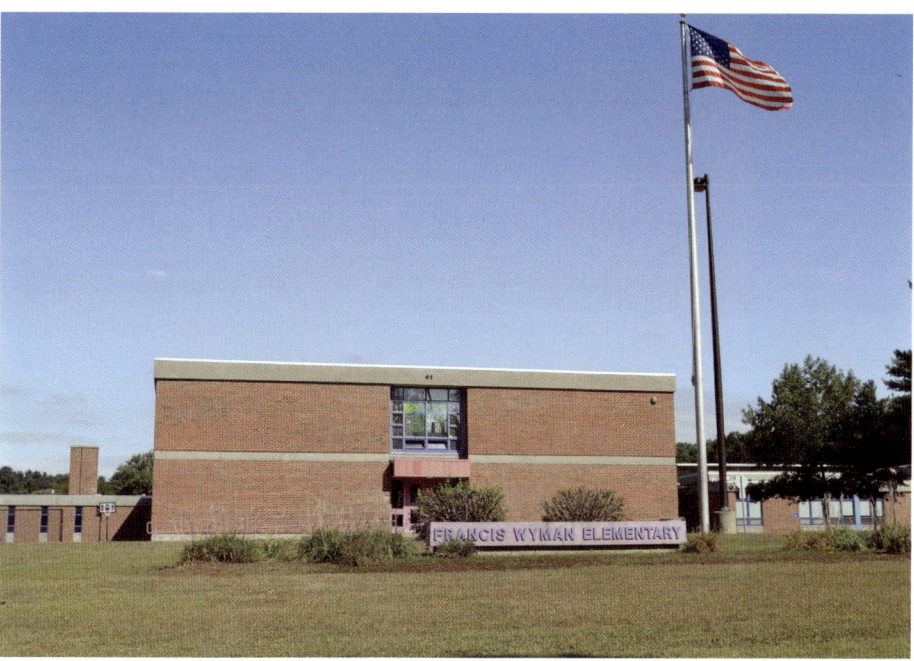

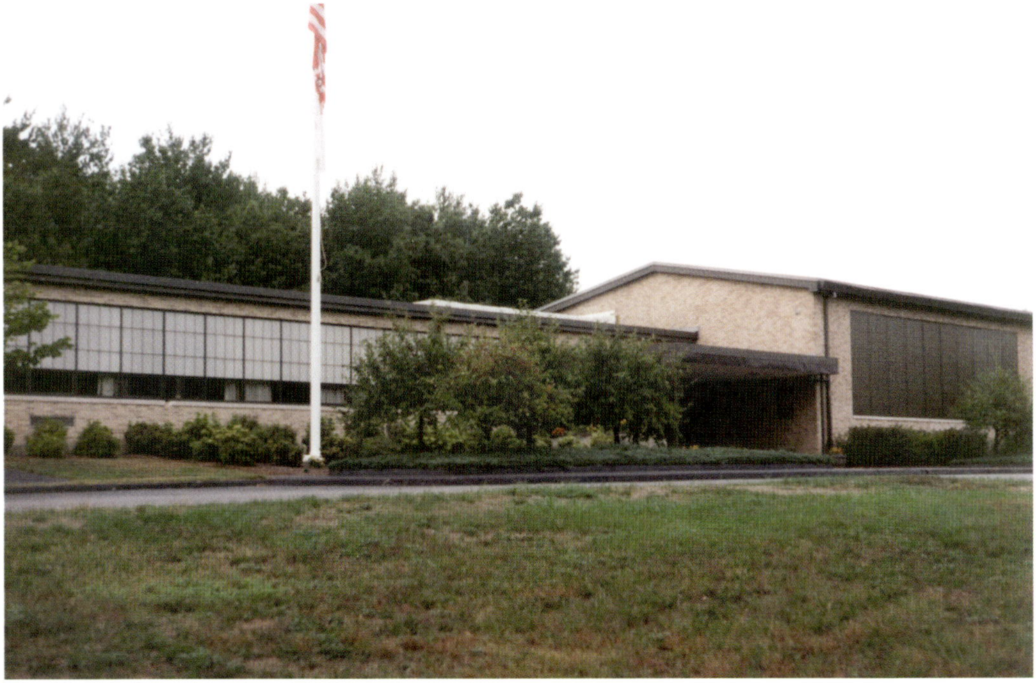

**MEADOWBROOK SCHOOL/MT. HOPE ACADAMY:**  Located off Lexington Street, adjacent to the playing fields of BHS, Mt. Hope Academy is the current occupant on the site of the former Meadowbook Elementary School. Built during a period of a great increase in Burlington's population, the Meadowbrook opened in 1959. It was one of the first elementary schools to close and the private school has occupied the site for many years. (SCAN + IMAGE/RJC)

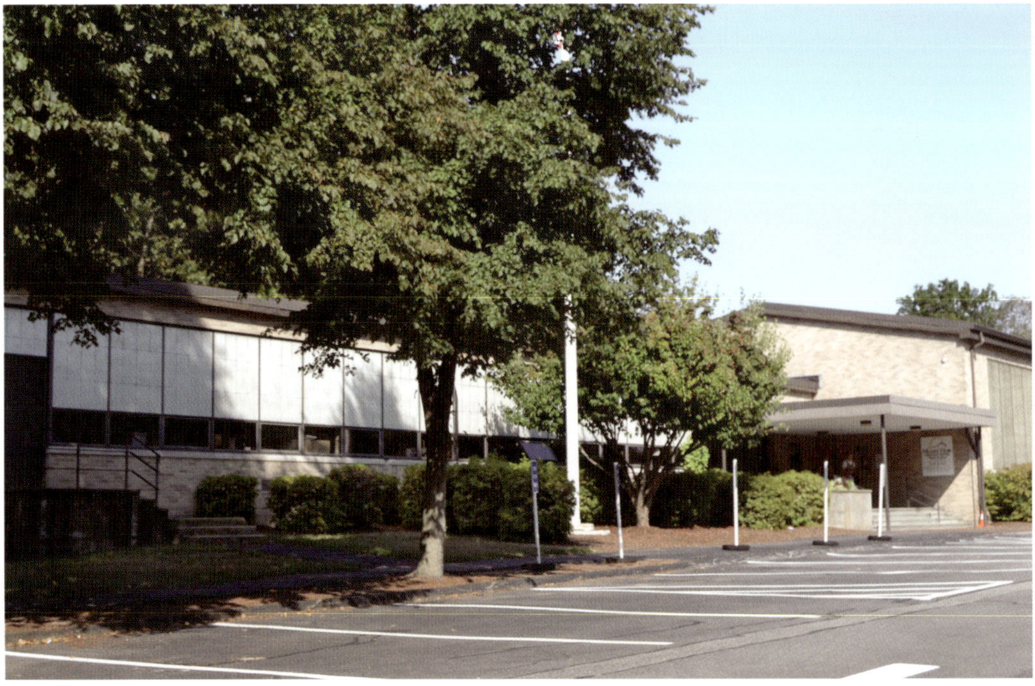

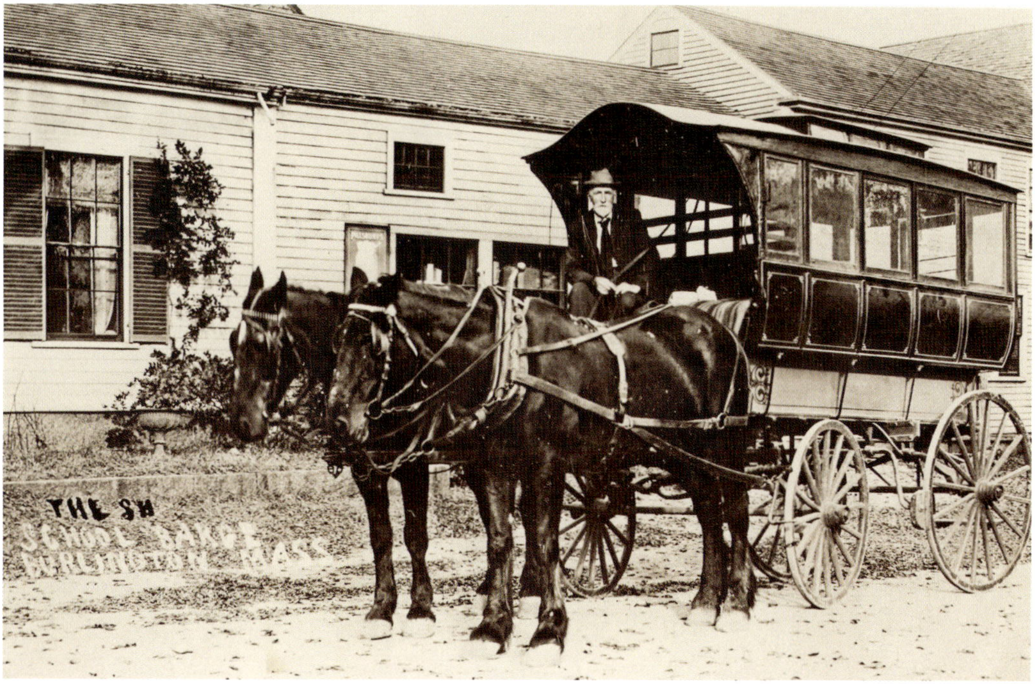

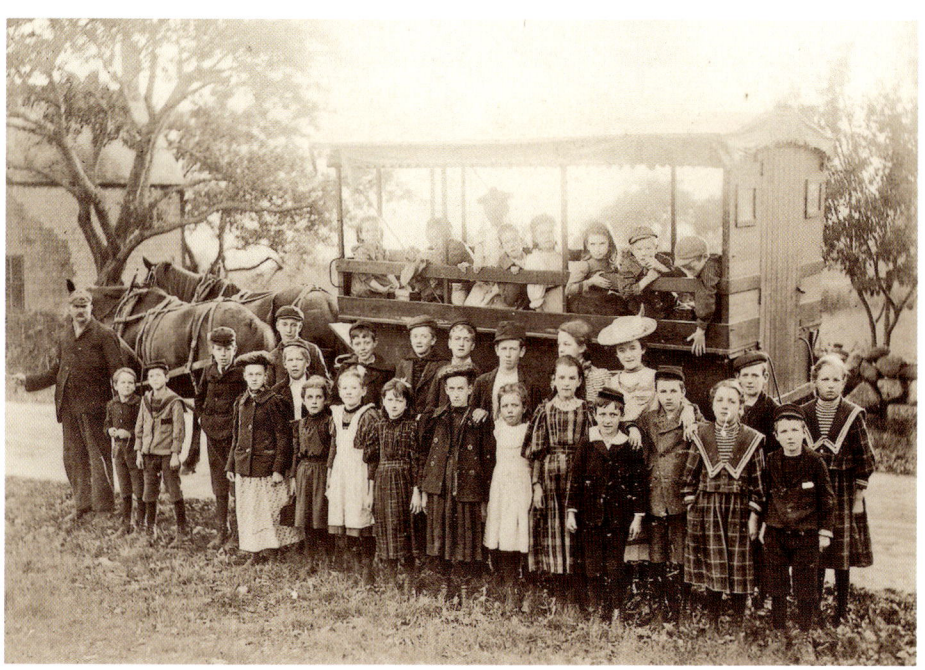

**"THE BARGE"**: "The Barge," Burlington's first school bus, stands ready to pickup its precious cargo, *c.* 1900. This location, near the General Store, seems to indicate that the bus driver's route was around the Union School. Frank Barnaby became one of the first bus drivers, when in March 1899, a town meeting approved $400 to provide a school bus service. In the *c.* 1902 image, very well dressed students and Mr. Barnaby stand proudly before and in "The Barge". (SCANS/BTA + HISTORICAL COMMISSION)

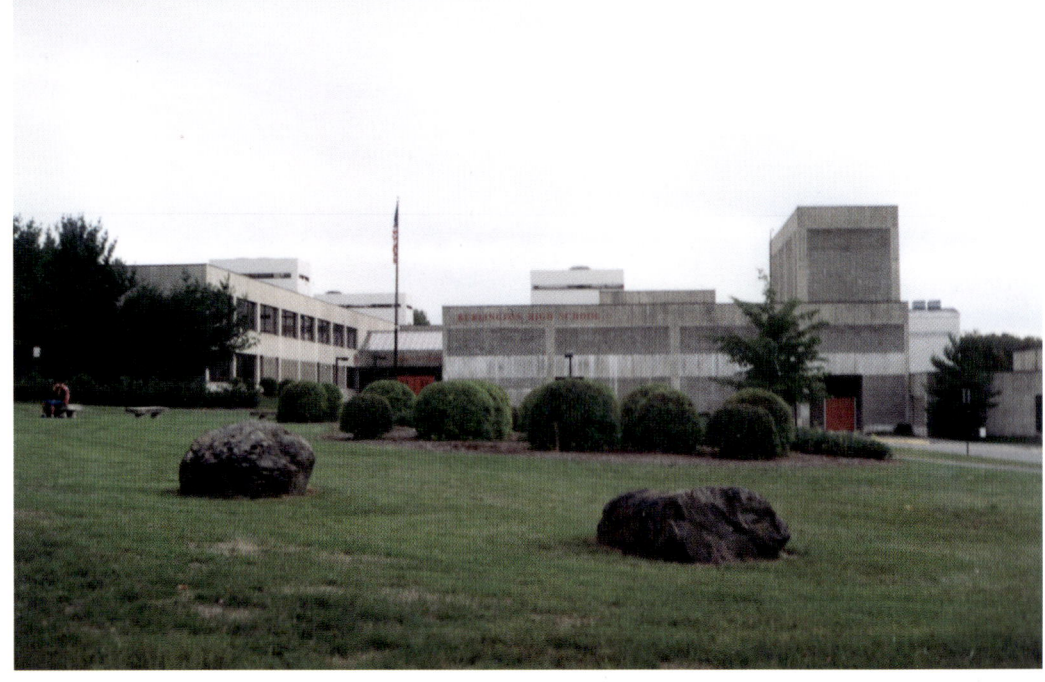

BHS THEN/NOW:   The third and present Burlington High School opened in the spring of 1973. The massive, concrete, modern design was built to house 2,100 students. Innovative programs were instituted, class sizes were very high and controversy surrounded the need, location, and cost of the building. This was the High School where the author taught History, especially Burlington History, for thirty-eight years. Today there are far fewer students and many organizations in the community use this large space. (SCAN + IMAGE/RJC)

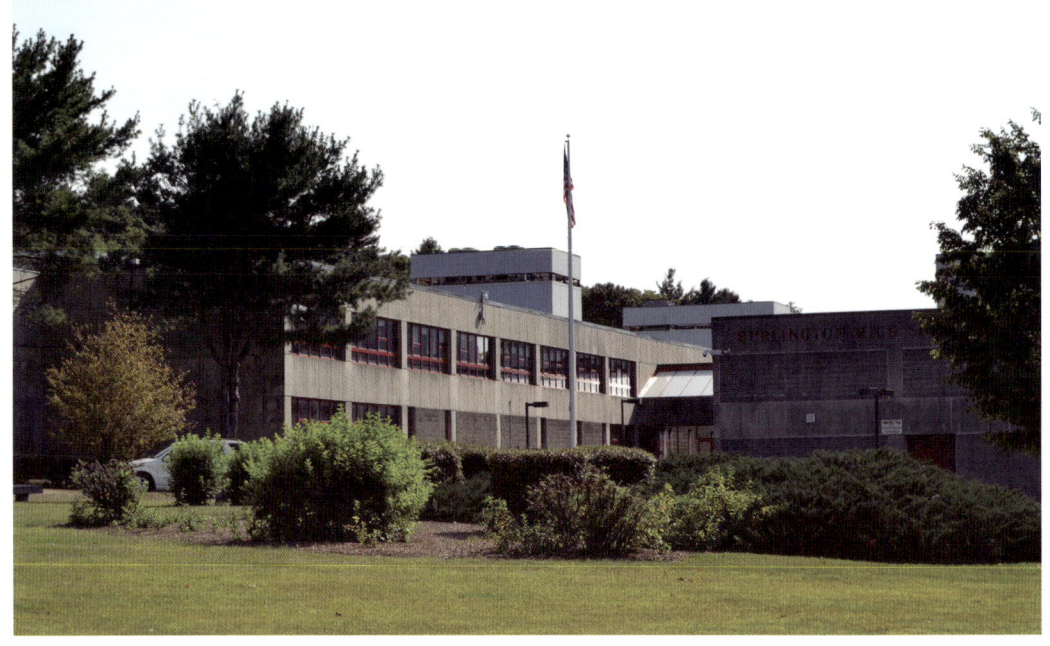

# SECTION 4

# LOST BURLINGTON

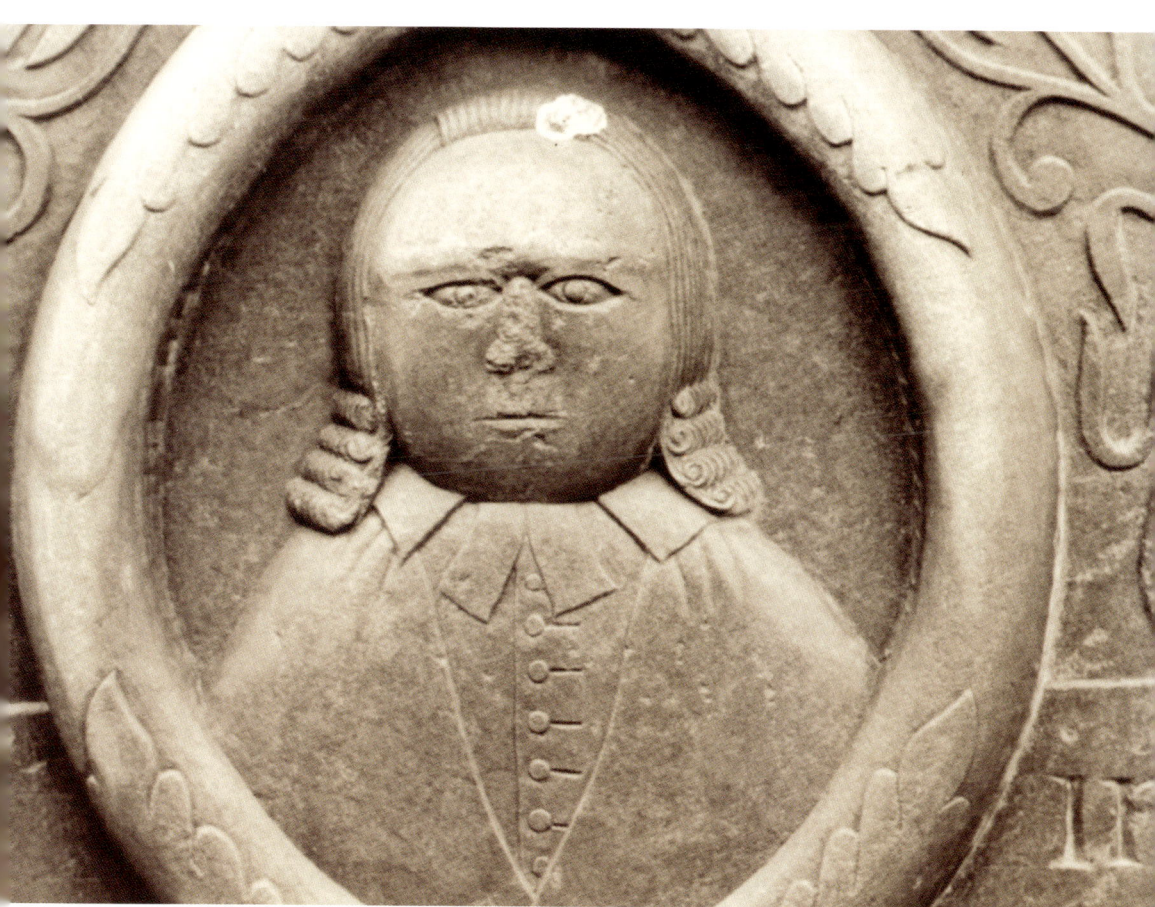

# SECTION 4

# INTRODUCTION

So much of Burlington History has been lost over three centuries due to progress and development but especially due to devastating fires. Since early records and artifacts were often housed in wood-framed dwellings, the fire risk was high. Many of our colonial documents were recorded and kept by the ministers of the town, usually in the Parsonage. In Burlington's case, the parsonage was the Sewall Mansion on Lexington Street, where John Hancock and Samuel Adams stayed for a short time at the outbreak of the American Revolution. In the seventeenth and eighteenth century, in New England, the government and the church were connected. Town documents were often times kept by the clergy. Since so much has been lost in time and history many mysteries remain about some key moments and events in the 330-year history of Burlington and the region.

*Previous page:* Detail from the headstone of the grave of Rev. Thomas Jones minister of the Second Parish Church from 1751–1774, in the Second Precinct Burial Ground.

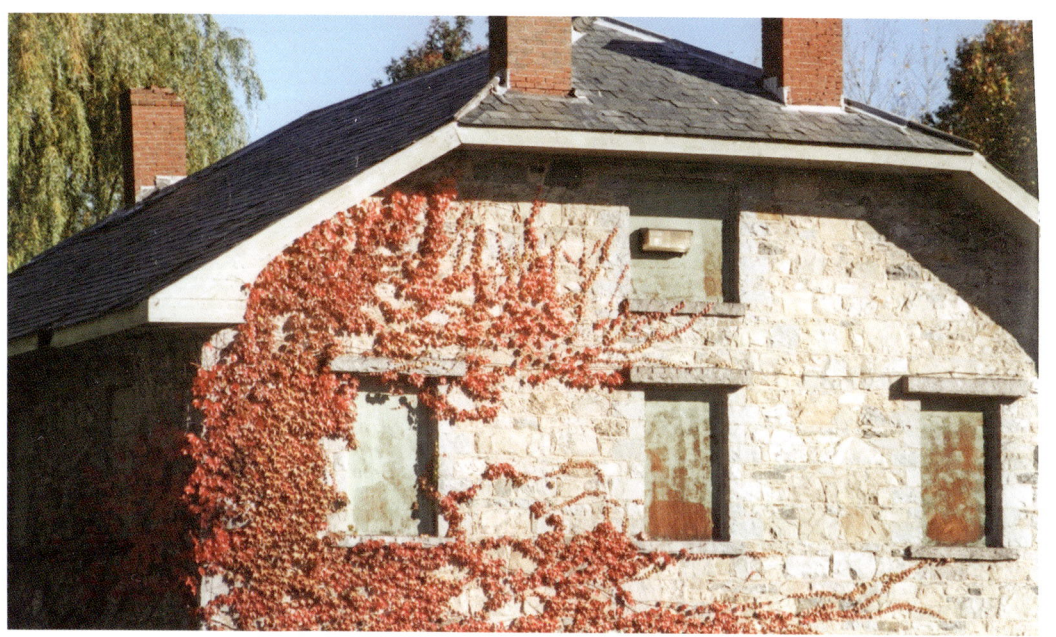

**KENT HOUSE:** A unique and somewhat mysterious Burlington structure, now owned by the private sector, is the Kent House. Standing abandoned off of Network Drive, the house was built *c.* 1850 for John Kent, an affluent brewer from Charlestown. James MacGregor Burns, prize winning historian and Franklin D. Roosevelt biographer, lived in the "Kent Cottage" for a time in the 1930s. Burns went to grade school in Burlington and graduated from Lexington High in 1935. Large corporations acquired the property by the end of the twenty-first century, and as of 2013 the fate of the former Kent House is unknown. (SCAN + IMAGE/RJC)

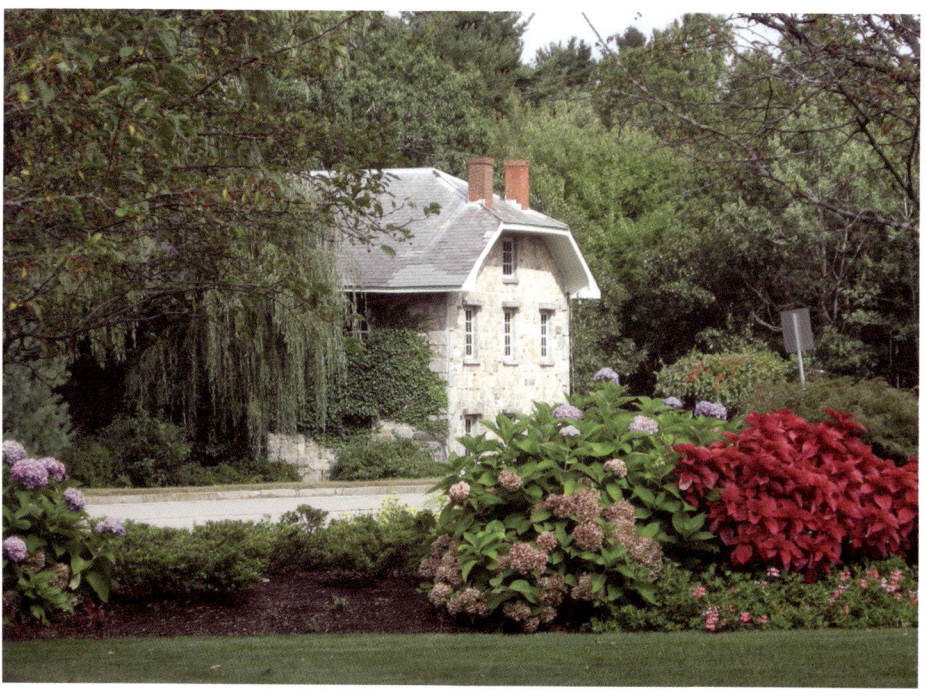

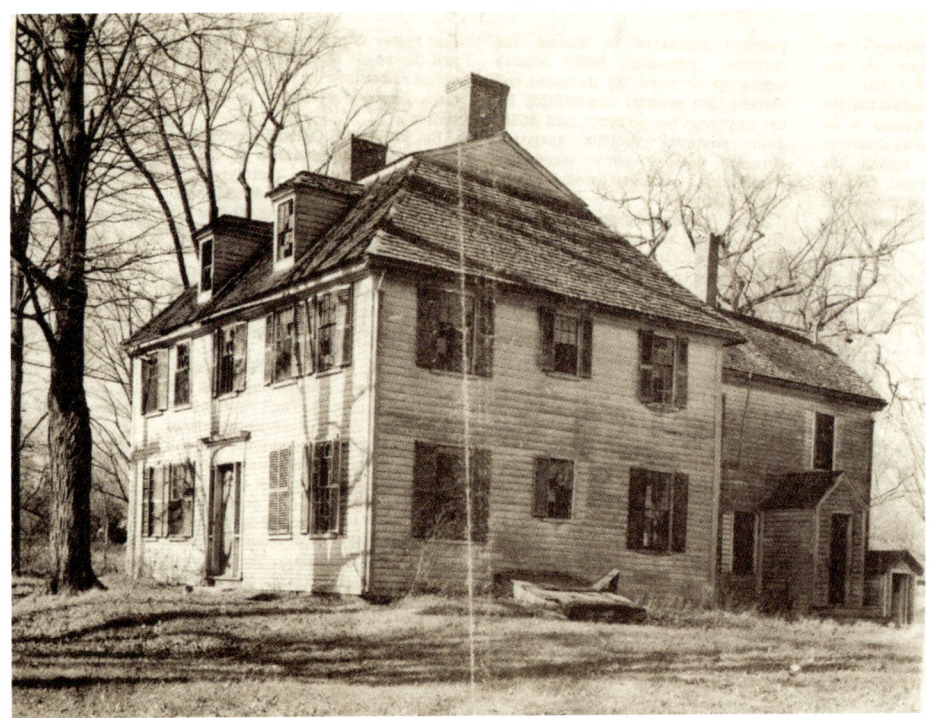

**THE WILLIAM WINN MANSION:** When the William Winn mansion was dismantled and carefully moved to stand in Wellesley, Burlington lost a historic gem. Timothy Winn, town father, state representative, and notable citizen, built this Georgian mansion, *c.* 1734, on the corner of Newbridge and Winn Street. It remained in the Winn family until the First World War era, when it was sold and used as a rooming house. It was purchased, dismantled, moved and reconstructed in Wellesley in 1938. (SCAN/BTA) (RJC/IMAGE)

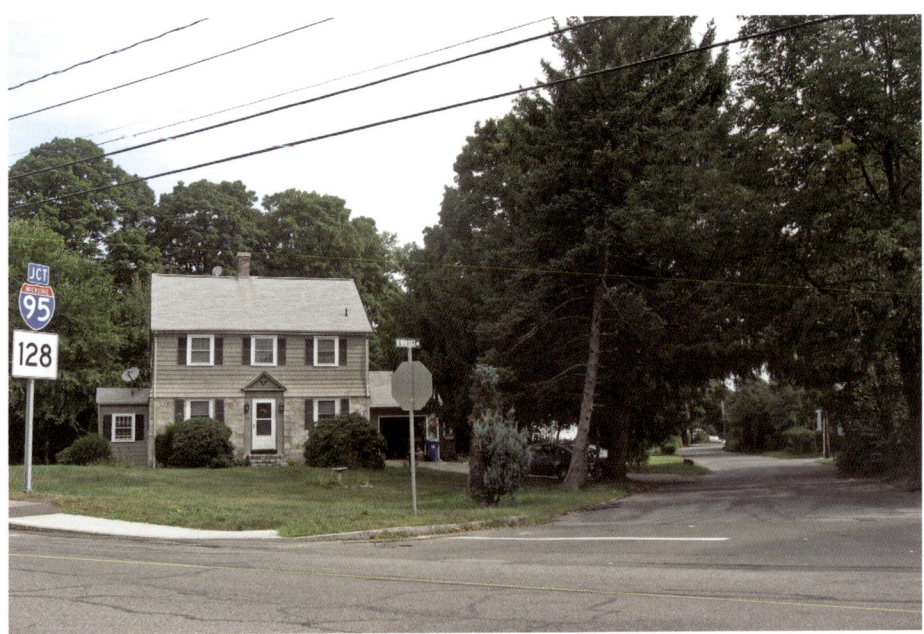

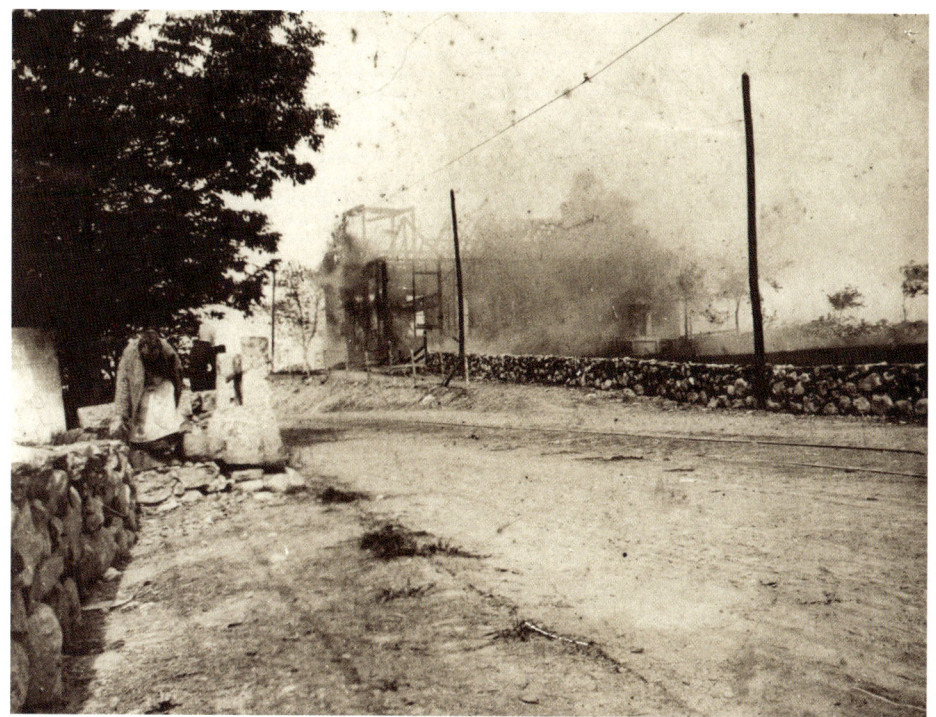

THE TOWN HOUSE FIRE: In 1902 Burlington history burned when the 1844 Town House (first Town Hall) was destroyed by fire on May 30, 1902. This image was reportedly taken the morning after the fire with embers still smoldering among the ruins. A close look at Bedford Street shows the trolley tracks that ran through to Winn Street, via Sears Street. Notice the older woman in the lower left, standing near the corner of the Old Burial ground. (SCAN/BTA) (RJC/IMAGE)

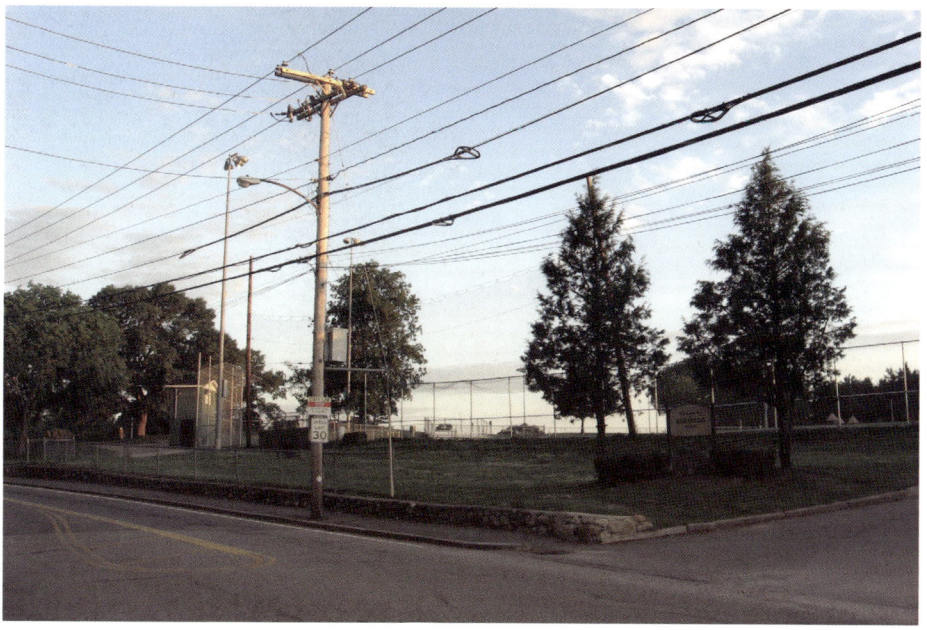

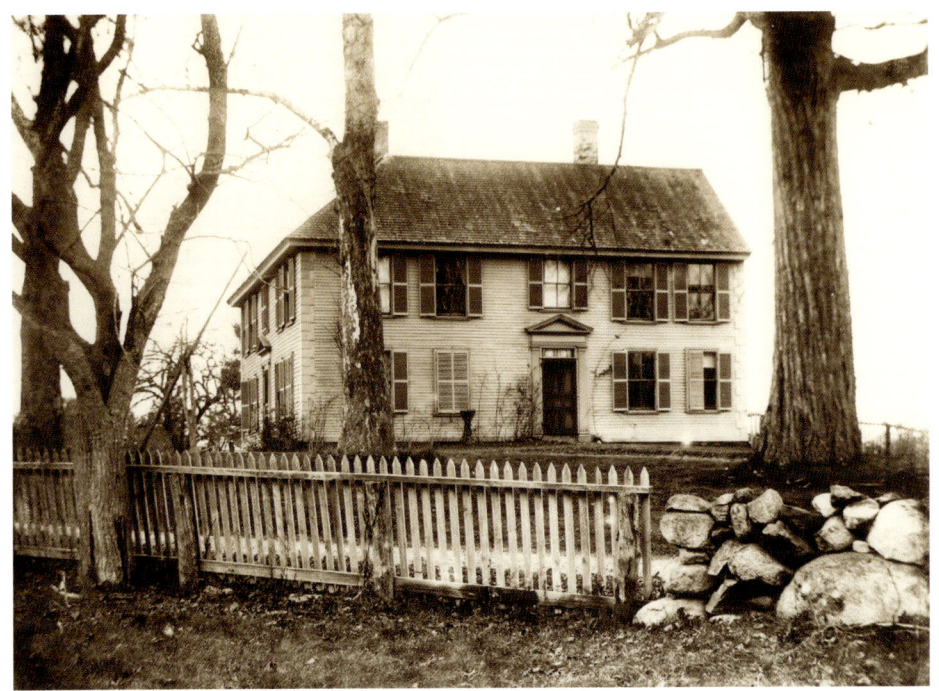

**THE SEWALL HOUSE FIRES:** Another tragic fire on April 23, 1897 destroyed the Sewalls' home and a great deal of the history of the local area. The L-shaped, sixteen-room mansion was the home of the Samuel Sewall family at the time of the blaze, but it had also been the Town Ministers' parsonage from 1751–1844. Since the minister was usually one of the most educated in the colonies, many early documents and artifacts were stored here and all were lost. A second house was built on the site and it also burned to the ground. (SCAN/RJC ) (RJC/IMAGE)

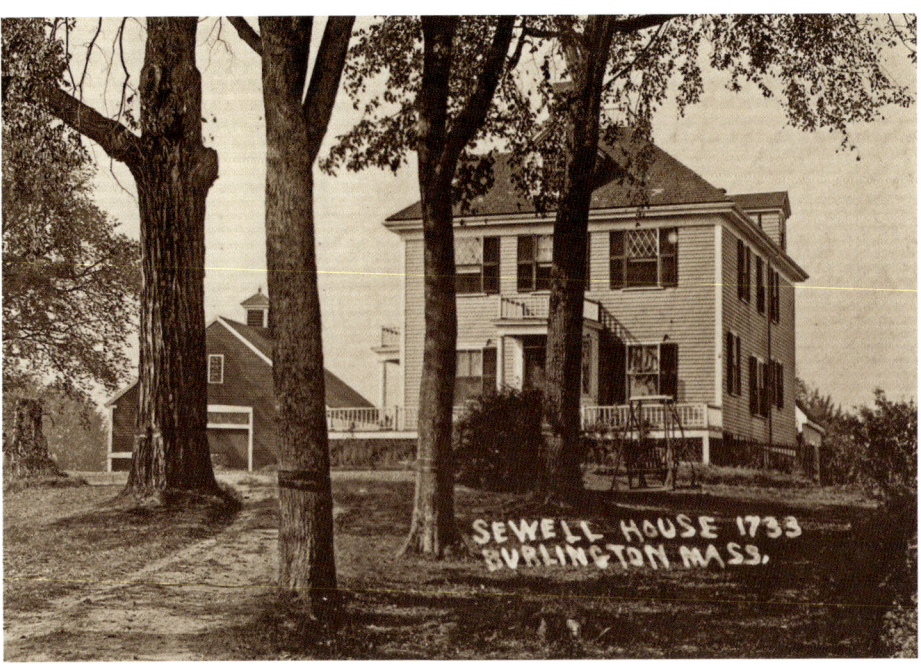

SEWELL HOUSE 1733
BURLINGTON MASS.

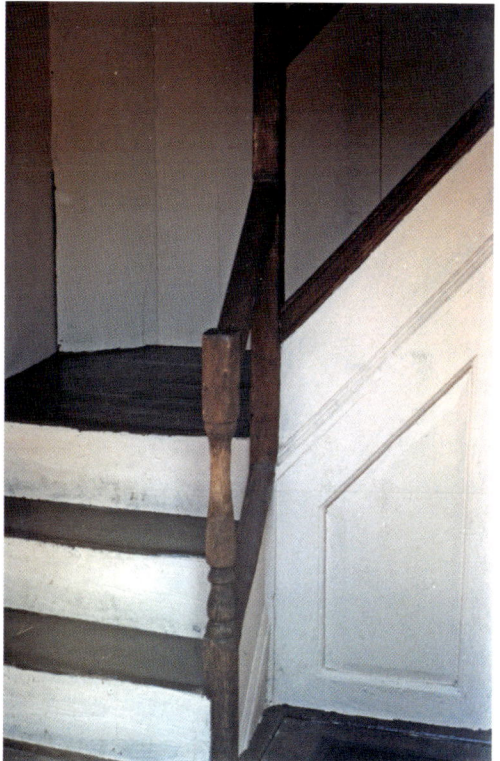

**THE FRANCIS WYMAN HOUSE FIRE:**
Once thought to be the oldest house in
Burlington, *c.* 1666, and an icon for the town
was the homestead of the historic Wyman
family which survived a terrible fire in
November 1996. Although many early colonial
architectural features were lost, details have
been carefully recreated and the structure has
been nearly restored as of 2013. Pictured are
the U-shaped staircase, newel post and some
paneling showing the extent of the damage.
(SCAN + IMAGE/RJC)

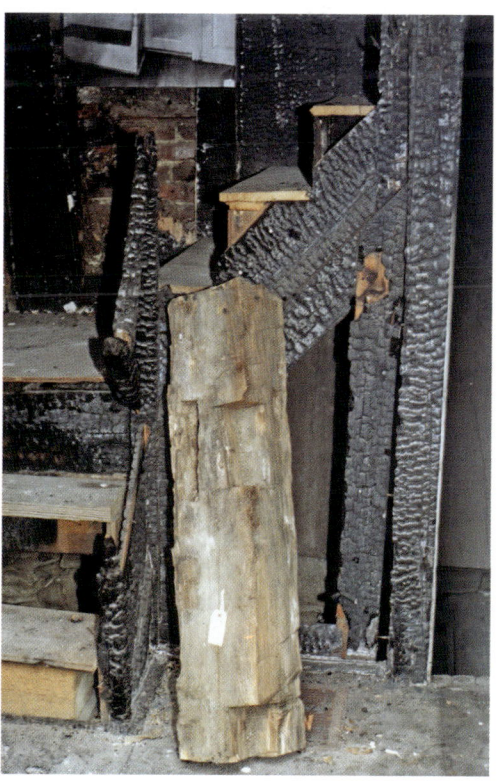

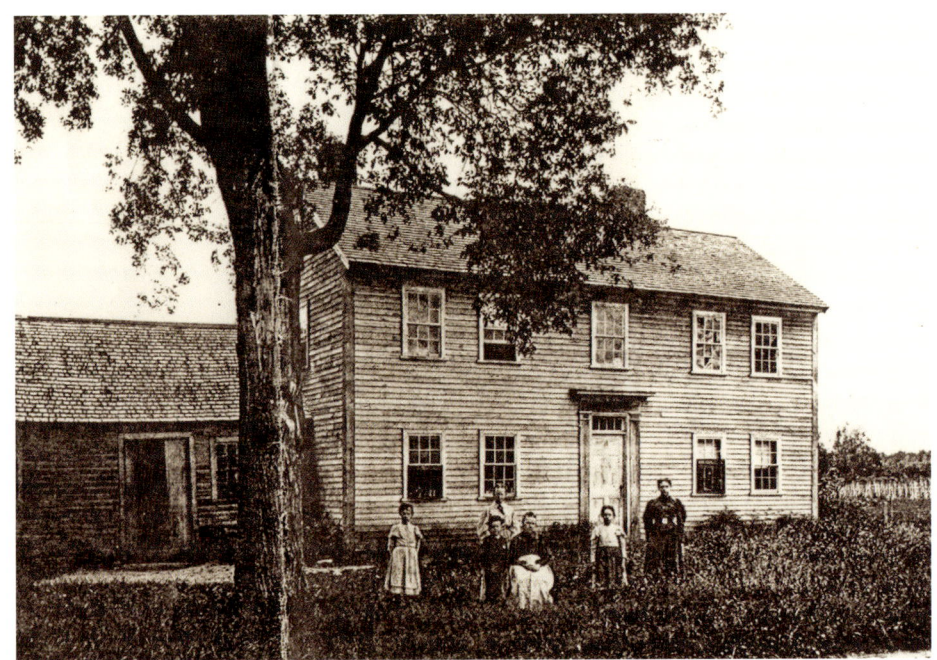

THE DAVID SKELTON HOUSE:   Several simple Burlington farmhouses built in the nineteenth century and earlier continue to be lost to modern development. Such was the case with the David Skelton house that was built on the corner of Bedford Street and the Middlesex Turnpike. Although not extremely significant in the history of the area, it was a good example of an 1830s rural farmhouse. A large private residence is located on the site today. (SCAN/TONI FARIA) (RJC/IMAGE)

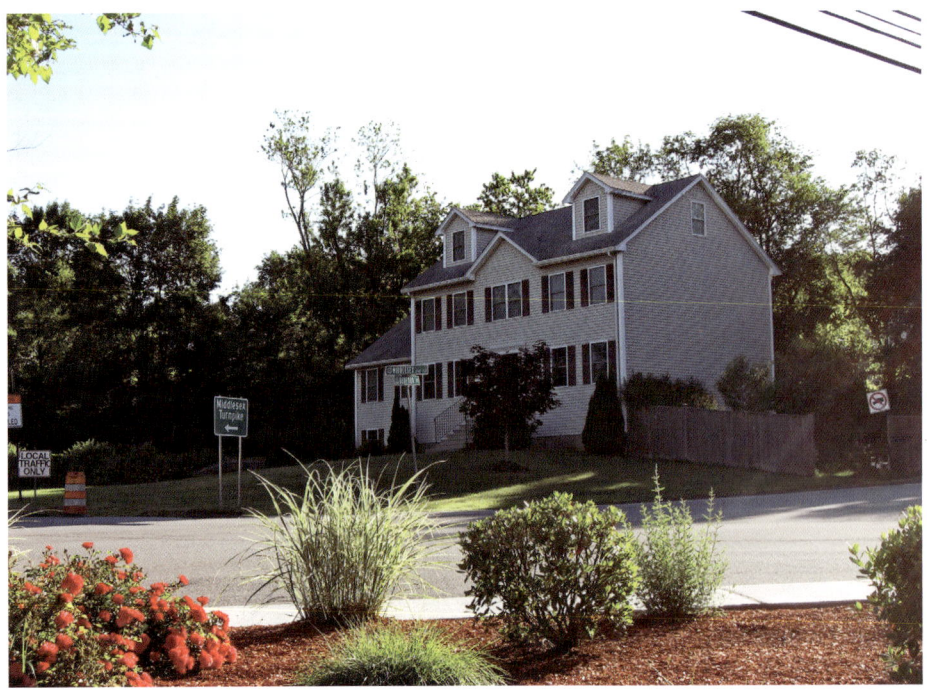

## WARD FROTHINGHAM/ MANSION:

Ward Brooks Frothingham was born in Boston on November 26, 1828, son of the well-known clergyman Dr. Nathaniel Langdon Frothingham and Ann Gorham Brooks. Ward served as a Lt. in the Civil War while his wife Franey worked as a volunteer nurse. The mansion that was built for Ward's father still stands on Spruce Hill Road. The image shows the mansion just before its restoration in the 1990s. (SCAN/BTA) (RJC/IMAGE)

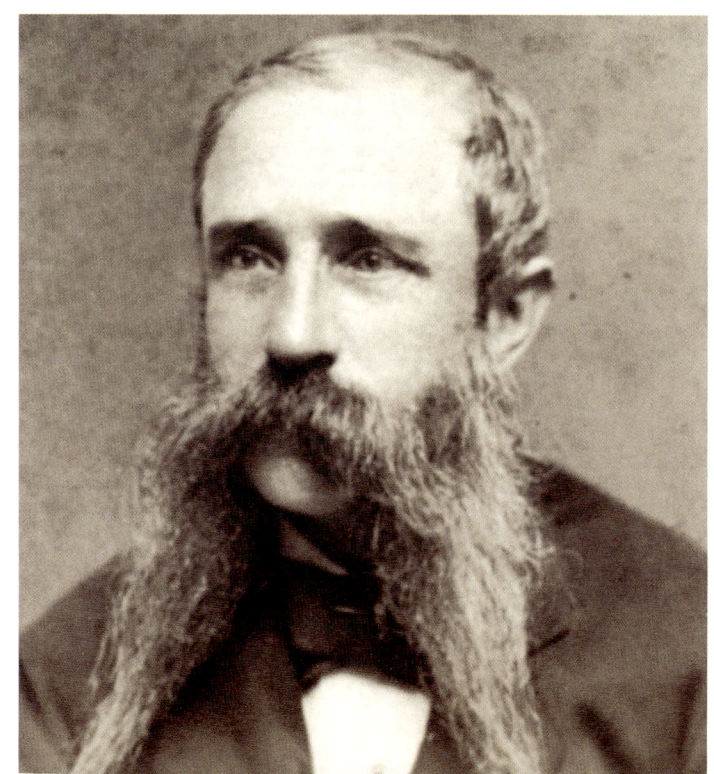

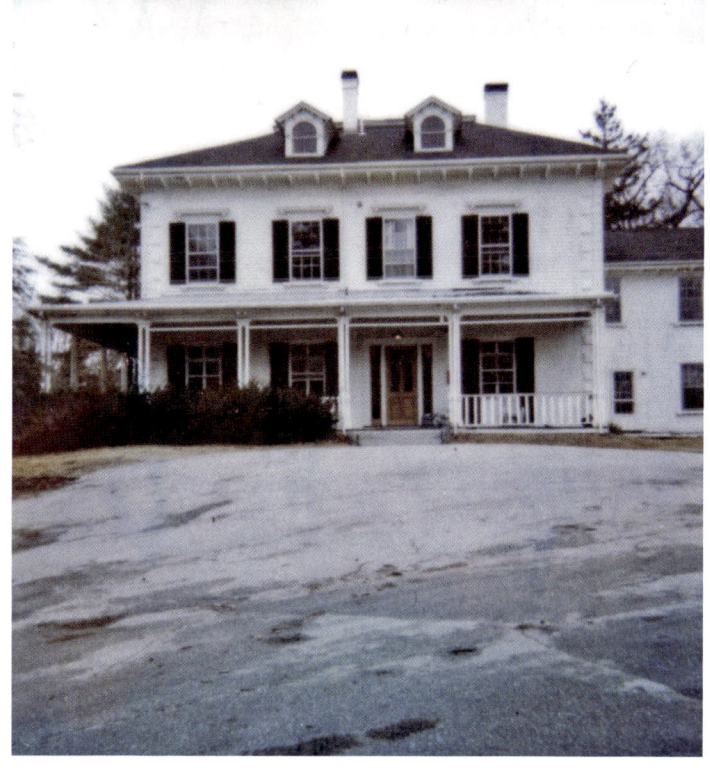

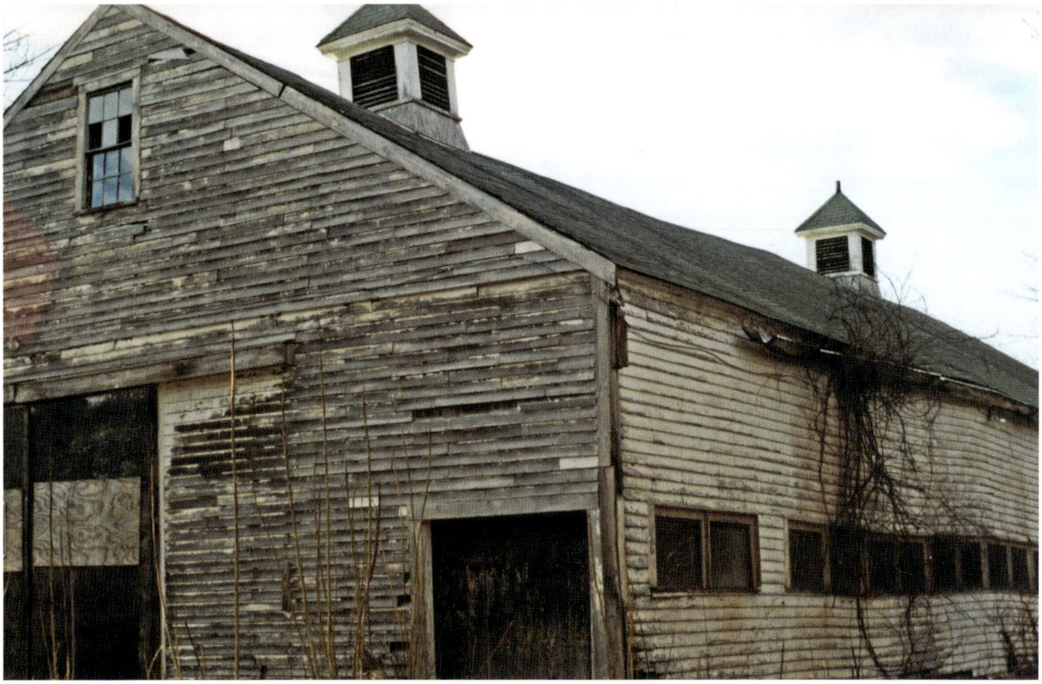

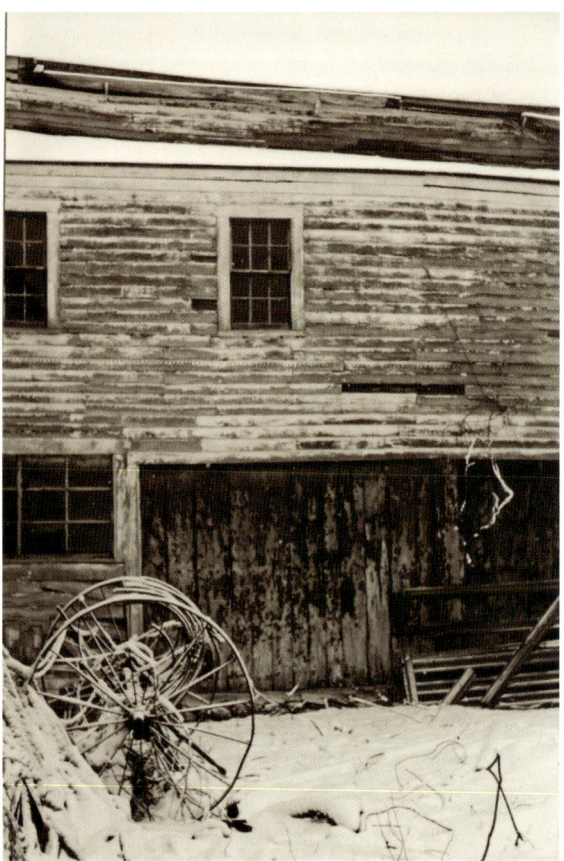

### GRAND VIEW FARM:

"The Grand View" in the late nineteenth century, was of Mt. Wachusett. Today the view is less inspiring, apartment buildings and condominiums. Saved by the town from development, it is being renovated for modern use. Many of the original features could not be saved, the best example being the architecturally significant rear barn (pictured). The remodeling is ongoing as of 2013. (SCAN + IMAGE/RJC)

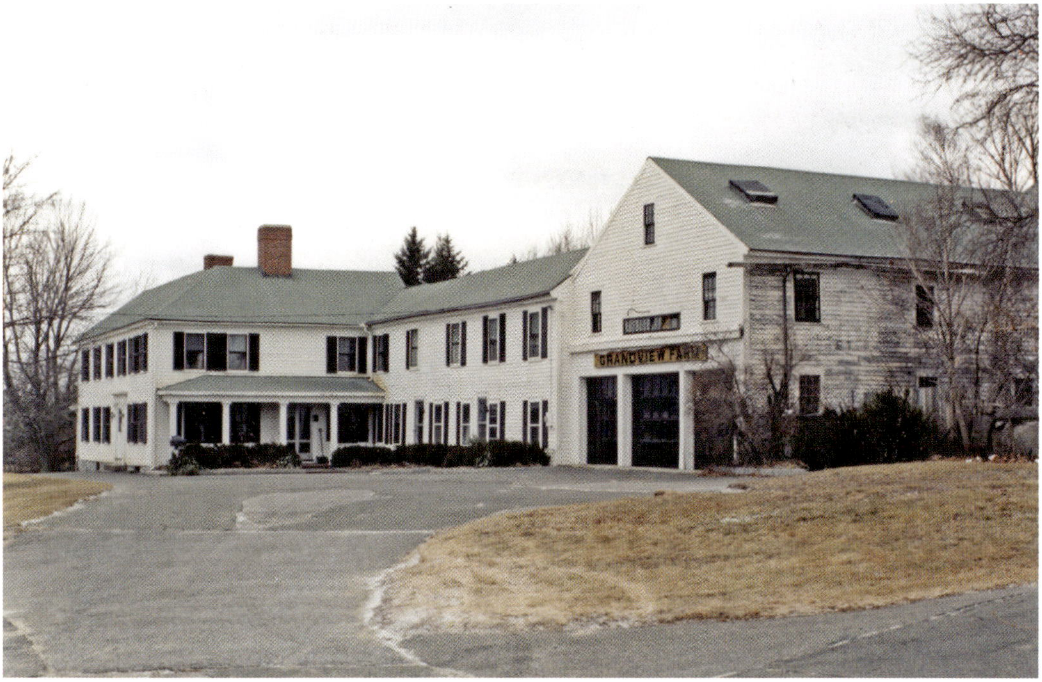

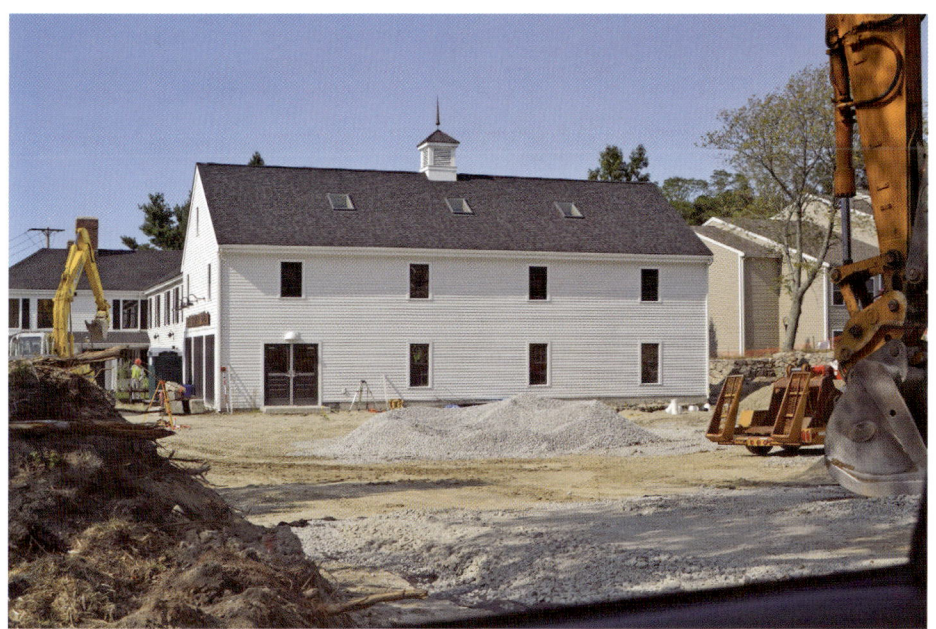

**GRAND VIEW FARM/REAR BARN WORK:** Now town-owned property, the distinctive Grand View Farm graces the entryway to Burlington's Town Common from the east. The site, also known as the Marion Tavern, was considered to be Burlington's finest example of a nineteenth century, connected farm. The complex consisted of five principle structures; two historic houses joined, and two barns, all connected in a concept conceived *c.* 1840 in the New England farm world. The architecturally significant rear barn could not be saved. (SCAN + IMAGE/RJC)

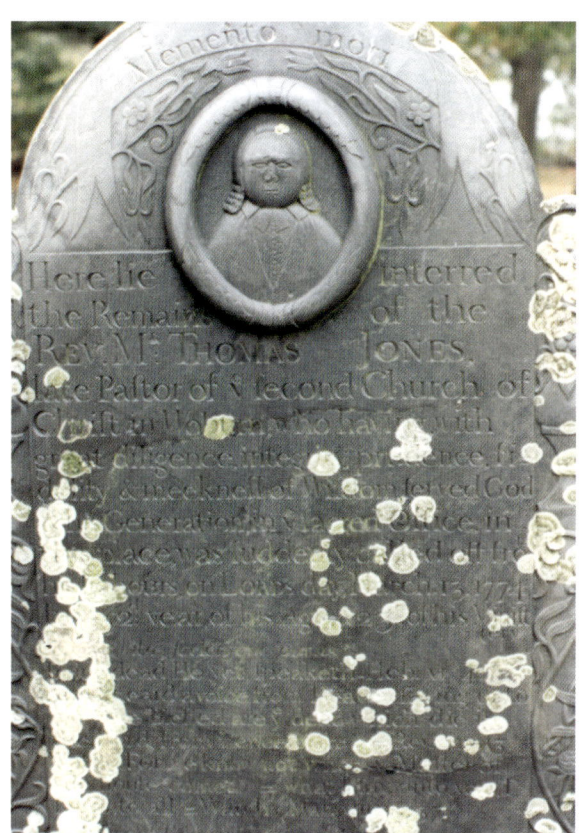

**SECOND PARISH BURIAL GROUND:**
In 1732, Benjamin Johnson donated land at the top of "Forest Field Hill" to the newly created (1730) Second Parish of Woburn, to erect a "Meeting house" and set aside land for a burial ground. The Second Precinct Burial Ground, is the final resting place of many notable Burlington citizens. Early settlers, four significant ministers, many Revolutionary War veterans, and two African slaves are among the illustrious. It is now part of the Burlington Museum Complex. (SCAN + IMAGE/RJC)

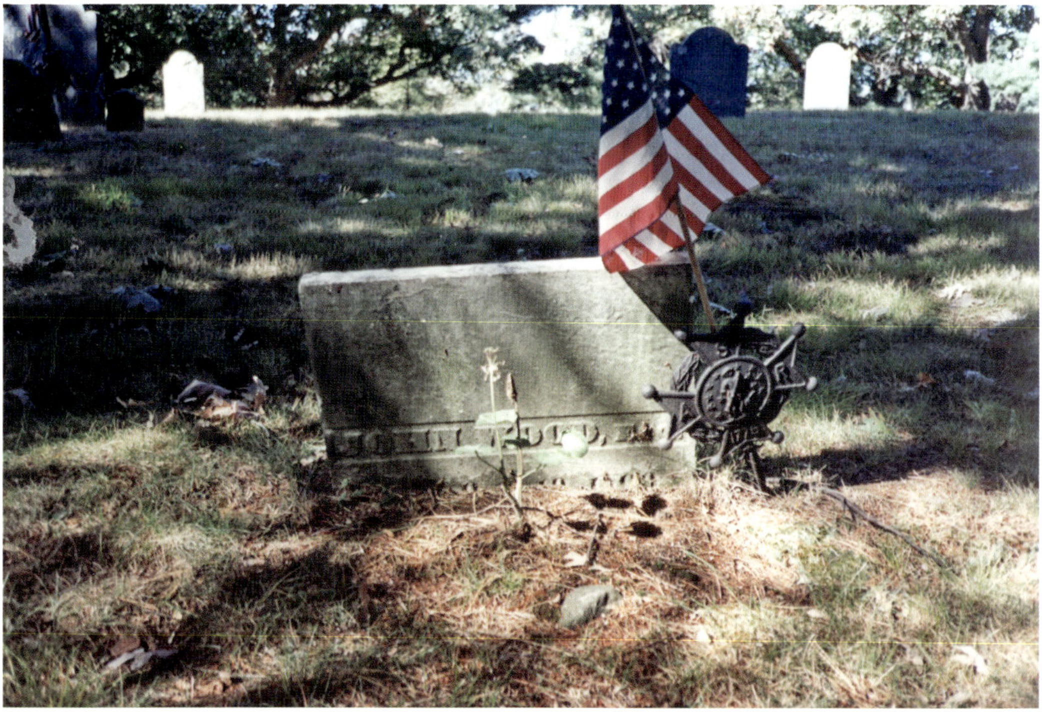